D0375016

FANNY
KEMBLE

FANNY
KEMBLE

Dorothy Marshall

ST. MARTIN'S PRESS

New York

Printed in Great Britain
Library of Congress Catalog Card Number: 77-3854
First published in the United States of America in 1978

Library of Congress Cataloging in Publication Data
Marshall, Dorothy.
    Fanny Kemble.

    Bibliography: p.
    Includes index.
        1. Kemble, Frances Anne, 1809–1893.   2. Actors—
Great Britain—Biography.
PN2598.K4M3   792'.028'0924   [B]   77-3854

ISBN 0-312-28162-5

Contents

	List of Illustrations	*vii*
	Introduction	*1*
	Note on Books	*4*
ONE	The Early Years	*6*
TWO	A Star is Born	*34*
THREE	The American Venture	*70*
FOUR	Marriage and its Problems	*96*
FIVE	Georgia and Slavery	*129*
SIX	A Clash of Personalities	*158*
SEVEN	Frustration and Divorce	*196*
EIGHT	Building a New Life	*222*
NINE	Peaceful Pastures	*244*
	Index	*273*

Illustrations

between pages 152 *and* 153

Fanny Kemble as Bianca by Thomas Sully (Courtesy of the Pennsylvania Academy of the Fine Arts)

Charles Kemble as Pierre in Otway's *Venice Preserv'd* (The Raymond Mander and Joe Mitchenson Theatre Collection)

Mrs Charles Kemble, née Maria Theresa De Camp (The Raymond Mander and Joe Mitchenson Theatre Collection)

Sarah Siddons, Fanny's aunt, as Euphrasia in *The Grecian Daughter* (The Raymond Mander and Joe Mitchenson Theatre Collection)

Fanny in her dressing-room at Covent Garden Theatre (The Raymond Mander and Joe Mitchenson Theatre Collection)

'The attitudes' adopted by Fanny Kemble in her role of Juliet (The Raymond Mander and Joe Mitchenson Theatre Collection)

Covent Garden Market in the 1820s (The Greater London Council Print Collection)

Butler Place (The Historical Society of Pennsylvania)

Pierce Butler (The Historical Society of Pennsylvania)

Fanny's daughters, Sarah and Frances (New York Public Library)

Fanny in America (The Historical Society of Pennsylvania)

Catherine Maria Sedgwick (New York Public Library)

Monument Mountain, The Berkshires (The Detroit Institute of Arts)

George Coombe (National Galleries of Scotland)

Henry James (National Portrait Gallery, London)

Fanny reading Shakespeare at the St James's Theatre (The Raymond Mander and Joe Mitchenson Theatre Collection)

Fanny as an elderly lady (New York Public Library)

Introduction

Because readers on each side of the Atlantic will probably react differently to this book, I feel that it should be prefaced by an introduction. English readers are likely to ask vaguely 'Fanny Kemble? Wasn't she a nineteenth-century actress? Why write her life?' or, more bluntly, 'Who was Fanny Kemble?' To such queries I would reply that Fanny Kemble was a complex and fascinating woman whose incident-packed life reads like a novel. In her twenties she was the pin-up girl of the London stage; then, married to a Georgian slave owner, she became a passionate opponent of slavery. Finally, in her sixties, her memoirs were among the best sellers of her day. In addition she wrote plays and poetry. In the course of her long life she knew many of the most interesting literary figures of the time, in both England and America. She saw enormous changes in society, and in the means of communication that bound it together as the steam engine replaced the horse and the sail. Such a woman has a right to be remembered. In the words of Henry James, 'Even if Mrs Kemble had been a less remarkable person she would still have owed a distinction to the far away past to which she gave continuity.'

Today her name is better known in her adopted country than in her own. American readers are more likely to ask not who was Fanny Kemble but why anyone should wish to write yet another book about her, because there are already well-documented biographies in existence. In addition to the older ones by Dorothy Bobbe, Leota Driver and Margaret Armstrong, all published in the thirties, two new ones based on more recent research were published in America in 1972 – Constance Wright's *Fanny Kemble and the Lovely Land* and Fanny

Kemble Wister's *Fanny; the American Kemble*. The latter, written by Fanny Kemble's great-granddaughter, contains many hitherto unpublished letters, which makes it of the utmost value to all Fanny Kemble's future biographers. Though it has not altered in any fundamental way my interpretation of her personality and matrimonial difficulties, this has been much enriched by the availability of this new material, particularly when dealing with the latter. The brief extracts quoted from Fanny's letters to Kate Minot, and some scattered allusions to letters in particular those written to Mrs Joshua Fisher, Mrs Follen and Mrs Henry Cleveland, from which I have not quoted, but to which I am indebted for information as to her moods and feelings where her husband was concerned, have been taken from this book. As a direct descendant of both Fanny Kemble and Pierce Butler, the authoress has treated the relations between them with a fairness and restraint that has not always marked some of Fanny Kemble's earlier biographers. Why then is there still a place for another biography? The answer must be that all biographies are interpretative as well as factual and hitherto her main biographers have been American while she herself remained impenitently English. Again to quote Henry James, 'The United States commended themselves to her liberal opinion as much as they disconcerted her intensely conservative taste; she relished every obligation to them but that of living in them.' What I have tried to do therefore is not to add to the factual knowledge of her life, or even to present it in meticulous detail, but to look at it from the English angle and against her English background. For this I can plead some modest qualifications. At the beginning of my academic career I was fortunate enough to spend a year as an Instructor at Vassar, and towards its end I was invited to become a visiting member of the History Faculty at Wellesley. Like Fanny I have the warmest feelings for America, but like her I remain impenitently British. Also, because for much of my academic life I have concentrated on the social history of the eighteenth and nineteenth centuries, this should help me to see Fanny against the background of her period. For both British and American readers, whether they are students of human nature or of history, Fanny Kemble has much to offer.

It gives me great pleasure to acknowledge all the help that I have received in writing this book, both from the previously mentioned biographies of Fanny Kemble and from the staffs of the various libraries in which I have been privileged to work. I am very grateful to those of the Manuscript Department of the National Library of Scotland for assistance when I was working on the George Combe papers and, as always, to the staff of the British Reference Library of the British Museum. I should also like to thank Wm Heinemann for permission to quote a passage concerning Fanny Kemble which had been omitted from the earlier editions of the Greville Diaries and which was subsequently included in that published by them in 1927, and to the Dr Williams Library for permission to quote from the Diary of Crabbe Robinson, edited by E. Brown. In America I received nothing but kindness. The Library of Congress, by supplying me with a photostat copy of Fanny Kemble's *Answer to the Libel of Pierce Butler etc.* saved me from the necessity of making a special trip to Washington to consult it in the Rare Book Room. To the Massachusetts Historical Society I am indebted for much courteous assistance and for permission to quote from Fanny Kemble's letters in their possession. I should also like to thank the staff of the Rare Book Room of Boston Public Library and of the Houghton Library, where I was able to examine her letters to Henry James and Sam Ward. For permission to quote from the latter my thanks are due to Mrs William D. Ticknor, and to Mrs Carey C. Chamberlain for permission to include an extract from Sarah Ellen Browne's diary now in her possession. Finally it gives me the greatest pleasure to thank my friends Professor and Mrs Ralph Beatley of Cambridge, Massachusetts, for their kindness and patience in acting as my host and hostess while I was working on my American material, without which this book could never have been completed. To them I am more than grateful.

Note on Books

In addition to the MSS. letters mentioned in my introduction the main sources for the life of Fanny Kemble are her own published works:

The Journal of a Residence in America (Paris 1835).
Poems (1844, 1866, 1883).
A Year of Consolation (London 1847).
Journal of a Residence on a Georgian Plantation 1838–1839 (London 1863).
Records of a Girlhood (London 1878).
Records of a Later Life (London 1882).
Further Records (London 1890).

With the exception of *Journal of a Residence on a Georgian Plantation*, which has been edited by John A. Scott with skill and devotion, and which was also published in this country in 1961, these are now only to be found in libraries. The British Library has a complete collection, but many must still be mouldering on forgotten bookshelves or in attics along with other Victorian books. Much scattered material concerning Fanny Kemble is to be found in contemporary diaries, such as *The Diary of Philip Hone* (1889), *Leaves from the Diary of Henry Greville* (1892) and Anne Thackeray Richie's *Chapters from some unwritten Memoirs*, but many of these are now out of print and in any case to search through them for passages that throw light on Fanny Kemble is often like looking for the needle in the proverbial haystack. More concentrated and revealing are the obituary appreciations of Henry James in his *Essays in London* (1894) and in Nathaniel Beard's *Some Recollections of Yesterday* which appeared in *Temple Bar* in the same year.

The main modern biographies of Fanny Kemble are:

Bobbe, Dorothy, *Fanny Kemble* (1931).

Driver, Leota, *Fanny Kemble* (1933).

Armstrong, Margaret, *Fanny Kemble; the passionate Victorian* (1938).

Gibbs, Henry, *Yours affectionately, Fanny* (1947). (This leaves out any discussion of her marriage, etc.)

Wright, Constance C., *Fanny Kemble and the Lovely Land* (1972, also published in England 1974).

Wister, Fanny Kemble, *Fanny; the American Kemble* (1972).

ONE

✦

The Early Years

Among the modern crowds surging up and down Oxford Street, once more romantically known as the Oxford Road, few of those who glance casually up Newman Street will remember that it was there, on 27 November 1809, that Fanny Kemble was born. Even they may only recall her vaguely as a nineteenth-century actress, well known in her day on both sides of the Atlantic. Frances Anne Kemble, to give her her full name, was much more than a youthful leading lady whose dramatic rise to stardom, coupled with the famous Kemble name, had captured the imagination and the hearts of both British and American theatregoers. She was in addition a passionate opponent of slavery, a talented authoress of memoirs, plays and poems, and a woman of such forceful personality that when Henry James met her in her later years he called her 'the terrific Kemble'. In her day she knew most people, both British and American, who were worth knowing. Sir Thomas Lawrence sketched her when she was barely twenty-one; Henry James attended her funeral. Her story, as it unfolds against the changing backgrounds of theatrical and fashionable London, Quaker Philadelphia, the deep south and her beloved Swiss mountains, reads more like fiction than sober fact. Throughout her life Fanny was fascinated by living writing:

I confess that family correspondence, even of people utterly unknown to me, always seems to me full of interest . . . they are life, as compared with imitations of it – life that mystery and beauty surpassing every other; they are morsels of that profoundest of all secrets, which baffles alike the men of science, the metaphysicians, artist and poet.

To record and as far as possible interpret this 'profoundest of all

6

secrets' with regard to Fanny herself must be the task of those who attempt to write her biography. It is a daunting but fascinating undertaking. Fanny Kemble was a creature of moods and of passion as well as of intellect. Like Byron, whose poetry fascinated her in her adolescence, she too had found herself lionized by London society almost overnight. She too made a disastrous marriage which clashing temperaments, and in her case clashing backgrounds, brought to shipwreck. She too escaped from an unbearable situation by flight. But there the resemblance ends. Fanny was made of tougher stuff. Divorced by her American husband for desertion, and separated from her beloved daughters for years, she built on the shattered foundations of her past, making a new career for herself and dying in her eighties, once more reunited with her children, an honoured and respected old lady. Though, unlike the fairy-tale promise of her early days, she and her Prince Charming did not 'live happily ever after', the end of her story was a happy one.

Though circumstances rather than desire determined that Fanny should become an actress, from a child the theatre had been the background of her life. She came of famous acting stock. The antecedents of her grandfather Roger Kemble are vague. Beyond the fact that he was born in Hereford in 1721 little is known of his doings before he joined a troupe of strolling players in 1752. His wife, Sally, Fanny's grandmother, was the daughter of a leading provincial theatrical manager, John Ward of Birmingham, and the young Kembles' married life was largely spent on the road. It seems to have been a happy partnership. Even religious differences were settled amicably. Roger was a Roman Catholic, Sally a Protestant and, as was often the case, the boys followed their father's faith and the girls their mother's. Twelve children were born to Roger and Sally, eight of whom reached maturity. Three of them achieved fame, Sarah, John and Charles, the youngest, who was Fanny's father, and another sister, Elizabeth, who married a theatrical manager, achieved a creditable reputation as Mrs Whitelock on the American stage. Sarah, the eldest daughter, was born at Brecon on 5 February 1755 and the eldest son, John Philip, at Prescott in Lancashire two years later. Sally and Roger Kemble themselves never achieved more than a respectable reputation in their chosen profession. They were content to play wherever a provincial audience could be found, sometimes in one of the new provincial theatres but more often in a suitable room at some well-known inn. Yet even at this early stage the Kembles were careful to dissociate themselves from the lax moral standards of many of their fellow players. They gave their children an education unusual among the travelling fraternity; both Sarah and John were sent to good schools in Worcester. Conscious as their parents were of the uncertainties and hardships of the strolling player's life which they did not wish their children to follow as a permanent career, for a time they were allowed to play such parts in their parents' company as were appropriate to their years. This was how Sarah first met the man she married, and whose name she made immortal, Henry Siddons. Sometime in her late teens she set her indomitable will to become his wife. Her parents did not approve of a marriage that would seem to commit their daughter to the life of a strolling player and they placed her as a companion to the widowed Lady Mary Greathead. Sarah was well treated and retained the friend-liest of feelings towards her patroness, feelings that were reciprocated, but she was not to be deflected from her Henry; they were married on 28 November 1773.

Nor were the Kembles any more successful in diverting their eldest son, John Philip from the stage. Their intention had been that he should study for the priesthood and for this purpose he was sent to Douai. By the winter of 1775 he was back in England determined to make the stage his career. Nevertheless his years at Douai were not wasted; they were to bear useful social fruit. Though, since the impact of David Garrick, acting was slowly becoming respectable, the average barn-stormer was definitely beyond the social pale. Persons of gentle birth would still have been horrified if a son, or even worse a daughter, had contemplated going on the stage, but they were prepared to receive the outstanding actors and actresses of the day on social occasions if they had the necessary poise. In the world of polite society John's education stood him in good stead; in 1785 Thomas Whatley published his essay, 'Remarks on some of the Caracters in Shakespeare'. Already a leading light at Drury Lane, John Philip thus secured recognition as a scholar and a gentleman and found open to him the doors of the great London Houses, including Carlton House, the residence of the Prince of Wales. The Kembles had arrived. This success had been slow in coming to both brother and sister. Sarah, now the mother of two children, had been lucky enough to be engaged by Garrick to play Portia at Drury Lane in the December of 1775, but she failed to im-press either the public or the critics. Her notices were bad, or at best indifferent, and she was not re-engaged. This may have been one of those proverbial blessings in disguise. Sarah was forced to return to the provinces where she spent two years on the northern circuit run by Tate Wilkinson, thus gaining further valuable experience. She then joined John Palmer's company at Bath. At the Royal Theatre Sarah had the stimulation of playing to the sophisticated audiences that were to be found only where polite society congregated, an experience by which she profited. When therefore she got a second chance to return to Drury Lane to play Isabella in *The Fatal Marriage*, later to be one of Fanny Kemble's great parts, she scored an instantaneous success. That was on 10 October 1782. Nearly a year later John Philip was equally widely acclaimed for his performance as Hamlet. The long pilgrimage was over.

The remaining member of the Kemble family to achieve stardom was Sarah's youngest brother Charles, born in 1775. He too, like John Philip, abandoned education for the stage and he too started his theatrical career in the provinces. Meanwhile his eldest brother had become manager of Drury Lane. Then in 1802, the year of old Roger Kemble's death, John Philip switched his interest to the rival theatre Covent Garden, in which he bought a sixth share, becoming its manager. It was to prove an unfortunate investment which hung round the necks of first John Philip and then Charles for over thirty years. The ill luck started when the theatre burnt down on 19 September 1808. Fire was a constant hazard in an age when lighting was provided by lamps and candles, fanned by draughts from the stage, where much inflammable material lay around, and Drury Lane soon suffered a similar fate.

By this time the Kembles had been established as the leading theatrical family, Charles having joined his brother and sister to play the juvenile leads, for which his good looks, elegant figure and graceful deportment make him particularly suitable. In 1825 a contemporary writer described him as 'elegant without affectation, learned without pedantry, witty without rancour, humorous without vulgarity'. It is not surprising that Fanny adored her father. Her mother was a more astringent person. She was half French, half Swiss, the child of an impecunious French officer and a Swiss farmer's daughter who, having lived for a time in Vienna, where Fanny's mother, called after the Empress Maria Theresa, was born, drifted to London. Her father, whose name was de Camp, had hoped to earn their living as a musician, but his health soon broke down. Possibly London smog and the London climate were too much for him. With no other means of support, and with even smaller children for whom to provide, the eldest of the stranded family, Fanny's mother Maria de Camp, found herself at the age of five its chief breadwinner. An entrancing fairylike figure, she became the star of a small troupe of child dancers and was lucky enough to attract the favourable attention of the Prince Regent and Mrs Fitzherbert. When she grew older Maria almost inevitably became an actress, though never quite achieving the status of her husband Charles.

The months preceding Fanny's birth were an anxious time for all the Kemble clan. Fortunately both John Philip's and Sarah's reputations were at their height and the money to rebuild Covent Garden was raised without too much difficulty. Nevertheless the new theatre was to prove financially their undoing. In the eighteenth century theatres were designed on a more or less common plan. They were either horse-shoe or rectangular in shape, with the elite accommodated in the stage boxes, and the main part of the audience seated on the hard benches that made up the pit, while the less socially eligible occupied the first and second galleries. The construction costs of the new Covent Garden had been heavy. John Philip had large ideas and spent lavishly, hoping to recoup his outlay both by increasing the number of private boxes, which could be rented out on a yearly basis, and by putting up his prices. This policy was not unreasonable. The new house in many ways was an improvement on the old and his costs were increasing under the pressure of wartime inflation, the result of the prolonged struggle with Napoleon's France. Nevertheless he ought to have expected trouble, particularly as the new seating arrangements had been carried out at the expense of the humbler patrons in the second gallery, who bitterly described their section of the auditorium as 'a pigeon-loft'. Eighteenth-century audiences were not the well-behaved patrons of the modern theatre; they were more like unruly football supporters on the terraces to whom violence was the normal way of giving expres-sion to their emotions. When a play displeased them they did not wait for the critics to pronounce its doom but broke into a fury of shouts, jeers and catcalls, the latter a particularly vicious form of whistle. Actors and actresses whose conduct in any way happened to offend their exacting patrons needed good nerves. When for any reason the management got across their audiences the trouble became more serious. On several occasions, sufficiently frequent to build up a tradition of violence, riots of a more destructive nature broke out when considerable damage was done. Any attempt therefore to put up the prices, or in any way to invade or curtail what the more plebeian parts of the house considered to be their rights, contained the seeds of potential trouble, trouble sometimes fermented by the young-man-about-town element, who were always ready for a rag.

This potential was dramatically demonstrated when the new Covent Garden opened on 18 September with *Macbeth*, John Philip and Sarah playing the leads. Lady Macbeth was one of Mrs Siddons' most acclaimed roles but on that night the audience heard not one of her great speeches, which were drowned in a crescendo of noise and calls of 'Old Prices! Old Prices!' that in volume were equal to any modern demonstration with its refrain of 'Out! Out!' Stoically the players continued to deliver their speeches in what to the audience must have been dumb show; not a word could be heard. After six nights of chaos a committee made up of independent members was appointed to examine the theatre's books and pronounce on the justification, or otherwise, for the new prices. The report was favourable to John Philip but the public, even *The Times*, refused to be convinced and when the theatre reopened on 4 October the rioters turned out in force. Public opinion was clearly against the new prices and John Kemble's position was made worse when his box-office keeper, Henry Brandon, dragged one of the rioters, Henry Clifford, who unluckily for Brandon was a barrister, before the Bow Street magistrates. The case was dismissed. Clifford then retaliated by bringing a charge of false imprisonment against Brandon and, though Justice Mansfield summed up in the defendant's favour, the jury returned a more popular verdict and awarded the plaintiff damages of £5. John Kemble was now doubly guilty in the eyes of the public; he was both exploiting them financially and threatening their liberties. The rhymesters got busy and their doggerel illustrates the strength of the public resentment. According to one it was a case of:

> *This is the manager full of scorn,*
> *Who raised the prices to the people forlorn,*
> *And directed the thief taker shaven and shorn,*
> *To take up John Bull with his bugle horn*
> *Who kissed the Cat engaged to squeal,*
> *To the poor in the pigeon-holes over the Boxes,*
> *Let to the great who visit the house that Jack built.*

The allusion to pigeon-holes was a reference to the fact that in order to increase the number of boxes the view of the patrons in the upper gallery had been impeded, hence their fury. Another would-be poet declared:

> John Kemble would an-acting go,
> Heigh ho says Kemble;
> He raised the price, which he thought too low
> Whether his public would let him or no,
> With his roly poly, gammon and spinach,
> And ho! says manager Kemble.

The forces against him were too strong. John had to give way. On 14 December the old prices were restored, the number of boxes reduced and the unfortunate Brandon dismissed.

The 'Old Prices' riots left John Kemble permanently financially crippled. Not only had business been lost; henceforth Covent Garden's manager was in an economic straitjacket, unable to take reasonable steps to keep his prices in line with rising costs. It was in this year that Fanny was born, and the last weeks of Maria Kemble's pregnancy were overshadowed by the worry of the confrontation with its threat of unemployment and financial stringency. Three years later the Kemble management suffered another blow. Sarah, who had grown stout and heavy with the years, decided to retire. For five more years John Kemble struggled to keep the theatre solvent but in 1817 he, like other actor-managers, decided that it would be prudent to extricate his personal fortune from the financial abyss of Covent Garden and retire to the safe haven of Lausanne. Accordingly he handed over his share in the theatre to his brother Charles. Henceforth the burden and responsibility were, as Fanny declared, to hang like the sword of Damocles over her family life. It was to be a constant source of anxiety to parents and children alike.

Fanny's childhood, however, was for the most part a happy one. The Kembles were a united and affectionate family. Mrs Kemble had the gift of home-making in spite of a compulsive need to rearrange her furniture when life got too much for her. According to Fanny her family 'never knew when we might find the room a perfect chaos of disorder, with every chair, table and sofa "dancing the hayes" in horrid confusion and with the furniture playing an everlasting game of puss-in-the-corner'. Possibly as the result of the pressures of her early childhood, Maria Kemble was a woman of moods, often suffering from depression and not easy to live with. Years later a niece declared that though she was sorry for 'poor Mrs Charles' she would be 'puzzled' to think her 'a delightful woman'. Her family, however, seem in the main to have put up with her nerves and foibles, for there were compensations. She was an excellent cook. She had the 'real *bon vivant*'s preference for the savoury to the sweet' and her store-cupboard was full of potted gravies, sauces, meat jellies, game jellies, and fish jellies. Indeed Fanny declared that the outside world was inclined to consider Mrs Charles Kemble to be an extravagant housekeeper because of the excellence of her table, whereas she was an extremely capable one. Moreover she was no mere housewife. Fanny, describing her mother, wrote 'Her figure was beautiful and her face very handsome and strikingly expressive; and she talks better, with more originality and vivacity than any English woman I have ever known.' In addition she was the possessor of a 'fine and powerful voice, and a rarely accurate ear'. Some of these qualities she passed on to her daughter. Fanny inherited her mother's expressive countenance and throughout her life was to show the same originality and vivacity in her conversation, which captivated people by its brilliance and variety. Fanny also inherited Mrs Kemble's love for music, but apparently not her accurate ear. Ruefully she recorded that her mother could hardly bear to be in the room when Fanny was practising.

The other permanent member of the Kemble household was Fanny's aunt, Mrs Kemble's sister Adelaide de Camp. After an abortive love-affair when she was young she had never married and, in the best Victorian tradition of spinsters, had devoted herself to her sister's children. Aunt Dall, their childish name for her, was a complete contrast to her more excitable sister Maria; her gentle patience and complete lack of self-interest provided an element of stability which Fanny's mother could never have supplied. It was to Aunt Dall that Fanny turned for understanding and practical advice, though it was not until after her aunt's death that she came to realize how much she had owed to that sweet unselfishness. During her life, though loving her deeply, the Kemble family took her very much for granted. She was just Aunt Dall.

The emotional instability from which Mrs Charles Kemble suffered was not only expressed in periodical rearrangements of her furniture. The Kembles were perpetually moving house; a characteristic which was to reassert itself in Fanny in her later years. There were other ways in which Mrs Kemble and her elder daughter were alike. Both at heart were country women, though most of Mrs Kemble's life had of necessity been spent in cities and towns. Both were capital horsewomen and both were devoted to the noble art of angling. As a consequence of these inclinations the Kemble household seemed to be in a state of perpetual migration between town and country, Mrs Kemble seizing every opportunity to live a rural life. For instance when Mrs Siddons, after her retirement, decided to move to what was then the rural area at Westbourne Green near the Paddington canal, Charles Kemble rented a house for his family next door. It was there that Fanny's younger brother Henry was born. By that time Fanny was an engaging imp of three. Her father spoilt her and she was rapidly growing into something of a handful, with an irrepressible buoyance of spirits that made her impervious to punishment and discipline alike. Even her formidable aunt Sarah could produce no effect. According to family tradition, afterwards recalled by Fanny, when Mrs Siddons took her erring niece on her knee and concentrated the full battery of her gaze on the young defaulter, preparatory to recounting her misdeeds, the only result was an engaging 'Aunt, what wonderful eyes you have got!' Even the great Sarah gave up the unequal contest. God was apparently no more successful. When, possibly as the last resort of her defenceless family, Fanny was told to ask God to make her better, all they got was the cheerful reply that, when she did, 'He makes me worse and worse'.

By the time that Fanny was five her family decided that something would have to be done to discipline their wilful daughter. Another sister of her father's, having had no success as an actress, had married a theatrical critic and, as Mrs Twiss, had retired from the stage and started an elegant school for young ladies at Bath. Accordingly Fanny was sent to Aunt Twiss to see what absence from home and school discipline could achieve. There Fanny remained for a year without any noticeable, or at any rate recorded, improvement. When she returned her family had moved back to London to be near the theatre, and it was at Covent Garden Chambers that her sister Adelaide, the future opera singer, was born. By now, at the age of six, the problem of Fanny's more formal education had to be faced. Her parents were determined that not even the slightest moral stigma that still clung to the acting profession should touch their daughter. The Kembles' private lives were exemplary, reflecting the values and out-look of middle-class England. This was part of the clash between the public image of the player and the new God of Respectability that the Evangelical movement was imposing on society. Writing later, but looking back to her girlhood, Fanny summed up the situation in these words:

The calling of the player alone has the grotesque element of fiction with all the fantastic accompaniments of sham splendour thrust into close companionship with the sordid details of poverty; for the actor alone, the livery of labour is a Harlequin's jerkin lined with tatters, and the jester's cap and bells tied to a begging wallet. I have said artist life in England is apt to have such characters, artist life everywhere probably. But it is only in England, I think that the full bitterness of such experience is felt; for what knows the foreign artist of the inexorable element of Respectability? In England alone is the prevailing atmosphere of respectability that which artists breathe in common with all other men – respectability, that English moral climate, with its neutral tint and temperate tone, so often sneered at in these days by the new German title of Philistinism so often deserving of the bitterest scorn in some of its inexpressibly mean manifestations – respectability, the pre-eminently unattractive characteristic of British existence, but which with all its deductions made for its vulgar alloys, is in truth only the general result of the individual self respect of individual Englishemen, a wholesome, purifying, and preserving element in the homes and lives of many, where without it, the recklessness bred of insecure means and obscure position would run miserable riot . . . a power which, tyrannical as it is, and ludicrously tragical as are the sacrifices sometimes exacted by it, saves especially the artistic class of England from those worst forms of irregularity which characterize the Bohemianism of foreign literary, artistic and dramatic life.

For the actor who wished to be received in polite society, respectability was essential. So was the kind of education which would enable him to move within it.

The elder Kembles therefore were determined to see that their children received such an education as would place them in the category of the gently born. Mrs Siddons had sent her two daughters, Sally and Maria, to a finishing-school in Calais and Fanny received all her formal education in France. At the age of seven she was sent to a boarding-school kept by a Madame Faudier in Boulogne where she stayed two years. They were not very happy years. It must have been a traumatic experience to be cut off from her family and plunged into a strange world. We have only Fanny's recollections, seen through the mist of years, and no doubt embroidered with stories passed on to her by her family at some later date, by which to judge. This is true not only of her first sojourn in France but of all her early life until her meeting with Harriet St Leger in 1825. After that date Fanny's letters to her friend have preserved the fleeting mood of the moment like a fly in amber. Before then, however, Fanny, looking back, tried to recapture her own past. Checking against the recollections of one's own childhood, one realizes how selective and even inaccurate these self-portraits can sometimes be. What we know about Fanny's childhood is merely how she herself assessed it sixty years later. Of her first two years in France some impressions have filtered through. It was not a period she remembered with much pleasure. She was full of energy, ill disciplined and high spirited, and Madame Faudier's methods would fill a modern psychologist with dismay, though it must be admitted that Fanny was hard to control. After one piece of naughtiness Madame Faudier locked the child in a cellar, where poor Fanny crouched on the top step, terrified by the darkness below. Once, having been confined to an attic, she managed to clamber out on to the roof, to the surprise of passers-by and the horror of her preceptress, who feelingly described her as a young devil. Even so there were compensations. On holidays she was free to roam the sand dunes, rejoicing in the sights and scenes of the countryside around her. Throughout her life Fanny had a tough resilience that helped her to accept the inevitable and to snatch at the good things that came her way. From early childhood she was a creature of moods, exuberantly happy or plunged into the depths of misery.

When Fanny returned to England she returned to yet another new home. The Kembles had left the smells and bustle of Covent Garden for the peace of Craven Hill. It was a welcome change to be once again in a rural setting. The front windows of her new home looked across the carriageway to a row of fine elms and to a large green meadow that lay beyond. The children each had tiny gardens and spent much of their weekly pocket money on what Fanny described as 'pots of violets and flower seeds and roots of future fragrance'. All her life Fanny was passionately fond of flowers. Nevertheless, even at Craven Hill life was not always peaceful, nor Fanny a well-behaved child. Looking back she remembered one occasion when out for a walk with Aunt Dall and the younger children she was told to go home as a punishment for some childish insolence. Her first reaction was to contemplate suicide by throwing herself into a nearby pond. As she confessed, her remedies 'always had rather an extreme tendency'.

However on closer inspection of the pond, she found it 'thickly coated with green slime, studded with frogs' heads, and looked uninviting' and decided to walk to London instead, where her father had a *pied à terre* in Gerrard Street, Soho, then still a fashionable quarter. Luckily her little legs soon grew tired and she took refuge in a nearby cottage which belonged to the family's sewing-woman and where Dall was relieved to find her sleeping peacefully. For this escapade she was locked up in the garden shed on a diet of bread and water. Though less frightening than the dark cellar of earlier memory Fanny found it intensely boring but, characteristically refusing to admit defeat, she sang at the top of her voice whenever she heard approaching footsteps.

By this time Fanny was twelve and it was becoming clear that she needed firmer handling, and possibly a more regular education, than Aunt Dall or her mother could provide. It was therefore decided to send her back to France, this time to Paris. The school to which she was to go was kept by an Englishwoman, a Mrs Rowden, who had previously had a school at Hans Crescent in London. There was a link between her and the Kemble family, and in particular with John Kemble, of whom she had been a devoted admirer, which was an added advantage in her parents' eyes; Fanny was very much happier then than she had been with Madame Faudier. The routine of Mrs Rowden's establishment with its ordered life provided an interlude of discipline that Fanny's tempestuous nature needed. Mrs Rowden had fallen under the influence of the Evangelical movement and the general tone of the school was one of sober piety which had a lasting effect on her young pupil. Years later Fanny declared that the intimate knowledge of the Bible that was then forced on her was 'the greatest benefit derived from my school training'. Throughout her life Fanny's letters reveal how deep this influence was; again and again there are evangelical undertones in them. The more immediate results of her education were cultural rather than religious. She studied the great French playwrights Racine and Corneille; she learnt to read Dante in the original; and she nearly became acquainted with the poems of Byron. One of the older parlour boarders lent her a smuggled copy which Fanny hid under her pillow, meaning to read it in bed at night. When however she confided in a fellow boarder the latter was so horrified that she infected Fanny with her sense of guilt and the volume of poems was handed back unread. This feeling of shame and guilt is a measure of the immoral aura that clung round the name of Byron. It is difficult to imagine the modern teenager being as shaken by being told that a book she proposed to read was 'porn'. Later Fanny was to fall very much under the poet's spell, but she never quite got rid of her feeling that to fall for his poems was to yield to temptation as well as to experience delight.

France was not all work. During the four years she spent there Fanny did not return to England, but on several occasions she had the very great pleasure of her father's company when he was in Paris. Then, with him as her mentor, she explored the more sophisticated Paris that lay beyond the confines of the schoolroom. Together they saw the sights, went to plays and sampled Parisian food. These were red-letter days, but her other vacations, which she spent with a French family in the country, were pleasant in a less stimulating way. When after four years Fanny returned to England, outwardly at least she was very different from the hoyden she had been when she left. She spoke French fluently, had a good knowledge of Italian and she was familiar with the great literature of both countries, thereby laying the foundation for reading that was to be a major resource and interest to her throughout her life. She had gained pleasure as well as profit, in that it was at school that she first discovered the exhilaration of dancing. This may have been to some extent a trait that she had inherited from her mother but until she grew too old, as Victorian England reckoned age, to indulge in it, Fanny remained passionately fond of dancing. It was in France also that she had her first experience of acting. The occasion was a school performance of Racine's *Andromaque* in which, probably because she was a Kemble, she played the lead. But, though she scored a gratifying success, this was an isolated incident without apparent influence on her future career. Nevertheless with hindsight her performance throws an interesting light on things to come, not because her experience convinced Fanny that she had the ability to follow the family profession, but because it foreshadowed the kind of actress she was to become. Fanny acted with her heart and with her emotions; unless she could live her part she was never happy in it, could never reach the heights. It was this quality that carried her through her first schoolgirl performance. While she was on the stage she was Andromaque and, swept away herself, she swept her audience with her.

During her years in France Fanny had learnt to live with a community and to some extent to accept discipline, though as an adolescent there were still tormenting moods to be faced. She had not yet come to terms with life. At her age – she was rising sixteen when she returned to England – it could hardly be expected that she should. Nevertheless some important foundations had been laid. Returning home brought its own fears with it. During her four years of exile she had seen her father at intervals; with him there was no gap to be bridged. With her mother the situation was different. At sixteen the four years that they had been parted seemed an eternity and Fanny was seized with a sudden fear that she might no longer recognize her own mother. She got out of the coach almost with terror but at the sound of the well-known voice all misgivings left her. Fanny rushed into her mother's arms. She was home again. It was not however the same home; the family had moved yet again and were now living at Eastland Cottage, near Weybridge, Charles joining them when his work at the theatre permitted him. Both Fanny and her mother were happy there. Days slipped away with Mrs Kemble spending hours absorbed in one of her favourite occupations, fishing, while Fanny lay under a tree reading anything that had come her way. To a modern sixteen-year-old many of the books that she devoured so eagerly would seem heavy going. Her reading was not entirely desultory; to some extent it was directed by her brother's schoolmaster, Dr Malkin. He was a fine scholar and when he and his wife paid a visit to Weybridge he had a stimulating effect on Fanny. It was he who suggested that she should attempt a translation of Sismondi's standard work *Les Républiques Italiennes*: no light task for a budding teenage scholar. At this time Fanny was also passionately interested in such German authors as she could read in translation. She was also immensely excited by the poetry of Byron, no longer out of bounds; and she revelled in Carlyle's *Sartor Resartus*. Again and again one cannot but be impressed both by the serious reading that absorbed her, and by the fact that such books were so readily to hand. Both imply a standard of culture not popularly associated with the acting profession.

Fanny's time was not absorbed by the pleasures of the mind alone. She loved what she called 'long rambling walks in the wild, beautiful countryside'. Crowds terrified her; she was always something of a solitary, arguing in a letter to George Combe that to absorb any scene or place completely one must be alone. Everything in nature fascinated her; the flowers, the trees, the changing seasons, the song of the birds but above all 'the charm and seduction of bright water which had always been irresistible to me, a snare and a temptation I have never been able to resist'. Any clear, running stream acted as a magnet. In her early days at Weybridge this was a harmless compulsion that she could indulge with impunity, wading and splashing in the water to her heart's content. Later it provoked some embarrassing situations. Once walking in the Catskills with her friend Catherine Sedgwick Fanny, deep in conversation, suddenly walked into the stream that ran beside their path, and sat down in it without once interrupting the thread of her conversation. This might be an instinctive reaction to Fanny, as instinctive as that of a dog who, seeing water, must plunge into it, but Catherine Sedgwick was so convulsed with laughter that when they got to their hotel the pair of them had the greatest difficulty in keeping straight faces when telling the staff that Fanny had fallen into the water accidentally. The sea had much the same fascination for her. 'I feel strong,' she once wrote, 'as I run by the side of the waves, with something of their strength, and the same species of wild excitement which thunder and lightning produce in me, always affects me by the sea shore.' After one unhappy experience, however, Fanny preferred not to trust her person to that exhilarating element. On this occasion she had begged some Scottish fishermen to take her out in their boat on the wave-crested Firth of Forth only to implore some minutes later to be delivered from the sea-sickness that resulted. Having only crossed he Channel in a packet vessel she had not realized the hazards of a small boat on a lively sea. Henceforth she preferred to glory in its strength from the shore.

It was at Weybridge that Fanny first became infected by her mother's passion for angling. Her attitude towards the disagreeable task of baiting her hook is revealing and characteristic:

It seems to me, that to inflict such a task on anyone, because it was revolting to me, is not fair or sportsmanlike; and so I went on torturing my own bait and myself; too eagerly devoted to the sport to refrain from it, in spite of the price I condemned myself to pay for it. Moreover if I have ever had female companions on my fishing excursions, I have invariably done this service for them, thinking the process too horrid for them to endure; and have often thought if I were a man, nothing could induce me to marry a woman whom I had seen bait her own hook with anything more sensitive than paste.

Later in life Fanny always cleaned out her own bird-cages, thinking it unfair to inflict such a task on her servants. Her views on sportsmanship may have been derived from her brothers, who when they came home from school insisted, like brothers the world over, that Fanny play a humble role in their games. Having once been painfully hit on the ankle by a cricket ball, cricket was a game for which she had no liking. At pistol-shooting she competed on more equal terms; she had a steady hand and eventually became a respectable shot. Fanny was devoted to her brothers. John was two years older and Henry three years younger, Adelaide was still the baby of the family. Both the boys were boarders at the school at Bury St Edmunds of which her mentor, Dr Malkin, was the head and, once they had gone back there, Fanny resumed her programme of solid reading and her routine of solitary rambles. In the absence of any close companion with whom to share the emotions to which these gave rise Fanny tried to enshrine them by scribbling verse in what she described as bad Italian and 'most indifferent English'. All her life Fanny was to find relief for her overcharged emotions, be they of joy or sorrow, exultation or despair, by exploding into verse, good, bad, and indifferent. During these early years her desire to become an author began to shape her hopes for the future.

For a sixteen-year-old she was leading a lonely life. Adelaide at ten was too young to be the companion she was later to become, her brothers were away at school, her father spent much of his time away from home, and her mother and Aunt Dall, loved though they were, could not supply the place of a confidential friend into whose ears all the hopes and dreams, woes and despairs, inseparable from growing up, could be poured. Then in 1825 Fanny met Harriet St Leger and everything was changed. It was an instantaneous friendship, one that was to last as long as life itself, though the meetings between them were less frequent than the letters which they interchanged. From the beginning it was an uninhibited correspondence, reflecting, in a way that no mere recollection of times past could do, Fanny's fleeting moods and emotions. Henceforth her biographer is on firmer ground; Harriet kept her friend's letters and many years later returned them to her. It was these letters that provided the raw material when Fanny came to write her own *Recollections* though unfortunately for posterity she at the same time destroyed any letter that she felt was too intimate to publish. Even so enough remain, particularly those written up to the time of her marriage, to see the events of these formative years through Fanny's own eyes.

Harriet St Leger was thirty years old when Fanny first met her. She

had been a close friend of Fanny's famous uncle John Philip Kemble
and his wife, known among her friends as 'Pop'. After John Philip's
death his widow had returned to England where she settled at Heath
Farm near Cassiobury Park, through the courtesy of Lord Essex.
Harriet had kept up her friendship with her and, while Fanny was
staying with her aunt by marriage, came on a visit to Heath Farm. The
friendship that blossomed between the thirty-year-old Harriet and
the sixteen-year-old Fanny was one of those unexplained unions of
heart and mind that sometimes occur for no apparent reason. All day
long they walked together through the beautiful springtide country,
talking, talking, talking. Half the night they sat up as if the day had not
been long enough; there still seemed so much to say. Harriet had an
exciting mind. Many years later Fanny described it as being 'of a very
uncommon order; she delighted in metaphysical subjects of the greatest
difficulty and abstract subjects of the most laborious solutions'. Fanny,
her head stuffed with German authors, found her new friend one of the
most exciting people she had ever known, while to Harriet Fanny's
own receptivity and sensitivity must have made her the most congenial
of listeners. Yet there must have been more to their friendship than
mental sympathy. A confidence maintained over forty years, in spite
of long absences, and dependent largely on the letters which they wrote
to one another, testifies to some interlocking of the spirit. Each had
much to give the other, though as Harriet's letters have not survived
her contribution to their friendship remains obscure. Fanny's description of her is a characteristic blend of hero-worship and amusement;
however deeply she loved she always had an eye for the comic and
absurd. Harriet, she wrote, was:

tall and thin, her figure wanted roundness and grace, but it was straight as a
dart, and the vigorous, elastic, active movements of her limbs, and the firm,
fleet, springing step of her beautifully made feet and ankles, gave to her whole
person and deportment a character like that of the fabled Atalanta, or the huntress
goddess Diana herself, Her forehead and eyes were beautiful. The broad white
pure expanse surrounded with thick, short, clustering curls of chestnut hair, and
the clear, limpid, bright, tender grey eyes ... were the eyes and forehead of
Aurora.

One can understand the enormous impression that Harriet made on
lonely Fanny at their first meeting. Harriet was not only striking in
appearance; she was clearly an eccentric. She affected a mannish,
austere style of dress, always wearing black or grey with skirts that

were noticeably short. Her footwear reduced Fanny, who said that her friend always wore boots 'made by a man's boot maker, and where there was only one place in London where they could be made sufficiently ugly to suit her', to comical despair. Under pressure she even had to admit that apart from such eccentricities Harriet was not quite perfect. Her valued friend George Combe having made some criticism of her, Fanny was forced to concede that 'She is my very dearest friend but there is much in her that I see with sorrow and anxiety as well as much, very much that I love and admire and respect.' This was written later, in 1834, but when they first met during that magical spring at Cassiobury these flaws, whatever they were, had not yet become apparent and for Harriet's oddities Fanny had nothing but affectionate amusement.

Those of her aunt 'Pop' Kemble were another source of amusement. The other permanent member of the household at Heath Farm was Fanny's aunt Elizabeth Whitelock, who also had returned to England as a widow at the end of her acting career in the United States. These two ladies had entertained the idea that they might set up house together and for this they were totally unsuited both in outlook and in background. According to her niece, Mrs John Kemble 'had lived in the best London society with which she kept up an intercourse by zealous correspondence; the names of lords and ladies were familiar in her mouth as household words, and she had undoubtedly an undue respect for respectability and reverence for titled folk'. Her sister-in-law was completely different. Fanny described her as simple hearted and simple minded. She had never mixed in English society. Her manners were odd – Fanny called them grotesque – she wore old-fashioned clothes, including a white flounced apron and a towering cap. For Mrs Kemble she was a continual social embarrassment. When the latter looked out of her window and saw a coroneted carriage approaching whose aristocratic occupants were undoubtedly about to pay her a call, the poor woman was torn both ways. Should she receive her visitors and face the social humiliation of having to introduce her peculiar sister-in-law, or deny herself the pleasure of the polite society that was meat and drink to her? Generally her apprehension won and breathlessly she would rush down to tell her maid to say 'not at home'. The strain soon proved too much and the two old ladies went their separate ways. Mrs Kemble chose Leamington and polite society, Mrs Whitelock a cottage near Addlestone in Surrey, where she lived in great content.

After her death she left it to Fanny's mother, who in her turn died there.

It was while the family were at Weybridge that Fanny's relationship with her brother John began to deepen as they matured. No longer was she merely regarded as a useful 'long stop' or 'short stop' – she was never quite sure which. She could now provide him with a sympathetic audience when he came home in vacations from Trinity College, Cambridge, where he had won an Exhibition in 1826. Distinction in education always meant a great deal to the Kembles, perhaps because it set them a little apart from the rest of their profession, and when the news of his success reached Weybridge Fanny told Harriet that 'We all, with my father at our head, looked more like hopeful candidates for Bedlam than anything else. My poor father jumped and clapped his hands, and kissed the letter like a child.' John Mitchell Kemble, to give him his full name, as a young man was, like Fanny, given enthusiasms for which Britain in 1826 gave much scope. Since the loss of the American colonies, almost unbelievable progress had taken place in the world of industry, while in the world of politics and constitutional reform stagnation still prevailed. But by 1826 men of business, industrialists and workers alike, were no longer content to see the affairs of the nation entrusted to the chosen few. When in 1827 Lord Liverpool, the Tory prime minister, died, his death seemed to bring the hope of change one step nearer. The cry for a wider representation in the House of Commons was increasing in volume year by year, mounting to the crescendo that led to the great Reform Act of 1832. In intellectual circles new ideas as to the way in which society should be run were fermenting and when John came down for the Christmas vacation, according to Fanny he could talk of nothing but politics with a 'passionate eagerness' which she described as 'a sort of a frenzy', telling Harriet, 'He is neither Whig nor Tory but a radical, a utilitarian, a worshipper of Mill, an advocate for vote by ballot, an opponent of hereditary aristocracy, the Church establishment, the army and navy, which he deems sources of unnecessary national expenditure.' The more things alter the more they remain the same; it is not only the modern students who attack the 'establishment' and long to put to rights the world by sweeping away the old and so creating a more just society. Fanny had her doubts as to the feasibility of her brother's sweeping programme of abolitions, asking 'who is to take care of our souls and bodies, if the three last named institutions are done away with,

I do not quite see?' In spite of John's eloquence Fanny remained un-converted and unconvinced. Five years later in a letter to George Combe she confessed, 'I am an anti-reformer of the deepest dye. I am a supersititious person and cling to all ancient worship, among which I hold a hereditary aristocracy which I think the present reforming and levelling spirit will soon overthrow. My reason may possibly be reformist but I am very sure my ideality is not.' If she could not agree with her brother's views neither did she think his devotion to them likely to forward his academic career. In her eyes to spend morning, noon and night writing volumes against the establishment was not the best way to obtain a degree. In this she was to prove a true prophet. When John Kemble presented himself for examination in 1829 he failed to persuade the examiners that his knowledge of Paley and Locke, with whose views he violently disagreed, was sufficiently sound. The University therefore decided to defer his degree until he could satisfy them on this point. His failure to graduate was a cause of deep distress to his parents, already sufficiently depressed by the financial tangle of Covent Garden's finances and the long-drawn-out law case in which it had involved them. They found it difficult to understand the pressures to which their son had been subjected during the last three years. At Cambridge he had been one of a brilliant circle of young men who in later life were, to some extent, to achieve national fame. Included among them was John Romilly, the son of the reformer Sir Samuel Romilly and himself to become Master of the Rolls; Frederick Maurice, whose name will always be linked with the Christian Socialist movement; the future novelist William Makepeace Thackeray; the poet Edward FitzGerald, who was to remain a lifelong friend of Fanny's; and the future Poet Laureate Alfred Tennyson. John's own mind was in a ferment. In a sonnet Tennyson described him as one who was 'spurr'd at heart with fieriest energy', and his early life was one of uncertainties and false starts. When he left Cambridge for Germany he had intended to study German philosophy and religion, apparently with the intention of eventually taking holy orders. In the same sonnet Tennyson declared

> *My hope and heart is with thee – thou wilt be*
> *A latter Luther and a soldier priest*
> *To scare church-harpies from the master's feast;*
> *Our dusted velvets have much need of thee.*

and ended with the lines

> *Thou from a throne*
> *Mounted in heaven wilt shoot into the dark*
> *Arrows of lightening I will stand and mark.*

The sonnet is interesting in that it reveals the feelings which his fellow students entertained about John Kemble at this time. Here was no young man content to take as certainties Paley's *Evidences of Christianity* or Locke's constitutional theories. He returned from Germany more interested in Teutonic philology than in German religious thought and, with a switch of interest, determined to fight as a volunteer for liberal principles in Spain, to the great anxiety of his family. Luckily the struggle was over before John managed to reach the scene of operations, to the very great relief of Fanny. Eventually, having completed his degree in 1830, he returned to academic life and became a recognized authority on Anglo-Saxon and, while he never made much money, did achieve a considerable reputation in his own field.

Fanny could sympathize with her brother's difficulties because she too was struggling to see some pattern in the years that lay ahead. Her future seemed appallingly shapeless, and her parents were very little help in that their attitude was negative rather than constructive. They did not want her to go on the stage; what they did hope for her was less clear. Fanny herself had no wish to be an actress. Her own aspirations were literary but, apart from a propensity to scribble verse, her abilities in this direction were an unknown quantity. She was still emotionally very immature, a bundle of vague ambitions, moods and romantic dreamings. She had been very little exposed to the outside world and had led a sheltered life both at school and as a member of a closely knit family. Her deepest affections were still bestowed on it and on Harriet. Sexually she was still unawakened. Her sentimental devotion for the German composer Weber, whose opera *Der Freischütz* was the rage of London, was that of a schoolgirl. Ugly though he was, Fanny wore an engraving of him contained in a small black silk case round her neck. The emotional outlet that she needed she found increasingly in her writing. French history fascinated her and her original plan was to write a novel set at the court of Francis I but, surrounded as she was by people whose lives lay in the theatre, it is not surprising that she turned to playwriting instead. Optimistically she hoped to kill two birds with one stone by doing so. A successful play might both further her own literary ambitions and also do something to help the family financially. Her father spoke of a possible fee of £200 if it were performed. Certainly Charles Kemble needed all the help of this kind that he could get. He had found the situation at Covent Garden, where, as well as being responsible for his own stake in the company, he was now manager, increasingly difficult. Faced with a mounting burden of debt he had refused to pay his leading actors and actresses the increased salaries which they were demanding and as a result lost such players as Kitty Stephens, Young and Liston to Drury Lane. Then difficulties occurred with Macready and he too left Covent Garden. By 1827 the situation was looking very black.

Fanny set to work with tremendous enthusiasm. She told Harriet that the project was not 'one of the soap bubbles which I am so fond of blowing, admiring and forgetting'. The first three acts were quickly written, the fourth more slowly, but the young authoress had difficulty with the fifth act, which the convention of the day required. Finally, in a mood of grim determination, writing furiously between six in the evening and eleven-thirty at night, Fanny finished her play. Next she had to brace herself for the ordeal of reading it to her parents, who, to her enormous joy, thought well of it. In the first flush of her achievement Fanny confessed to her friend that she was 'puffed up and elated in spirit'. Who, having written their first play or novel, would not feel the same glow of excitement? Her father suggested the possibility of its being produced at Covent Garden but Fanny favoured its being published by a bookseller, then the recognized channel through which authors hoped to place their work. Fanny's preference, somewhat surprising to the modern reader, was very much in line with current thinking in literary circles, Byron being one of its exponents. The popular theatre with its demand for mysteries and melodramas offered little scope to the serious dramatist. Byron's own plays *Manfred* and *Cain* he declared were not intended for dramatic presentation. His proclaimed aim was to create a 'mental theatre' and he told his publisher, John Murray, that his historical dramas were intended not to be acted but to be read. It was as an authoress rather than as a dramatist that Fanny hoped to make her reputation, and she feared that the mangling necessary for the stage might destroy whatever literary value her *Francis I* might possess, though, as she confessed to Harriet, it would have given her much happiness to see her father in the leading part wearing the costume that he had just brought back from Paris.

Fanny's mood of self-satisfaction did not last long; the inevitable reaction followed. Nothing that she did pleased her. She had finished her play on 5 October 1827 and by the January of 1828 she was in the grip of an attack of 'blue devils' and as a result had thrown 'between seven and eight hundred pages (about a year's work) into the fire', which, she told Harriet ruefully later, 'now seems to me rather deplorable. You will perhaps say that the fire is no bad place for some seven or eight hundred pages of my manuscripts, but I had spent time and pains on them, and I think they should not have been thrown away in a fit of despondency.' Fanny was going through a bad patch. She complained of headaches and a pain in her side, ailments that may well have been psychosomatic as she was also suffering from sharply alternating moods, at one moment in a state of feverish excitement and the next low-spirited and nervous. Looking back with the wisdom of old age she described her general condition in the March of 1828 as 'difficult and troublesome and unsatisfactory to myself and others. My mind and character were in a chaotic state of fermentation that required the wisest, firmest, gentlest guidance. I was vehement, and excitable, violently impulsive and with a wild, ill-regulated imagination.' The tension in the family, while waiting for the result of an appeal against the unfavourable judgement given against Charles Kemble in the Covent Garden litigation in the previous April, made Fanny's moods more difficult to endure. Her general restlessness may well have been augmented by the fact that financial stringency had forced the Kembles to give up their cottage at Weybridge. Because they could no longer afford to keep their younger son Henry at Bury St Edmunds they had moved back to London in the autumn of 1827 so that he could go to Westminster as a day boy, and were now living in Buckingham Gate. This meant that Fanny could no longer get rid of her energy and pent-up feelings by taking her long, solitary rambles. Because her restlessness was making her a misery to herself and her family it was decided to see what a change of scene would do; she was sent to Edinburgh to stay with her cousin by marriage, Mrs Henry Siddons.

Mrs Henry Siddons was the widow of Sarah Siddons' youngest son. Unlike the rest of her children he had maintained the family tradition by going on the stage. Unfortunately he had not inherited his mother's talent and, having little success as an actor, he had gone into management in Edinburgh. There he married a Scottish woman, Hannah Murray, the sister of the actor William Murray who, in Fanny's later judgement, was one of the best actors that she had ever seen. Mrs Henry herself was very much the star of the local theatrical firmament. Edinburgh was proud of her, calling her 'our Mrs Siddons' to distinguish her from her more famous mother-in-law. When her husband died, leaving her with four children to support, she assumed the management of the old Edinburgh theatre as joint proprietor with her brother William Murray. They were a very successful team. Fanny, critical even of those she loved, never considered her cousin a great actress. In her opinion Mrs Henry's most successful parts were those in which she was called upon to portray her own natural qualities of grace, beauty and sheer goodness. It was for these qualities that Fanny came to love her cousin most dearly. Mrs Henry Siddons lived in an aura of tranquillity, very soothing to Fanny's taut nerves. Mrs Kemble was often irritable with her daughter, criticizing her habit of shutting herself away in her room scribbling instead of making an effort to be sociable downstairs. Fanny's reaction was characteristic. After one such rebuke she retreated to her room and there, as she told Harriet, she sat 'looking at the moon and thinking of my social duties and then scribbled endless doggerel in a highly Byronic mood', after which she confessed to going to bed and sleeping soundly. She was never easy to discipline. Too immature as yet to take charge of her own destiny, nevertheless Fanny resented parental, or perhaps it would be more accurate to say maternal, interference. Mrs Siddons had that rarest of all qualities, the knack of 'all but imperceptible control'. It was her personality, not the advice she gave, that had such a profound effect on her young guest, who repaid her with the romantic hero-worship of the adolescent. Each night Fanny would pick a sprig of myrtle from the garden and hand it to her divinity who tucked it into her sash during dinner, returning it to the donor before she retired for the night. To Fanny such relics were too precious to be thrown away; each night the little sprig was placed in a special drawer in her bedroom. When that threatened to overflow Fanny used to light a sacrificial fire and burn her cherished mementoes. This nightly routine, all but absurd in its dramatic, romantic devotion, meant a great deal to Fanny at the time, though looking back as an old lady it seemed to her what indeed it was, the act of someone still emotionally immature and very, very young.

Mrs Henry Siddons and Edinburgh between them provided exactly he background that Fanny needed. Her visit was intended to last two or three months; she stayed a year. It was one of the most important and perhaps happiest years of her life. Writing from Manchester two years later, when her theatrical triumph had changed the whole pattern of her life, she declared 'I truly believe that much happiness is yet in store for me in this world; but a period of such utter repose and yet real enjoyment will never I think fall in my way again.' In Edinburgh Fanny was able to enjoy a new kind of freedom. At Weybridge she had always been free to wander at will but in London, the only city she knew, convention dictated that young ladies did not go out unaccompanied. Edinburgh imposed no such restraints. Often in the early morning she would climb Carlton Hill, revelling in having it to herself. Sometimes she went as far afield as Newhaven, chatting to the fisherfolk. With one woman, whom she once described as her 'yellow-petticoated fishwife', she struck up a friendship that was to last for years. Whenever she returned to Edinburgh Fanny tried to see her and sometimes sent her money to help with her brood of children – she was never quite sure whether there were twelve or thirteen. It was with the fishermen of Newhaven that Fanny had her first experience of what it felt like to be tossed on the lively waters of the Forth in a small rowing-boat.

Fanny was grateful for this lack of restraint. Looking back over the years and remembering the freedom of her Edinburgh days, she commented that 'more harm is frequently done by over culture than by under culture in the training of youth. Judicious letting alone is a precious element in the training of youth, and there are certain chords which often touched and made to vibrate too early, are apt to lose instead of gain power.' In this atmosphere of trust and affection Fanny began to mature. Hitherto religion seems to have made little impact on her. It was not that the Kemble household was irreligious; indeed by any but nineteenth-century middle-class standards the reverse was the case. In the matter of religious observance the Kembles did what any 'average English Protestants of decent respectability' did. The children were brought up on the improving literature of Mrs Trimmer and Mrs Barbauld. Mrs Kemble read the Bible to them before breakfast, they learnt their catechism and the Collects, they went to church on Sundays. The youngest member of the family always said grace before meals. When Charles Kemble was home before they went to bed, the children knelt round his chair to hear him say 'God bless you, make you good, happy and wise.' Nevertheless, as Fanny came to realize, such observances were more a tribute to the God of Respectability, so devoutedly worshipped by the Kembles, than an outpouring of the spirit. In this sense they did, as she described them, no more than was expected of English Protestants of decent respectability. The attitude of the Edinburgh household was different. Mrs Siddons did not so much preach Christianity, she practised it with grace and gentleness, and by her conduct turned Fanny's thoughts increasingly towards religion.

Influenced by this deepening religious awareness, Fanny struggled to control her over-active romantic imagination by denying it one source on which it fed. She determined to conquer her addiction to Byron. Once free of the restraints of school she had read both his peoms and his plays avidly, though even then some slight sense of forbidden fruit, born of Byron's reputation, had led her to a moral compromise. Fanny read Byron one day and the devotional works of Jeremy Taylor the next, a typical example of the mass of contradictions that character-ized her. But during her time in Edinburgh this compromise no longer satisfied her awakening religious conscience. *Cain* and *Manfred* in particular aroused in her emotions which she felt were morally wrong. As she wrote, 'the noble poet's glorious chanting of much inglorious matter did me no good'. Accordingly she decided to renounce the disturbing pleasure that he gave her. It was a hard fight. For two years the desire to read and reread Byron persisted. When four years later she read the biography of her erstwhile enchanter during her first voyage to the United States her reactions were very different. She found him 'too much of an egotist. I think I never read anything pro-fessing to be a person's undisguised feelings and opinions, with so much heartlessness – so little goodness in it.'

Edinburgh had provided Fanny in the interim with more solid food for her mind. In the early decades of the nineteenth century some of the most outstanding thinkers and writers of the day came from Glasgow and Edinburgh, including John Mill, whose radical thought had so fascinated young John Kemble at Cambridge, and Sir Walter Scott, the great novelist. In Edinburgh in the dramatic, literary and artistic groups the Siddonses had many friends of merit and distinction with whom Fanny came into contact. Among these were the two brothers Andrew and George Combe, who became valued and lifelong friends. Both brothers were men of distinction who achieved national and even international recognition. George, the elder, was forty when Fanny first met him, and Andrew thirty-one, the former still practising law, the latter medicine. George had already shown an interest in the subject for which he is best known, phrenology, on which he had already contributed a couple of books, but it was his *On the Constitution of Man*, published in the year that Fanny came to Edinburgh, that laid the foundation of his reputation. Andrew was less well known. It was not until 1836 that he was appointed physician to Queen Victoria's uncle, the King of the Belgians; later when the breakdown of his own health necessitated his return to Britain he became one of her own physicians. Sometimes Fanny drove with him on his rounds and her parents apparently became somewhat perturbed by the friendship that developed between them, and indeed had he not been a man of delicate health, he may have entertained some matrimonial ideas. In a letter written to Fanny while she was in America George hinted as much, to which she made the laughing reply that, 'I certainly never suspected him of having any matrimonial designs, or any intention of becoming himself an inmate of Bedlam which such a plan carried into effect could not I think have failed of rendering him.' Andrew was no dancer and Fanny did apparently make a pact with him that he would be her dancing partner sixty years hence. By that time he was dead; his death occurred in 1847 but until then Fanny in her letters to George, who married her cousin Cecilia, Mrs Sarah Siddons' daughter, in 1833, continued to make the most affectionate inquiries about 'the dear doctor'. On one thing all who knew him were agreed, and that was the strength, goodness and sweetness of his nature.

The Combes' house – they were both bachelors when Fanny first knew them – was the centre of a group of brilliant men, including Duncan McLaren, the editor of *The Scotsman*, and the sculptor Lawrence Macdonald. It is a tribute both to Fanny's charm and to her intelligence that she was privileged to spend so many evenings with 'these grave men', as she called them. None of them would have willingly borne with the presence of some empty-headed teenager, however charming. Fanny, remembering with affectionate nostalgia the hours she had spent in their company, declared 'it was undoubtedly a great advantage to an intelligent girl of any age to hear such vigorous manly clear expositions of the broadest aspects of all the great political and governmental questions of the age'. For too long Fanny had read at random almost every type of book that had come her way and had fed her more than vivid imagination on the disturbing Byron. Now, at a vital stage in her intellectual development, she had come within the orbit of disciplined first-class minds and the benefit to her was incalculable. It left her with a permanent desire to cultivate her own mind and when the pressure of her theatrical life prevented this she grieved.

There was a lighter side to Fanny's life in Edinburgh. She went regularly to the theatre where Mrs Henry Siddons was acting and once later, in a letter written to George Combe when she was on tour in Manchester, sent him an interesting comparison between her own conception of Juliet and her cousin's. Fanny loved music and became enthusiastic about Scottish ballads. 'The dew of heaven on the mountain,' she felt, 'is not more limpid than their diction, nor the heart's blood of the lover more fervent than the throbbing intensity of their passion', a description that is as revealing of Fanny herself as of the ballads that had enthralled her. Yet moved though she was when she heard them sung with 'a clear, high, sweet, passionless soprano, like the voice of a spirit' one evening at a friend's house, her sense of the ridiculous contrast between the song and the singer, whom she described as having 'a dull brick coloured long, thin face and dull pale green eyes like boiled gooseberries', could not be stifled. The year in Edinburgh passed all too quickly. In her letters written to George Combe from America she constantly recalled those happy days, telling him 'Edinburgh and the happy time I lived there is shrined in my head and visited in constant pilgrimage by grateful recollections and pleasant happy thoughts.' The Edinburgh that she remembered so affectionately was the old, grey city of history, still wedded to the leisurely ways of the past. The New Town with its elegant wide streets and crescents was still being built and no one could dream of a railway chugging parallel to Princes Street. In the course of her life she was to see many changes in the place where she had been so happy; they were changes she regretted. Because of her year there when Fanny returned to London she had gained a new tranquillity and a new stability. It was a year in which she grew more able to face the challenge that lay ahead. Her girlhood and her youth were nearly over. Full of trivia as in the telling of them they seem to be they are not unimportant even though in them so little seemed to happen. The girl who baited her own hooks, who renounced Byron, who found her greatest pleasures in the beauty of the countryside, in reading and in the companionship of men who typified 'the Scottish Enlightenment', the 'grave men' of Northumberland Street, and whose greatest ambition was to win a literary reputation for herself within two years, was to be lionized by London society as the newly risen star of the London stage.

TWO

♣

A Star is Born

Fanny returned to a gloomy home. Her father's financial troubles were approaching a climax and her brother John's future was causing serious concern, since he failed to take his degree. In 1829 everything seemed uncertain. John's parents, who had built their hopes on their son's academic success, were disappointed and distressed by what seemed to them his failure. Fanny found herself pulled in two directions. She sympathized with her parents' disappointment; she admired her brother, believing him to be doing what to him seemed right. Nor was there any comfort to be found in the situation at Covent Garden. So desperate had its financial position become that a writ on behalf of the parish of St Paul's for £896 for the non-payment of rates, and another for £600 owing to the collectors of revenue, were taken out against the theatre. This disaster played a major part in shaping Fanny's future. To understand why this should be it is necessary to turn away from Fanny herself and to examine first the state of the English stage and secondly the special relationship between the Kemble family and Covent Garden.

To do this one must go back to the time of Sir Robert Walpole. As the King's leading minister he was hated and lampooned by some of the most brilliant wits and writers of the time. The stage in particular was a favourite medium for such attacks. In 1737 Walpole hit back, steering with his customary skill a bill through Parliament which enacted that no plays could be performed except on premises licensed for this purpose by the Lord Chamberlain. In addition new plays had also to be licensed by him. This act governed the public performance for money of all plays in England until it was repealed in 1968. The result was to put the theatre in a straitjacket of government censorship. At the beginning of the nineteenth century there were only three licensed theatres in London, the King's Theatre in the Haymarket, which was largely given over to opera, and two houses devoted to drama, Drury Lane and Covent Garden, though the little theatre in the Haymarket was licensed for summer productions when the two main theatres were closed. Outside London there were a handful of licensed theatres, such as the Theatre Royal at Bath, in the provinces. In practice these restrictions could be, and were, circumvented. As concerts did not require a licence the main device was to charge for a concert and, between the two parts, present a play which the programme described as free. By employing such expedients companies of strolling players, such as Roger Kemble's troupe, had been enabled to continue their precarious existence. In London similar devices were used when new places of entertainment, which in response to local demand had been built in the less fashionable parts of London, began to put on plays. So long as these did not seem a serious menace to the established theatres these were usually left alone but were always in danger of facing a prosecution if they began to tempt audiences away from Drury Lane and Covent Garden. The result of the 1737 act had in essence, as far as London was concerned, been to confer a privileged position on these two theatres. This inevitably sharpened the rivalry between them; each struggled to employ the most popular players and thereby attract the larger audience.

Though licensed by the Lord Chamberlain, and thereby enjoying all the security and prestige of a shared monopoly, both theatres were privately owned, financed and managed. Had the Kembles been content to remain players, financial ruin would not have been threatening Charles Kemble in 1829, but from 1802 his brother John Philip had involved himself increasingly in the complicated arrangements by which Covent Garden was financed and managed. No one man could command sufficient funds to do this alone; the necessary resources were provided by a group of proprietors. At the beginning of the century the largest proprietor was a Mr Thomas Harris, who owned about half the investment of some £138,000 at which the theatre was valued. Of the remaining proprietors the stage manager, a Mr Lewis, owned a sixth which John Kemble bought for £23,000. When the theatre was rebuilt after the fire, he contributed another £80,000. Had the 'Old Prices' riots not been successful the investment might have proved a sound one, but the result of not being able to raise prices or extend the profitable box accommodation left the theatre with permanently crippled finances. When on his death Thomas Harris was succeeded by his son Henry, difficulties were increased by clashing personalities. There was as yet no limited liability act and, faced with the possibility that his private fortune might become liable for the debts of the theatre, John Kemble, to borrow a phrase from the world of politics, handed 'the poisoned chalice' to his brother Charles, retiring to the haven of Lausanne. There he died in 1823. Charles, who seems to have had more enthusiasm and optimism than prudence, cheerfully accepted the apparently magnificent gift and threw himself into the negotiations, which he hoped would give him practical control of the theatre. Unfortunately he made a bad bargain with Henry Harris, taking on contractual obligations which later were to prove financially impossible. When he, and the group of proprietors who were acting with him, tried to repudiate them Harris took legal action. In addition there were other legal complications concerned with the settlement of old theatre debts, and from 1824 Charles found himself involved in a long-drawn-out legal battle, with the fortunes swinging first one way and then the other.

Charles Kemble has frequently been criticized for the financial difficulties which dogged him and Covent Garden but the London theatre as a whole was going through a difficult time. Tastes were changing and the old recipes for success were no longer working. The English stage had always been closely associated with the patronage of the court, which had been responsible for much of its earlier development. Theatres had been small because the people from whom audiences had been mainly drawn were limited in number. In London certainly there had always been some popular element, Shakespeare's groundlings, but the main financial support had come from the aristocracy and the gentry. It was they who in the eighteenth century had occupied the boxes and the pit. The unfashionable had been relegated to the first and second circles, as readers of *Evelina* will remember. For the same reason in the heat and stench of the summer, when Parliament was not sitting, both Drury Lane and Covent Garden were closed. Even theatre hours of opening were fixed to suit the convenience of their fashionable patrons. Performances started at six, a time too early for the average citizen. At eight-thirty people were admitted at half price. To attract this class of patron it became customary to put on a farce, or some sort of 'afterpiece' at the conclusion of the main drama. The result was inordinately long theatrical performances. By the turn of the century the type of audience was changing, a change associated with the growing commercial and industrial wealth of England. There were far more of the middling sort with money to spend on amusements. Originally they had been content with such places as Astley's Amphitheatre near the Surrey side of Westminster Bridge, or the theatre that had grown out of the pleasure gardens at Sadler's Wells. Such places provided a varied bill made up of stunts, spectacles and music, more reminiscent of the circus and the fair with their monstrosities than of the legitimate stage. Now their patrons began to frequent the royal theatres, reinforcing the smaller numbers of those citizens who, even in the seventeenth and eighteenth centuries, had patronized the legitimate theatre. Unfortunately for the older conventions these newer patrons brought their cruder taste with them.

The position of the Kemble management had already become precarious when the writs were pinned up on the theatre doors. They were merely one step further along the road to bankruptcy. As Covent Garden was already closed for the summer and Charles Kemble touring in Ireland, it was his wife and daughter who took the first shock. Fanny's immediate reaction was to suggest that she should cease to be a burden on the family resources. She wrote to her father asking his permission to look for a post as a governess, then one of the very few respectable employments open to a woman of some education. Her qualifications, which included a fluent knowledge of French, some Italian, English literature and considerable musical ability, were excellent. However her independence of mind, embattled sense of justice and an approach to people that was direct rather than pliant would have fitted her much less well for that submissive role. Mrs Kemble had other ideas. She did not veto the proposal to Fanny but wrote privately to her husband asking him to defer any decision until his return home. Fanny was a Kemble, her mother too had been an actress; there was at that moment a great dearth of new young leading ladies. It seemed that it might be possible to take advantage of this situation. Though neither Mrs Kemble nor Charles had welcomed the idea of Fanny's following their example, she must have been aware of her daughter's potential. Moreover the Kemble name still had a magic; the publicity that would surround the debut of the next generation of Kembles might bring back the dwindling audiences to Covent

Garden. Almost inevitably Fanny herself had earlier speculated on the possibility of adopting the family profession. Before she had gone to Edinburgh Fanny had heard her father giving it as his opinion that there was 'a fine fortune to be made by any young woman of even decent talent' and this was not without its attraction. Her own ambition, then and always, was to be a writer; the stage merely represented a means of earning her bread and butter while giving her enough leisure in which to pursue a literary career. The stage as such held no glamour for her. As she wrote to Harriet, 'I have no fear of looking only on the bright side of the picture, ours is a house where that is very seldom seen.' Nevertheless she was shrewd enough to realize that if she did go on the stage she would have definite advantages. As in the same letter she pointed out to Harriet, 'No girl intending herself for this profession can have had better opportunities for acquiring just notions on the subject of acting. I have constantly heard refined and thoughtful criticisms on our greatest dramatic works and on every rendering of them on the stage,' adding that lately she had been frequently going to see plays. Fanny had another advantage of which she was equally conscious. Young unknown actresses, however talented, were often forced to achieve stardom by dubious moral means. That could not happen to a daughter of a Kemble. Indeed, so anxious were her parents to shield her from any possible moral contamination that when she did become Covent Garden's leading lady she was never allowed to mix with the rest of the company in the Green Room.

When on that occasion Fanny had discussed the subject with her father he had not been enthusiastic. The most he would concede was that 'should our miserably uncertain circumstances finally settle unfavourably, the theatre might be an honourable and advantageous resource for me, but that at present he should be sorry to see me adopt that career'. Now circumstances were forcing him to change his mind. By this time, the August of 1829, any lingering inclination on Fanny's own part to become an actress had vanished but it did not occur to her to question her parents' decision. The question still remained, however, whether Fanny had the necessary requisites for success. Good looks are a useful asset for any actress; her contemporaries disagreed as to Fanny's. In the many portraits subsequently painted of her she could pass for a beautiful woman. She had lovely, dark hair, good teeth, and fine eyes. She also had something still more important; an expressive face that changed with every changing mood. At one moment she seemed the epitome of plainness, the next almost beautiful. In addition her voice had a quality that both in private life and in the theatre was one of her greatest assets. Unfortunately her complexion was bad. It had not always been so. In the early nineteenth century, in spite of Jenner and his method of vaccination, smallpox was still a menace. To some extent this was due to the fact that it had not yet been fully realized that immunization did not last for ever. The Kembles had been sufficiently progressive to have their children vaccinated but when, the period of immunity having expired, young Adelaide had a mild attack, Mrs Kemble lost her faith in Jenner. Fanny was away at the time and need never have come in contact with her sister had not her mother deliberately sent for her to come home. Her thinking was like that of many a modern mother who believes it prudent to subject her daughter to German measles while she is still young enough to obtain immunity before marriage. Mrs Kemble argued that as Adelaide's attack was mild Fanny's would be equally so, and that she would then be safe from further attacks. Unfortunately these calculations went wrong. Fanny developed a virulent form of the disease. Her face was not pitted but the smallpox left her with a thickened, muddy skin and coarsened her features. Fanny tried to be philosophical about this but it is clear that throughout her life she was sensitive about her appearance, affecting an indifference that she did not feel.

Fanny's figure was on the short side and she was inclined to be stocky. In later life she put on weight and was definitely stout, but as a young woman she managed to give an impression of slimness that was somewhat misleading, as one young admirer discovered. When gallantly lifting her down from a small height, he exclaimed in surprise, 'Oh, you solid little lady!' If her figure was unimpressive it was redeemed by her excellent carriage. It had not always been so. By her own confession, when she first returned from Paris she stooped, 'slouched, and poked, stood with one hip up and one shoulder down, and exhibited an altogether disgracefully ungraceful carriage'. Her parents were appalled; they were both noted for the elegance of their deportment. At first they resorted to the usual remedies, in this case a formidable contraption of steel and leather, resembling some medieval instrument of torture, which they made Fanny wear. The results of this discomfort were imperceptible and to Fanny's infinite relief she was turned over to an enterprising sergeant of the Horse Guards who employed the more modern techniques of drill and exercises. So successful was he that Fanny emerged with 'a flat back, well placed shoulders, an erect head, upright carriage, and resolute step'. Her grati-fied instructor declared her 'fit to march before the Duke of York'. This was an asset that never left her until she became old and frail. Physically therefore her appearance could be described as adequate, though her mother informed her, with her usual critical honesty, that nobody could say she had become an actress because of her looks. Possibly the remark rankled; as an old lady of over seventy Fanny made some caustic remarks about the influence of the shape of Lily Langtry's nose on her career on the stage. More important than her looks was the question of whether Fanny had that 'decent talent' with-out which even the name of Kemble could not hope to bring success. Mrs Kemble, whom her daughter always declared to have been one of the finest critics of acting that she had ever known, set Fanny to study the part of Portia. This was one of Shakespeare's heroines with whom Fanny felt herself to be most in sympathy, she was 'so generous, affectionate, wise, so arch and so full of fun, and such a true lady', indeed the prototype of what Fanny would herself like to be. Neverthe-less Portia made her appeal to Fanny's head, not her heart; she was never to become one of her more famous roles.

As Fanny came to realize later, to play comedy needed more skill and experience than the portrayal of rip-roaring emotion; Portia was too well balanced a character for the inexperienced Fanny to tackle. With more success her mother then told her to study Juliet, a part in which Fanny's inexperience mattered less. This time Mrs Kemble approved of her daughter's reading, murmuring 'Very well – very nice, my dear.' To modern ears this hardly sounds like excessive maternal praise, but in spite of her mother's low-key reaction, Fanny, her ordeal over, fled out of the room and sat weeping on the stairs with what she later described as 'repressed nervous fears'. In choosing Juliet as a test of her daughter's potential as an actress Mrs Kemble showed herself to be a realist. However great Fanny's innate talent, though all her life she had lived in the atmosphere of the theatre where the art of acting was under constant discussion, she had no knowledge of the technique by which effects were produced nor, apart from her own appearance at her Paris school, any stage experience. All that she could rely on was her own emotional response to the situation in which Shakespeare had placed Juliet, a girl as inexperienced as herself and even younger. She had to feel herself to be Juliet, torn between her romantic love for

Romeo and her duty to her family, as Fanny herself might have been torn – and later in life by an irony was so torn. The immature Fanny who could sit at an open window, gazing at the moon and scribbling Byronic verse, would have no difficulty in feeling herself to be Juliet on the balcony communing with the night, experiencing all youth's heedlessness of consequences and passionate response to life. To Charles when he returned from Ireland his wife, in spite of her cool words of commendation to her daughter, suggested that he should subject Fanny to a more rigorous test. In the drawing-room she had seemed to her mother to be potentially excellent raw material, but to read Juliet in a drawing-room was one thing; to fill the auditorium of Covent Garden, capable of holding some three thousand, another. Microphones were an invention of the future and Fanny's voice, though later described by Sir Thomas Lawrence as 'sweet but powerful', was untrained. In an empty theatre she passed the test with flying colours. Later she described how 'I was seized with the spirit of the thing; my voice resounded through the great vault above and before me, and, completely carried away by the inspiration of the wonderful play, I acted Juliet as I do not believe I have ever acted it again.' Delighted with his daughter's performance, Charles Kemble fixed her debut as Juliet for three weeks ahead. The prospect gave Fanny no pleasure. She confided in Harriet that the theatrical profession was 'utterly distasteful' to her and that in adopting it as a career she was acting in accordance with her parents' wishes as filial affection bound her to do. For the next three weeks her mind was in a daze and life assumed an almost dreamlike quality.

The play was rehearsed for three weeks, which today would seem a frighteningly short time in which to equip an untrained girl to undertake the leading role in a London theatre. In the conditions of 1830 it was less outrageous. Repertory rather than long runs was the order of the day. In the course of a season a well-known actor or actress expected to play all his or her favourite parts. Once a player had made a success in any particular role then nobody else in that company would be given a chance to do so. A part became almost a personal property; an actor's 'freehold'. To accommodate this system productions were largely standardized, so that a couple of rehearsals were all that were thought necessary when a newcomer joined the cast. One Romeo, one Juliet could be substituted for another at short notice. Moreover Fanny's lack of experience and of technical expertise were not the handicaps that they would be today. What audiences demanded from an actress was emotion, not technique. Theatregoers of the day wallowed in vicarious emotion; they wept and swooned. When Mrs Siddons, then an unknown actress, appeared in Otway's *Venice Preserv'd* at Cheltenham the ladies of the party, who had gone to laugh at what they supposed would be a company of ranting players, wept so much and were so disfigured with red eyes and swollen faces that they could not appear in public next morning. To such audiences it did not matter how Fanny got her emotional effects so long as she wrung their hearts. This her ability to identify with Juliet and her imaginative, highly strung nature enabled her to do. One vital question remained that could not be answered until the night itself: knowing how much depended on her success, would Fanny be paralysed with fright?

Fanny, like her aunt Sarah, was a quick student, and had little difficulty in learning her lines. Nevertheless, rehearsals must have been a strain since she knew none of the people with whom she had to act. There had been some difficulty in finding her a Romeo. Normally this part at Covent Garden belonged to Charles Kemble, but it was feared that the audience might see something incestuous in father and daughter enacting the roles of lovers; a new Romeo had to be found. At one time the Kembles considered pressing Henry into service; apparently incest was not felt to apply in this case, but, unlike his sister, when dragooned into reading the part he displayed a ludicrous lack of acting ability. Finally the somewhat solid William Abbott was given the part. Rehearsals occupied the mornings; the evenings were taken up with discussions on costume. Here too theatrical conventions were changing. David Garrick had played Lear in a tie-wig and brocaded coat, Othello in English regimentals, but by the time of Fanny's debut there was a movement abroad to substitute historical for contemporary costume. Charles Kemble himself when he produced *King John* in 1823 had done so. Mrs Jameson, the Irish authoress whom Fanny had first met and liked in Edinburgh in 1828, belonged to the historical school; she was anxious that Fanny should be garbed in authentic medieval Veronese style. Mrs Kemble thought otherwise. The medieval garments would only impede her daughter's movements on the stage and she had already enough hazards to face without being encumbered by unwieldy garments. So it was decided that Fanny should make her first appearance in a simple white ball-dress that any young girl among her contemporaries might have worn. To help her daughter further, Maria

Kemble, who had long retired, decided to play Lady Capulet herself. At Juliet's first entrance her mother would be there to give her courage.

On the morning of her first night, 5 October 1829, there was no rehearsal. Fanny spent the morning trying to feel that this was a day like any other. She practised the piano, she walked in St James's Park opposite her home, she read the chapters on St Peter and Jacob in Blunt's *Scriptural Characters*. Then she was driven early to the theatre, accompanied by the comforting presence of Aunt Dall. Once dressed, and with nothing to do but wait for her call, Fanny was in a pitiable state of nerves, feeling, she later told Harriet, like a victim 'ready for execution, with the palms of my hands pressed convulsively together' and tears streaming down her face, as she lay back in her aunt's arms, almost unconscious with fright, while the latter tried to repair the damage of her niece's trickling tears on her make-up with the skilful application of a hare's foot. The roar of applause that had greeted her mother's appearance merely intensified Fanny's panic. Then the dread moment came. The call-boy summoned her to the wings where she stood waiting to make her entrance. Keely, the actor who played Peter, did his best to steady her, saying, 'Never mind 'em, Miss Kemble, never mind 'em. Don't think of 'em any more than if they were so many rows of cabbages.' When her cue came poor Fanny had to be pushed on to the stage. There she was 'stunned by the tremendous shout' that greeted her, so that the mist before her eyes made it seem as if the green baize that covered the stage were rising against her feet. In her own words, 'I got hold of my mother and stood like a terrified creature at bay, confronting the huge theatre full of gazing human beings.' In her terror her opening lines were all but inaudible, but she had the house with her; the preliminary 'puffing', as publicity was called, had been skilful. During the ball scene Fanny began to lose herself in the part and in the balcony scene she was so carried away that, as she told Harriet, 'I did not return to myself till all was over.' The applause was tremendous and her success assured. Her day ended on a happy domestic note. Home at last, Fanny sat down to supper with her 'rejoicing parents, well content, God knows, with the issue of my trial'. Her father marked her triumph with the gift of a Geneva watch, encrusted with gold and jewels, a gift which Fanny said meant more to her than all her success.

There is no doubt that Fanny had scored a personal triumph. An anonymous writer, probably an American, as his pamphlet 'Memoir of the Dramatic Life of Miss Fanny Kemble' was published in Boston after her first appearance there, gave a rave account of that memorable evening as seen from the other side of the footlights:

The feeling of the audience and her reception cannot be better described than in the graphic words of one of the most eminent poets of the age [whom unfortunately he omitted to name]. Even in our young days we have never shared in so anxious a throb of expectation as that which awaited the several appearances of these persons on the stage. The interest was almost too complicated and intense to be borne with pleasure, and when Kemble bounded on the scene, gaily pointing at Romeo, as if he had cast all his cares and twenty of his years behind him, there was a grateful relief from the first suspense, that expressed itself in the heartiest enthusiasm we ever witnessed. Similar testimonies of feeling greeted the entrance of Mrs Kemble but our hearts did not breathe freely until the fair debutante herself had entered pale and trembling, but resolved, and had found shelter and encouragement in her mother's arms. But another and happier source of interest was soon opened, for the first act did not close till all fears for Miss Kemble's success had been dispelled. The looks of every spectator conveyed that they were electrified by the influence of new tried genius and were collecting emotions as they watched its development swell its triumph with fresh acclamations.

As if this eulogy were not enough, Fanny's unknown admirer also quoted from what he called 'one of London's most eminent prints', again unnamed, as saying,

We dreamt for a while of being able to analyse her acting, and to fix in our memory the finest moments of its power and grace, but her attitudes glided into each other so harmoniously that we at last gave over our enumerating how often she seemed a study to the painter's eye and a vision to the poet's heart.

Exaggerated as such flowery tributes may have been, the fact that they could be made is itself a testimony to Fanny's triumph.

It was a success that transformed her life. The connection between the stage and society was close; the Kembles were well respected both for their talents and for their characters. Well-educated and well-mannered, they had the entree to the best social circles. The nineteenth century had seen the last flowering of that aristocratic domination that had marked the eighteenth century. Power was still in the hands of those who possessed rank and landed wealth. Other forms of wealth were slowly coming to be accepted and society, though exclusive, was not excluding. Men of brains and ambition could still gain admission to it if they were prepared to play the political game. Lord Liverpool's father had been the confidential adviser and man of business of Lord North, Lord Melbourne's grandfather had laid the foundations of the family fortune with money amassed in the law and then by a pliant parliamentary career. Nevertheless the centre of political power was still the House of Lords, which could block and amend anything but money bills and whose tentacles extended through the eldest sons, relations and clients who sat in the House of Commons. Even the licensed theatres opened only when Parliament returned to London after the summer. Certain features distinguished this aristocratic society. It was both political and rural. One aspect of its power was national, expressed through Parliament and through the King's ministers. Non-well-born members of the Cabinet were very few; titles and eldest sons predominated among the English members though an O'Connel might stand out among the Irish members. The other aspect of aristocratic power was local and rural. The great landed houses were still immensely wealthy and their wealth came largely from their estates, not just from agricultural rents but from the exploitation, in the economic sense of the word, of the resources of timber, minerals and even building land in the larger towns and particularly in London. This dual interest was expressed in their life style. Town houses such as Holland House and Bridgewater House were centres of culture, as well as of political power and intrigue. Though not all the members of the aristocracy were either intelligent or sophisticated the tradition had been established of the Grand Tour, of an appreciation of literature, of an appreciation of painting and sculpture, and the hostesses of the day delighted to gather round them men of learning, men of brilliant conversation, men of wit. Before the days of organized entertainment there was little beyond the theatre and musical concerts to fill the empty hours that had to be passed indoors and society made its own amusements. Among these, good conversation at the dinner table, amateur plays and individual musical contributions by the invited guests were important. Leading society figures at intervals gave more splendid entertainments, balls, routs, card parties, concerts, and more sophisticated amateur dramatic performances. When the London season was over and the aristocracy departed to their country seats a new facet of their lives was displayed. This was the era of the stately home, where among beautiful and lavish settings house-parties that lasted weeks rather than weekends were the order of the day before the railways made rapid transport available. Here the gentlemen shot or hunted during the daylight hours while the women rode or drove or walked in the shrubbery, and at night dancing, talking, gossiping, music and cards conformed to a conventional pattern. Later Fanny described the elegance of the Duke of Rutland's place at Belvoir. Though grander than most it was yet typical of the life of a great country house before modern transport and modern industrial society had made its impact on the pattern of the past. Here is Fanny's description of it:

It is a beautiful place; the situation is noble, and the views from the windows of the castle, and the terraces and gardens hanging on the steep hill crowned by it, are charming – The interior of the house is handsome, and in good taste; and the whole mode of life stately and splendid, as well as extremely pleasant and comfortable. Every morning the duke's band marched round the castle, playing all sorts of sprightly music, to summon us to breakfast, and we had the same agreeable warning that dinner was ready.

She then went on to describe how when the dessert was put on the table this was accompanied by more music, this time songs. Then the ladies retired. Later in the evening there was more music and one evening there had been a ball which, as the Duke of Rutland led the country dances and in which the housemaid and male cooks also joined, looks as if it was one of those servant balls that occurred from ime to time in the routine of these great country mansions. The tradition of the 'great house', be it castle, mansion or manor, still dominated the English countryside, and the good landowner felt a personal responsibility for all the people on his estate, always provided that they refrained from poaching and behaved with due deference. But though Belvoir was impressive Fanny's especial affection was given to Oatlands, the country home of Lord and Lady Egerton; to Hoo, Lady Dacre's place; and to the smaller Bannisters, the home of her great friend Emily Fitzhugh. These are the places and the names that occur so frequently in her letters and memoirs.

Fanny's success had transformed her overnight from what she called 'an insignificant schoolgirl' to a little lion in this society. Though in her memoirs and letters it is clear that she never genuinely liked her new profession and declared that 'all the tinsel sudden success and popularity' was to prove a 'pitiful preparation' for the duties and trials of her future, it is probable that Fanny enjoyed her success more than she thought consistent with her own picture of herself to admit. Indeed she half excused herself by pleading 'If I was spoilt and my head turned, I

can only say I think it would have needed a strong head not to be so.'
After a winter of adulation, in the March of 1830 Fanny confessed to
Harriet, who was clearly worried about the effect that this might have
on her young friend, that though her profession was still not attractive
enough to engross her mind yet she had become aware that 'admiration
and applause, and the excitement springing there from, may become
necessary' to her, though she assured Harriet that she was determined
both to watch and pray that this might not happen. Meanwhile
materially the fruits of success were sweet. It is the little things Fanny
records that are so revealing. Instead of an annual allowance from her
father of £20, she was now earning £30 a week, and had the prospect
of an income of around £1,000 a year, wealth indeed in 1830. She
could buy fashionable clothes instead of having to wear 'the faded,
threadbare, turned and dyed frocks' that had been her lot in the past.
She could afford a carriage and 'a charming horse'; she could enjoy the
filial pleasure of providing her beloved father with a mount. Fanny
adored riding; horses and riding occur again and again in her letters
and she became a very fine horsewoman. All this new affluence is
thrown into sharp relief by a tale that Fanny recalled of the days of her
penury when having 'sorrowfully concluded myself penniless until
the next allowance day' she had experienced what she called 'the
ecstasy' of finding an unexpected sovereign which had been wedged
at the bottom of the money drawer in her desk.

During that winter, life for Fanny was delightful. She could have
gone to parties every night had she so wished. She became the idol of
the young men about town, who made a point of sitting in the front
row of the pit night after night and who schemed and plotted to
secure an introduction to her. Among these was Augustus FitzClarence,
William IV's son by Mrs Jordan. He dangled after her for some time
and did manage to secure an introduction, but so carefully was Fanny
chaperoned in the theatre, not even being allowed to use the Green
Room, that for some time their acquaintance went to further. Finally
he managed to meet Fanny at a ball and was able to dance with her.
The impression that he made on her was mixed. She pitied him for
having been forced into the Church; he was the most unsuitable vicar
of Maple Durham, but she disapproved most strongly of his uncon-
cealed dislike for his royal father.

Young FitzClarence was only one of many admirers. From her first
initiation in France Fanny loved to dance; like riding, it was one of her

major joys. Balls delighted her but more stuffy social occasions she found boring, and throughout her life when she was bored she made little attempt to conceal the fact. In congenial company she was at her best. Sir Thomas Lawrence, who in these last months had been seeing much of her, described her manner in private as being 'characterized by ease and that modest gravity which, I believe, must belong to high tragic genius'. He was hardly an unprejudiced judge. His connection with the Kemble family, and in particular with Fanny's aunt Sarah, went back to the days when, as a child artist, he had painted several portraits of Mrs Siddons before he was thirteen. They did not meet again until the 1790s. Then Lawrence was in his mid twenties and making a great reputation for himself as a painter of portraits. But from his boyhood she had cast her spell over him. In spite of the four-teen years between them and the fact that Sarah was a married woman with no intention of becoming involved in any scandal, there was a strong link between them. Lawrence in many ways seems to have been an odd character. He never married; possibly he never pursued any of his involvements to their normally accepted conclusion; nevertheless to believe himself to be passionately in love appears to have been emotionally necessary for him. His manner towards women made it fatally easy for them to think that he was deeply attracted to them, possibly because, though emotionally fickle, he was also emotion-ally intense. He was seeing a good deal of the Siddonses; in 1797 he painted the portrait of Sarah now in the National Gallery. As she had two attractive daughters, Sally who was 22 and Maria 18, the inevitable happened. The romantic devotion that as a boy he had felt for their mother was transferred to the daughters. All might have been well had Lawrence been able to make up his mind between them. Unfortunately his first choice was Sally, with whom he seems to have had an under-standing without being officially engaged. This was in 1797. In the next year Sally fell ill. Maria contrived to supplant her and early in 1798 she and Lawrence became formally engaged. Too late he then realized that after all it was Sally whom he loved. The strain and difficulty of this situation can easily be imagined. Lawrence broke his engagement to Maria and began to make desperate suit once again to Sally. Her own feelings are obscure; it seems likely that secretly she still cared for Lawrence in spite of the fact that she was by now disillusioned. A sweeter person than Maria, she did not feel that she could hurt her sister by marrying Lawrence herself. The situation was further complicated in that both sisters were delicate. Maria had consumption and Sally asthma. By the end of 1798 Maria was dead, but before she died she exacted the most solemn of deathbed promises from Sally that she would never marry Lawrence. Sally did not die until 1803. During these bitter years Sarah was torn between her devotion to her daughters and her deep affection for Lawrence. In spite of these unhappy events the friendship between the actress and the painter was renewed and after Sarah's retirement Lawrence continued to visit her.

To what extent Charles Kemble and Lawrence had been in touch during Fanny's girlhood is not clear. From her account of her brief but valued friendship with the artist it would appear that it was an accidental meeting, shortly after Fanny's debut, that renewed the old connection between them. By then Sarah was an old lady, and for years she and Lawrence hardly seem to have met, though a few letters that passed between them survive to show that each cherished memories of the other. Sarah died in 1831. This background makes it easy to understand how to Lawrence, now over sixty, Fanny seemed the reincarnation of his youth. He told one friend that 'she has eyes and hair like Mrs Siddons in her finest time'. When he was in London he never missed a performance of hers, sitting in the stage box. Next morning he used to send her a detailed criticism of her performance the previous night. He had already made a pencil sketch of her and was preparing to paint a full-length portrait of Fanny as Juliet when he died. As she sat for him, did he remember with nostalgia how often he had painted her famous aunt? In a letter written only three days before his death he described his feelings by saying, 'I have almost a Father's interest in her, and a Father's resentment towards those who will not see the promise of almost all that genius can do, because they have seen the unequall'd power, the Glorious countenance and the Figure of Mrs Siddons.' His death was a shock to Fanny but, looking back forty years later, she could not help acknowledging that it might have come in time to save her from what could not have been anything but a most unfortunate entanglement. Lawrence was exercising his old spell. Fanny had been too conscious of what she described as the 'melancholy charm of his countenance, the elegant distinction of his person, and exquisite refined gentleness of his voice and manner'. Added to which attractions were the flattery of his expressed admiration and the still more subtle flattery of his interest in her. He was not only charming and intelligent; he was a celebrity. It would not be the first time that a girl of twenty-one found a sixty-year-old man of the world dangerously attractive. As Fanny herself admitted, she was 'a very romantic girl with a most excitable imagination' and in spite of all that she had heard about his disastrous love-affairs with her own cousins, now long dead, there had been a genuine danger that she too might have lost her heart to him.

Meanwhile family tradition and theatrical convention alike were forcing Fanny to follow in her aunt's footsteps in other ways. As the leading lady at Covent Garden, and as a Kemble, she was expected to play the roles in which Mrs Siddons had once excelled. This was hard on Fanny. During the arduous grind of playing the provincial theatres, Mrs Siddons had acquired the technique to back up her natural tragic genius; Fanny had been launched on the London stage virtually untrained. Yet inevitably those who were not enchanted by her youthful grace or moved by her gallant attempt to retrieve the family fortunes were bound to compare her unfavourably with her aunt. This was something that Fanny accepted. She even told Harriet that though the years might give her the technique which at present she lacked, she could never hope to compare with her aunt's beautiful face and magnificent voice. Indeed she cheerfully admitted that the public had overpraised her and that she had benefited from the lack of good actresses, subsequent to Mrs Siddons' retirement, when the competition had not been great. Nevertheless Fanny was determined that if she were destined to be an actress she would be as good a one as she could, telling Harriet, 'It is very true that to be the greatest actress of my day is not the aim on which my happiness depends. But having embraced this career, I think I ought not to rest satisfied with any degree of excellence short of what my utmost endeavour will help me to attain in it.' She was coming to believe that 'the talent I possess for it was, I suppose, given to me for some good purpose, and to be used'. Even as soon as December 1829 Fanny was wrestling with the problem of 'controlling the very feeling one has, in order to manifest it in the best possible way to the perception of others'. She was discovering that it was not enough to live the part, as she had lived Juliet when she had first stood alone on the vast Covent Garden stage with her father and, unknown to her, his old friend Major Dawkins as her sole audience. Certainly an actress needed imagination but she also needed, as Fanny struggled to explain to Harriet 'a sort of viligant presence of mind – almost a split mind – one half living in the character, so as to produce real grief in an unreal situation' and yet to be aware, when playing Juliet one must not lean on the canvas balcony even when 'one's soul is on one's lips'. Fanny held very definite views on how the part of Juliet should be played. While in Edinburgh, when there seemed no likelihood that Fanny would ever play the part herself, she had reacted against Mrs Siddons' interpretation as 'pure, intellectual and comparatively cold'. Later, writing to George Combe from Manchester, where she was playing Juliet, remembering her aunt's playing of the part she compared her Juliet to a lovely white rose with just a hint of pink at its heart. This, Fanny contended, was wrong. Juliet was the damask of a red rose 'full, rich and glowing'. She was a passionate Italian, redolent of the south, not the conventional young lady of early nineteenth-century English society. No woman, she argued, who fell passionately in love with a handsome face and a sweet voice and who, but a few hours later, discovered that he was the son of a family in deadly enmity with her own, would have continued the wild course of her love if she had been ruled by reason. An intellectual perception of Romeo's qualities and virtues could have meant nothing to Juliet; two short conversations, one in a ballroom, had given her no chance to form a judgement on these. Though Fanny admitted readily enough that had she met Juliet in the flesh she would have thought her ill adapted for the society of nineteenth-century Britain, yet on the stage, she contended that to present her otherwise was to betray the character Shakespeare had created. Juliet should come before the audience like 'a vision of the warm South', and so Fanny intended to portray her.

Later, as a more experienced actress, Fanny confessed to Harriet that 'acting seems to me rather like dancing a hornpipe in fetters. And by no means the less difficult part of the business is to preserve one's own feelings warm, and one's imagination excited, while one is aiming entirely at producing effects upon others; surrounded moreover, as one is, by objects which, while they heighten the illusion to the distant spectator, all but destroy it to us, the *dramatis personae*.' Almost inevitably during her first season, though her split consciousness might make her automatically guard against catching her sleeve in the flame of a nearby candle, her interpretation of the role she was playing depended to a large degree on her emotional response to it. To have no sympathy with her character made Fanny's task doubly difficult. Shakespeare never presented her with this problem; his verse carried her along instead of her lines being a stumbling block to her imagination.

It was the non-Shakespearean plays that caused her so much trouble. Here too she was haunted and dogged by playgoers' memories of Mrs Siddons, whose reputation had been based as much upon her playing the tragic parts in the popular melodramas of the day as on her interpretation of Shakespeare's heroines. Even the great Shakespearean roles with which her aunt was most closely associated in people's minds Fanny felt to be, as yet, outside her range. The thought of having to play Lady Macbeth was horrifying; that of Constance in *King John* equally so. The day before her first appearance in this part she experienced a sharp pain in her side and when she made her first entrance the next night she confessed to being 'half wild with terror'. Nevertheless, because of her love for Shakespeare, there was satisfaction as well as terror in having to play even those parts which she felt that both her youth and inexperience made her ill fitted. For the melodrama which the public taste demanded she had nothing but dislike. For Fanny there was no satisfaction to be got from audiences who demanded emotion, retribution and despair expressed in grandiloquent verse or exaggerated prose. Otway's *Venice Preserv'd* was the first non-Shakespearean play in which Fanny played the lead. The plot is typical of the genre. Jaffier, a nobleman of Venice, has secretly married the disowned daughter of a leading senator and has become involved in a conspiracy against the State. This was engineered by one Renault, who tries to seduce Jaffier's wife, Belvidere. When she learns of the conspiracy she persuades her husband to betray the plot to the Senate on the understanding that the lives of the conspirators will be spared. When Jaffier learns that they have in fact been condemned to death he threatens to kill Belvidere in remorse unless she can persuade her father, the senator, to secure their reprieve. This she does, but in the best traditions of melodramatic tragedy the reprieve comes too late. The conspirators are executed, Jaffier commits suicide and Belvidere goes mad and kills herself. Fanny disliked both the play and its heroine. Belvidere she described as 'a sort of lay figure in a tragic attitude, a mere "female in general" without any particular or specific characteristics whatever'. In spite of its improbable plot and lack of characterization, Belvidere had been one of Mrs Siddons' most acclaimed roles. Critics had praised the melting tenderness of her voice, the amazing versatility of her expression, and found in some of her scenes 'a horror that chilled one's blood'. It was a part which Fanny could only tackle by working herself into a state of hysteria which sent her shrieking from the stage with screams that she could not control as she rushed away.

The Grecian Daughter, by Arthur Murphy, Fanny disliked even more, condemning the language as so poor and bombastic that she had great difficulty in learning her lines. The scene of this particular drama was set in Syracuse. The heroine, Euphrasia, having had her baby torn from her, suckles her starving father, who is threatened by a wicked usurper, who is also the enemy of her husband Phocion. It is all very complicated but finally to save her father Euphrasia stabs Dionysius, the usurper, which is the climax of the play. As the audience knew that Fanny herself had just rescued her own father from financial ruin this role had an added pathos for them. For Fanny having to act her way through this mass of drivel the only consolation was that as Euphrasia she had an especially lovely costume to wear. Once again Fanny was playing a part that Mrs Siddons had made famous but by now she was beginning to escape from her aunt's shadow. When Euphrasia stabs Dionysius, instead of flinging the dagger away in horror at her deed, as Mrs Siddons had done, Fanny, while shielding her eyes with one arm from the sight of the man she had just killed, with the other held the dagger aloft almost in exultation.

The part of Mrs Beverley in *The Gamester*, yet another part made famous by Mrs Siddons, gave her no pleasure to play, and she criticized it on the ground that it lacked 'the indispensable attribute of all works of art – imagination'. Moreover, it was written in prose. Once again the plot is complicated. The male lead, Beverley, is a gamester who squanders his own fortune and sells his long-suffering wife's jewels, having been led astray by a false friend named Stukeley, who is scheming to win Mrs Beverley for himself. The plot then becomes still more involved by the appearance of a Mr Lewson who is in love with Beverley's sister. When the virtuous Mr Lewson discovers Stukeley's villainy the latter attempts to murder him. Meanwhile Beverley, languishing in a debtor's prison, takes poison in despair, only to discover too late that he has inherited another fortune! His wife then dies of grief. In spite of her dislike for the part Fanny played it with great success. The diarist Charles Greville, after seeing her in it, wrote, 'She had a very great success – house crowded and plenty of emotion – but she does not touch me, though she did more than in other parts, however she is very good and will be much better.' His first impression, when he had seen Fanny in earlier roles, had not been favourable. In his diary he described her as 'short, illmade, with large hands and feet', thought he did allow that she had:

an expressive countenance, though not handsome, fine eyes, teeth and hair, not devoid of grace, and with great energy and spirit, her voice is good though she has a little of the drawl of her family. She wants the pathos and tenderness of Miss O'Neill, and she excites no emotion; but she is very young, clever, and may become a very good, even a fine actress. Mrs Siddons was not so good at her age. She fills the theatre every night.

Even when they became friends Charles Greville always had his reservations about Fanny, far more so than his brother Henry, who admired her enormously.

Fanny was learning all the time. When Greville had first seen her she had only been acting for a month, when he saw her next as Mrs Beverley she had three months' experience behind her. A year later still, in 1831, Crabbe Robinson, the dramatic critic, who had been abroad when she had first appeared at Covent Garden, saw her play Bianca in *Fazio*. He wrote:

F. Kemble is certainly a superior actress – And I should think the best we have and this in spite of her small figure and insignificant face . . . she plays Bianca the wife of Fazio, who from jealousy accuses her husband of murdering a usurer whom he in fact only robbed after he had come for refuge to his house, being mortally wounded by robbers. Fazio is executed and Bianca dies of grief. In the alternation of love and jealousy [is] ample room for the display of passion and on several occasions she reminded me successfully of her illustrious aunt, Mrs Siddons.

This was praise indeed.

Fanny's last new part during her first London season was that of Isabella in *The Fatal Marriage*, written by Thomas Southerne in 1694, revived by Garrick in his own version in 1757, and again by Sarah Siddons in 1782, since when it had become a hardy annual in the repertoire of popular plays. The plot is the usual farrago of intrigue and mystery in which Isabella, believing herself to be the widow of Biron, cast off by her father and pressed by creditors, marries the wealthy Villeroy to whom she is growing attached when Biron reappears. Isabella is plunged into an agony of despair, Biron is killed in a brawl and dies in the arms of his wife who then, in the best tradition of melodrama, goes mad and kills herself. No wonder Fanny turned with relief to Shakespeare. She disliked 'both the play and the part extremely' and took some credit for the fact that she thought she had played well on the night of her father's benefit. Benefits were important to actors and actresses because on such occasions they had the sole profits of the house, which was some compensation for low and often irregularly paid salaries. Fanny found some consolation also in the fact that 'the whole thing is over'. In May Covent Garden closed for the season and Fanny and her father, with Aunt Dall as her companion and chaperon, began the customary tour of the provincial theatres. It was a new and interesting experience for Fanny; though the plays were the same the places and the supporting actors were different. So, she soon discovered, were the audiences, many of whom came in a critical mood to assess for themselves this new London star. At Covent Garden Fanny had been able to take for granted the support of her fans. Now in each place she had to woo fresh audiences and her comments on their reactions are interesting. Their tour started in Bath, where Mrs Siddons had first established her reputation. Here Fanny found 'much less fervid enthusiasm' and also 'a far less eulogistic tone in the provincial press with regard to my performances'. She was also amused by provincial prudery. In Bath Mercutio, on first sighting Peter and the Nurse after calling out 'A sail, a sail,' had merely been allowed to mutter the succeeding allusion to the shirt and the petticoat; body linen was not something that could be mentioned before 'a truly refined Bath audience'. Fanny found Edinburgh ones difficult, reporting that though they had played to full houses 'our audiences (as is their national character) very cold'. She found 'The deathlike stillness of the audience, as it afforded me neither rest nor stimulus, distressed me a good deal.' The reference to rest is interesting. As Fanny explained elsewhere, applause did rest as well as stimulate the player in so far as it gave a moment or two in which to gather strength to continue to attack the part. The Glasgow audiences she liked better, finding them less unresponsive.

Her reception in Ireland, where the Kembles went in July, was an enormous contrast to that in Scotland, with its undemonstrative audiences, though even there eventually Fanny thought them in fact 'well pleased with us' in spite of a hostile press which had concentrated on her 'diminutive stature and defective features'. In Dublin, where the Kembles were appearing at the new theatre which Henry Harris had built in 1820 in Hawkins Street, her reception was overpowering in its enthusiasm. After the performance some two hundred Irishmen, all shouting and hurrahing like mad had followed the Kembles' carriage back to the hotel, and when Fanny alighted several of her fans 'dropped on their knees to look under my bonnet, as I ran laughing with my head down'. She confessed that 'I was greatly confused and a little frightened as well as amused and gratified by their cordial reception.' On the second night the enthusiasm was as great. The crowd called for three cheers first for her father and then for Miss Fanny, and compliments on her looks as well as her acting hurled through the air. Socially she and her father were much in demand. Lady Morgan, the eccentric novelist and friend of Lady Caroline Lamb, gave a grand party for them. The Irish tour was a heart-warming experience, and Fanny's happiness was complete when she was able to spend some time with Harriet at Ardgillan before returning to Liverpool and the industrial north. During August and September the Kembles played in Liverpool, in Manchester and in Birmingham, dividing their time between them with such rapidity that their movements are not easy to trace. Fanny was fascinated by everything she saw in what was to her a new England: the docks at Liverpool; the power-looms, spinning jennies and cotton factories at Manchester; the 'button making, pin making, plating, stamping' at Birmingham. While she was in Manchester, staying with Lord and Lady Wilton at Heaton Park, she had been taken over one of the large ironworks where she had seen what she described as 'a number of astonishing processes, from the fusing of iron in its roughest state to the construction of the most complicated machinery'. Of all these processes the one that had most intrigued her was that of casting iron. 'Did you know,' she asked Harriet in a letter of 3 September, 'that the solid mass of iron work which we see in powerful engines were many of them cast in moulds of sand? Inconstant, shifting, restless sand?' It was a juxtaposition that fascinated her, as did much of the strange new world of industry which she saw around her. In a letter to George Combe she wrote, 'These manufacturing towns have afforded me much pleasure and information and as I am rather desirous at present to acquire some knowledge on scientific subjects Liverpool and Manchester and Birmingham have been like the pictures in the children's spelling books, illustrations and encouragement.'

The highlight of Fanny's exploration of this world of iron and steam and power was her meeting with George Stephenson and her first introduction to the new kind of transport, the railway. The construction of his famous engineering feat, the railroad between Manchester and Liverpool, was nearing completion when Fanny was taken to see it.

She was thrilled and excited both by the marvel itself and by its author. In a letter to Harriet, too long to quote in its entirety, she described the carriages and engine as 'a long bodied vehicle with seats placed across it back to back, the one we were in had six of these benches . . . the wheels were placed upon two iron bands, which formed the road, and to which they are fitted, being so constructed as to slide along without any danger of hitching and becoming displaced'. The engine she described as 'a little fire horse' with wheels instead of feet moved by 'bright steel legs called pistons' while the 'reins, bit and bridle of this wonderful beast is a small steel handle which supplies or withdraws the steam from its legs or pistons so that a child might manage it. This snorting little animal which I was rather inclined to pat, was then harnessed to our carriage.' Having completed this dedicated horse-woman's charming description of the new locomotive, she then went on to describe its designer. It was a tribute to her fame or her charm that Stephenson allowed Fanny to ride with him in the cab and he assumed a heroic stature in her eyes. Indeed she confessed to Harriet, 'He has most certainly turned my head' and that she was 'most horribly in love with him', telling her friend that he was 'a man of fifty to fifty-five years of age; his face is fine though careworn and bears an expression of deep thoughtfulness, his mode of explaining his ideas is peculiar and very original, striking and facile.' In this age of speed it is thought-provoking to study Fanny's reaction to what was then a totally new experience for the human race in western Europe when the machine replaced the horse as the fastest form of land transport. 'You cannot imagine', she wrote, 'how strange it seems to be journey-ing thus without any visible cause of progress other than the magical machine, with its flying white breath and rhythmical, unvarying pace.' It is with something like awe that Fanny described the homeward journey. 'We set off at its utmost speed thirty miles an hour, swifter than a bird flies (for they tried the experiment with a snipe). You can-not conceive what that sensation of cutting the air was.' Fanny was entranced and delighted that in spite of the enormous demand for invitations the Kembles had been given three to the formal opening of the railway on 15 September by the Duke of Wellington, an occasion that was marred by the tragic death of Huskisson, who stepped into the path of an oncoming train. Of this too, though at second hand, because she did not see the actual accident, Fanny gave a long description much quoted by historians.

Mrs Kemble had joined her husband and daughter in Manchester for the opening of the new railroad and the three returned together to London for the new season, stopping for a few days in Buckinghamshire where they had arranged to met Dall and Fanny's younger brother, Henry. Once again though the Kembles returned to the familiar scene it was to yet another new house. Now that Henry's school days were over the Kembles moved from Buckingham Gate and took possession of John Kemble's old house in Great Russell Street. It was a comfortable house. Fanny had her own room upstairs which she told Harriet 'thanks to my mother's kindness and taste, was as pretty a bower of elegant comfort as any young spinster need have desired'. Here she could entertain her friends, and she hoped to persuade Harriet to pay her a long visit. When later the Kemble family moved again this memento of the Kembles was incorporated into the British Museum, providing houseroom for the librarian Panizzi. In Bloomsbury the pattern of Fanny's days began to take shape. She had a key to the gardens in Russell Square and planned to walk there every day for an hour in pursuit of exercise. Wherever possible Fanny lived by routine. As she explained she was so prone to give way to emotional tension that she found routine necessary to give her some measure of stability. Breakfast was over by ten and, as she had given up paying or receiving morning calls, still a feature of London social life, on the days when she was not acting she did not dine until six in the evening. This gave her a 'tolerably long day' in which to follow her other interests. Her literary aspirations still meant much to her and she was enormously excited when John Murray showed an interest in her poems and in her youthful attempt at playwriting, *Francis I*, which later he published. Fanny was already working on another play, *The Star of Seville*, which was based on *La Estrella de Sevilla* by Lope de Vega. By December she was copying out her fourth act. As well as all this literary activity Fanny had also hoped to take up the study of German but that, not surprisingly, got squeezed out.

She was certainly living a full life during her second season at Covent Garden. There were new parts to be learnt, including Bianca in Milman's *Fazio*. She found it an improvement on some of the melodramas that she had played in during her first season, telling Harriet that it was 'very powerful, and my part is a very powerful one indeed. I have hopes it may succeed greatly.' It must have been a relief to be able to create her own role instead of being condemned to play the parts that her aunt had made so famous. Crabbe Robinson thought she played the part well, and so did Mrs Kemble. Fanny was delighted that the performance had gone so well but, as she told Harriet, her chief pleasure was certainly her mother's approval, saying, 'She is a very severe critic, and as she censures sharply I am only too thankful when I escape her condemnation.' Fanny was not always so fortunate. She had been delighted in the February of 1831 to be given the chance to play Beatrice, declaring that 'it will be the second part which I shall have acted with real pleasure'. Alas, her mother informed her that she played Beatrice 'like the chief mourner at a funeral' in her early performances, though later she did admit that her daughter was improving.

It was during this season that Fanny created one of her most famous roles, that of Julia in Sheridan Knowles' play *The Hunchback*. This was a new play, and the management of Covent Garden hesitated to put it on. Though it was full of dramatic situations it actually had a happy ending; the heroine finally married the man she loved instead of killing herself in despair or dying of grief or remorse. Fanny was confident that it would succeed, and she was right in her opinion that 'the great merit of the piece as an acting play covers all its defects', adding that 'it is a very satisfactory play to *see*, but let nobody who has seen it well acted attempt to read it in cold blood'. Fanny herself grew bored with the part. Once she declared that though she could act Juliet a hundred times and still revel in its glorious poetry she wearied of Julia after half that number. Crabbe Robinson liked both the play and Fanny in it. He admitted to seeing it with 'more than usual pleasure' and that 'Fanny Kemble played the character better than any I have ever seen her in and it included every variety of tragic passion – and gentle vivacity.' Fanny still found comedy difficult. She could draw on her emotions for drama and tragedy but, as she realized herself, comedy called for more skill and experience than she as yet possessed. Once when forced to dash to a rehearsal of *A School for Scandal* she told Harriet that the experience had been 'horrible but not so horrible as my performance of Lady Teazle promises to be'. Lady Townley in *The Provoked Husband* was another character which she had difficulty in playing.

Success meant that Fanny belonged to two worlds, the world of the theatre and the world of aristocratic London. It was this mixture that brought her in her own words 'an ephemeral love' which was, she later confessed, the source of 'some pain'. Private theatricals were very popular and nothing was more natural than that Lord and Lady Francis Egerton should press Fanny to take the lead in a version of Victor Hugo's *Hernani*. The Egertons were old friends. Lord Francis Egerton was the second son of the Duke of Sutherland, and his wife a Greville, the sister of Henry and the diarist Charles. Their country seat, Oatlands, was near the Kembles' cottage at Weybridge, and Fanny had known them since she was sixteen. When she was asked to help by playing the lead Fanny felt that she could not refuse. She told Harriet that she thought it might be amusing but would certainly be time-consuming because they would need endless rehearsals. It was to prove more than time-consuming; for the first time the flames of love gently licked at Fanny's heart, leaving her to imagine that the burn was permanent. Though the final production was to be at Bridgewater House in London the preliminary rehearsals were to be at Oatlands where a merry party assembled. Here, reading between her very discreet lines, Fanny seems to have fallen in love. The details are wrapped in careful obscurity; even the name of the man who for a time won her heart is uncertain. Among the cast there are two possibilities, one of whom was Augustus Craven, who played the lead. Later he married a charming Frenchwoman, and an extract from one of Fanny's letters to Harriet, written in 1836, suggests that he was the mystery man:

Who do you think Adelaide and I went to dine with last Friday? You will never guess, so I may as well tell you. The Cravens. The meetings in this world are strange things. She sought me with apparent cordiality and I had no reason whatsoever for avoiding her. She is very handsome, and appears remarkably amiable, with the simple good breeding of a French great lady and the serious directness of a devout Roman Catholic. They are going to Lisbon, where he is Attaché to the Embassy.

When Fanny wrote this she was herself married, hence her detachment at meeting this ghost from the past. That Oatlands was the venue of this romance is clear from another extract. When later in the year she had been asked and could not accept the invitation from the Egertons to stay with them at Oatlands, Fanny had told Harriet, 'Everything is winter now, December within and without me; and when I was last there it was summer, in my heart and all over the world.'

Fanny could always find relief in her overstrained nerves in either tears or verse. The following lines, though included in a volume of poems published in very different circumstances in 1844, may well mirror this early heartbreak. The title is merely 'To—'.

> *Is it a sin to wish that I may meet thee?*
> *In that dim world whither our spirits stray,*
> *When sleep and darkness follow Life and day?*
> *Is it a sin that there my voice should greet thee*
> *With all the love that I must die concealing?*
> *Will my tear laden eye sin in revealing*
> *The agony that preys upon my soul?*
>
> *Is it not enough through the long loathsome day*
> *To hold each look and word in strict control?*
> *May I not wish the staring sunlight gone*
> *Day and its torturing moments done*
> *And prying sights and sounds of men away?*
> *Oh still and silent Night when all things sleep*
> *Lock'd in thy swarthy breast my secret keep;*
> *Come with thy vison'd hopes and blessings now!*
> *I dream the only happiness I know.*

Why Fanny's happiness faded with the year is pure speculation. Private theatricals are a well-known breeding-ground for quick, but often transitory, romances, and Oatlands provided an ideal setting for young love. Fanny's letters show how she revelled in its beauty, its gardens, its glorious woods when she wandered out in the early morning while the dew still lay heavy on the grass and all around her was the ordered loveliness of its grounds. By now Fanny was well used to the civilized routine of country house-parties. She had become a great favourite with Lady Dacre and a close friend of her granddaughter Barbarina, and was always a welcome visitor at Hoo, their place in Hertfordshire. There she met, among other distinguished men, the elderly Lord Grey and his son Lord Howick and little Lord John Russell, as well as such wits as 'Bobus' and Sydney Smith. What most appealed to her in such company, she told Harriet, who feared that Fanny's social success might be turning her into a head-hunter, was that 'extraordinary capacity was never an excuse for want of urbanity or the absence of a desire to please'. She acknowledged that 'When fine people seek me it is a decided compliment by which my vanity is flattered', but went on to argue that she had better reasons for enjoying this aristocratic world, writing 'In the common superficial intercourse of society, the minds and morals of those you meet are really not what you come into contact with half the time, while from their manners there is of course no escape, and therefore those people may well be preferred as temporary associates whose manners are most refined, and easy and unconstrained, and the refined people have all the advantages and background to secure this.' Nevertheless there were hidden dangers. Fanny was living on familiar terms with people to whose society her talent, not her birth, had given her access. This may have been one reason why her first romance faded with the year. It was not unknown for a man of title to marry an actress, even in the early nineteenth century, but it was unusual. Birth was still the main criterion and only a very strong attachment, a very clever woman, or the fortune of an heiress would induce a gentleman to marry beneath him. Fanny's unknown admirer may have been greatly attracted to her, may have paid her a misleading amount of attention, taking every opportunity that rehearsals offered and yet, this pleasant interlude once over, have looked for a wife whose birth matched his own. Only one thing is certain; he made Fanny very unhappy.

Though it had ended sadly, Fanny's second season, both professionally and socially, had been a brilliant success. She was young enough, blessed as she was with enormous energy, to burn the candle at both ends. Here is a sample of her engagements for one week, based on her letters to Harriet. On Monday she went to a party, on Tuesday to the opera, on Wednesday she acted Isabella, Thursday saw her dining with the Harnesses, Friday she acted Bianca, Saturday the Kembles themselves gave a dinner-party. Sunday Fanny liked to keep free of engagements but on Monday the round started again with a performance of Constance in *King John* and on Tuesday she went to the Fitzhughs' ball. Fanny always loved to dance and the combination of dancing and romance cast a special glamour over the ball at Bridgewater House which was held to celebrate the second performance of *Hernani* in May. Fanny described it with breathless excitement to Harriet, writing that they

had had a very fine ball; that is to say, we had neither room to dance, nor space to sit, nor power to move . . . certainly *a good* ball is a pleasant thing, and in spite of the above drawbacks I was enchanted with everything. Such shoals of partners! Such a delightful floor! Danced until the day had one eye open, and then home to bed.'

Next day Fanny paid for her pleasure; her feet ached so badly that she could hardly bear to stand. Not all the parties she attended drew from her such paeans of pleasure. On one evening spent at the house of the aged and eccentric Lady Cork she furnished Harriet with a much less enthusiastic report, writing,

Such rooms, such ovens! Such boxes full of fine folk and foul air! in which we stood and sat and looked and listened, and talked nonsense, and heard it talked and perspired and smothered and suffocated half an hour in the heat and another half hour in the freezing cold of the hall waiting for the carriage and got to bed at 2 am with face ache and tooth ache and caught a cold.

In the theatre things were not going quite so prosperously. In 1831 England in general, and London in particular, was in the grip of a political crisis and audiences were falling off. The aristocratic world was being increasingly challenged by that new world whose fascination had so caught Fanny's imagination, the world of Brunel, of Stephenson, of cotton-mills and ironworks. The social structure was under pressure; the middle income groups – perhaps a safer term than the more familiar but ambiguous 'middle classes' – were increasing. There were more manufacturers, more middlemen, more engineers, more professional men, doctors, lawyers, schoolmasters to cater for their needs, more substantial shopkeepers, more importers and exporters. All these groups had interests to protect and this could only be done if they too had a share in political power. In the growing towns, themselves a symbol of the new England, a new type of worker was congregating, mill-hands and ironworkers who suffered loss of wages when times were bad. Even when they were prosperous and industry was booming the hours worked by men, women and children were unlimited and the towns in which they lived filthy and disease-ridden. From the underprivileged, whether they were educated and moneyed or illiterate and poor, came increasing demands for a share in political power. This meant vital changes in the traditional structure of Parliament or, to be more accurate, in that of the House of Commons. Since the French Revolution the pressure had been building up against the dam of privilege and tradition, not always equally but, like the waves of an incoming tide, gaining a little after each seeming retreat. In 1830 the movement for parliamentary reform came to a head, partly because the death of George IV meant a new election, possibly encouraged by the replacement of the old Bourbon line in France by Louis Philippe after a bloodless revolution. These two events gave to the Whigs, long exiled from power, a chance to unseat the uncompromising government of the Duke of Wellington. In theory the Whigs believed in parliamentary reform, though not in the popular brand, and with public pressure behind them their leader, the elderly Lord Grey, was able to drive Wellington into resignation. This was in the autumn of 1830. In March 1831 Lord John Russell, one of Fanny's fellow guests at Hoo, introduced a Reform Bill into the House of Commons. On the 22nd it was passed, but only by one vote, and then ran into difficulties at the committee stage. The new king, William ɪv, agreed to an appeal to the country which in the general election of 1831 rang with the cry 'The Bill, the whole Bill and nothing but the Bill!' In June Lord John introduced another Bill which, having passed the Commons, was thrown out by the Lords to the fury of the reformers, a fury expressed in demonstrations and riots. This was the background of Fanny's professional career. Somewhat ruefully she told Harriet that she did not expect a good benefit as it would clash with the second reading of the Reform Bill. Theatrical business everywhere was bad, which was one reason, indeed the main one, why Fanny and her father decided on an American tour in 1832.

Both as a Londoner and as a frequenter of Whig political circles, Fanny could not but be interested in the current political turmoil. Though she never wished personally to be involved in politics she found employment for her pen in giving Harriet a slightly caustic account of the excitement around her, writing of one pro-reform demonstration, 'the streets are thronged with people and choked up with carriages and the air is flashing and crashing with rockets and squibs and crackers to the great discomfort of the horses. So many Rs everywhere that they may stand for reform, revolution, ruin, just as those who run may chuse to read.' On the dissolution of Parliament the Lord Mayor ordered illuminations and the mob followed its old tradition of breaking the windows of those who either failed to comply or did so insufficiently, so that Fanny declared, 'Sundry were the glass sacrifices offered at the shrine of consistent Tory patriotism in the West End of the Town.' It is not only modern football supporters who express their loyalties by breaking windows. In the face of this exuberant enthusiasm Fanny wondered with a touch of political realism what the government would be forced to do once people realized that the Reform Bill would not bring them 'immediate bread, cheese and beer'. Her letters to Harriet emphasize the increasing tension that was everywhere marking London life. 'Party spirit here has reached a tremendous pitch,' she told Harriet. 'Society is becoming a sort of battle field, for every man (and woman too) is nothing if not political.' Even Fanny could not resist the prevailing atmosphere and when the Lords rejected the second Reform Bill by 41 votes she admitted that 'this universal political effervance has got into my head', declaring that she really could not foresee the next move but that 'You cannot create forty-one peers; the whole book of Genesis affords no precedent,' a fact of which the noble House and the King himself were painfully aware. By December Fanny was reporting that 'rumours are rife that the Ministry dare not make the new batch of Peers, cannot carry the Bill and must resign. To whom?'

Apart from her theatrical interests Fanny had other reasons for wishing that the excitement would die down and London return to normal. She had been working hard on the criticisms that John Murray had made on the metre of her verse in *Francis I* and had written a new last scene. When she submitted the new version to him her labours were rewarded. He told her that he was not only prepared to publish it but would give her £250 for it. Fanny was overjoyed. She told Harriet, 'I am so happy, so thankful for this prosperous result of my work, so delighted at earning so much, so surprised and charmed to think what gave me nothing but pleasure has brought me such an after harvest of profit.' But though the play was accepted Murray had told Fanny that he intended to hold over publication 'until after this reform fever has a little abated'. When *Francis I* appeared the majority of the literary critics were kind. Arthur Hallam pronounced it 'a remarkable production for seventeen. The language is very pure, free, elegant English and strictly dramatic.' With this last opinion Crabbe Robinson was not in agreement. When the play was finally produced at Covent Garden, with Fanny in the part of Francis I's mother, in the April of 1832, he wrote in his diary 'A sad disappointment it would have been if I had expected anything from a girl of nineteen who aspired to write a Shakespearean historical play.' (Fanny's debut at Covent Garden was at the age of nineteen, although she wrote *Francis I* two years earlier.) As Fanny's own aspirations were literary she professed herself delighted with the reviews, declaring that she thought the one in the *Quarterly Review* was very handsome and that it should satisfy 'my most unreasonable friends. It more than satisfied me, for it made me out a great deal cleverer than I ever thought I was, or ever, I am afraid, shall be.' If the praise was valued the money was welcome. In spite of her personal success, funds in the Kemble family were still short, and her brother Henry's future presented problems. He had shown none of the academic quality that had distinguished John nor the dramatic quality of his sister. His own inclination was for the army but in the days before Cadwell's reforms commissions had to be purchased and Charles Kemble was in no position to do this. Now Fanny was able to help and a combination of influence and cash launched young Henry on a military career. To Adelaide, whose musical talent was already showing itself, Fanny gave a guitar with 'a low soft voice'. It is possible that her present to herself was riding lessons with the great Fozzard, who afterwards taught the young Princess Victoria to ride.

By the time that Fanny's second London season had come to an end and she and her father embarked on their provincial tour, Fanny was becoming an experienced actress and her letters to Harriet give a good picture of the pains and pleasures of going on tour in the eighteen thirties. One of the chief hazards was the uncertainty as to the capabilities of the supporting cast. It was possible for London actors on tour to move rapidly from one theatre to another, playing for a few nights here and a few nights there, because they had to transport neither scenery nor a full company but only themselves and their own wardrobe so long as they toured with standard plays which required the minimum of rehearsal. This could lead to difficulties; for instance, throughout her stage career Fanny found herself afflicted with a series of inadequate Jaffiers, the male lead in *Venice Preserv'd*. In Bristol, where the Kembles' tour of the western counties opened in July, Fanny was cursed with a Jaffier who did not know his lines and had to make them up as he went along. Moreover he was a ham actor 'who bellows low in his throat like an ill suppressed bull; he rolls his eyes until I feel they're flying out of their sockets at me, and I must try to catch them'. In Plymouth also she was unlucky and had to prompt her Jaffier through every scene. Moving from place to place meant not only getting used to unfamiliar players, it was also exhausting before the days of speedy and comfortable railroad travel. At Dorchester, for example, the Kembles seem only to have played for a single night before moving on. It was a relief to arrive at Bristol, the metropolis of the west, where the population was large enough to support a three-week season. Fanny liked Bristol; she loved the market piled high with fruit and was inclined to envy the buxom farmers' wives. A greater pleasure was that, because no leading actress was expected to appear every night, she and her father were able to explore the surrounding countryside on hired horses. But financially Bristol was something of a disappointment. Trade was bad, some of the leading mercantile houses had failed, and houses were thin in consequence though the theatre was crowded for Charles Kemble's own benefit. The manager of the theatre was less fortunate. Due to the appalling financial position of the theatre he was imprisoned for debt and the company left unpaid. This was something with which Charles Kemble could sympathize, and with genuine generosity he played for an extra night without a fee so that the salaries of the rest of the company could be paid. On 23 July he and Fanny left for Exeter. They had meant to sail down the Bristol Channel to Ilfracombe but the weather was bad and the wind contrary so they were forced to go by coach. After a week at Exeter they went on to Plymouth. Here their arrival was complicated by the fact that through some mischance the lodgings that they had bespoke had been let to someone else, so that Charles had to find fresh quarters for himself, Fanny and Dall, who once again was chaperoning her niece. Fanny liked the theatre at Plymouth, which she described as 'a beautiful building for its purpose, of a perfectly discreet size, neither too large nor too small; of a very elegant shape, and capitally constructed for the voice'. The provincial theatres in which Fanny and her father appeared have fallen victims to time and the developer, but one small gem, carefully and successfully restored, remains at Richmond in Yorkshire. Within its walls the modern theatregoer can enter the world that once was Fanny Kemble's. There seems to be no record of her having played there herself but certainly Mrs Siddons and John Philip did in their time. The first night that Fanny played in Plymouth she had liked the theatre better than her audience, reporting 'I played abominably ill and did not like my audience who must have been very good natured if they liked me.' The next evening things went better. There was however one aspect of the Plymouth theatre that drew loud complaints from Fanny. This was the lack of green baize which was normally laid down on the stage when tragedies were played to soften the falls of the unfortunate actresses who so often had to fling themselves down in their death agony. As a result of its absence Fanny declared 'my unhappy elbows are bruised black and blue with their carpetless stage, barbarians that they be'.

Plymouth had an attraction much greater for Fanny than the possession of a delightful theatre; it was on the sea. At seven in the morning she slipped down to enjoy a morning bathe. At Weymouth, where her mother had once acted before George III in a theatre so tiny that there was hardly room to move on the stage, Fanny again heard the call of the sea. She had been so terribly tired after the performance that she had had to be carried back to her dressing-room, where she almost fainted from weariness. Yet on reaching her lodgings the sea uttered its siren note, and in spite of her exhaustion she tried to persuade Dall to go with her down to the shore. Her aunt, always a practical person, refused to indulge her niece and Fanny was promptly sent to bed. Next day she had her reward. The trio hired a rowing-boat and went to Portland Bill, where she and her father climbed to the top. Here Fanny found the perfect stillness and solitude was like a spell. It nearly turned out to be an evil one for their audience that night. While they were climbing their boatman was imbibing and they only just managed to get back to the theatre in time. After the show Fanny went down to the shore again for one last look at the compelling sea. In spite of its discomforts touring had its brighter side. It was pleasant to be out of London in the summer, not only because all her friends and acquaintances were away but because in hot weather the capital stank. To read Fanny's letters and memoirs is to get an impression of elegant and civilized life, and it is easy to forget that the London of her day was the London of Dickens, in whose slums and alleys filth accumulated in antiquated drains and overflowing cesspools and where the Thames could smell so foul that Members of Parliament had to keep the windows closed. It is true that in the West End the more unsightly sanitary horrors were kept out of sight but only people who could not get away stayed in London during the summer heat. The more prosperous middle class acquired villas and summer quarters in the surrounding villages and even the craftsmen and the artisans got out on Sundays to the tea gardens that ringed the city. Even when the Kembles' tour took them to inland towns they could hire horses and enjoy the clean air and peace of the countryside. Nevertheless in spite of such compensations Fanny, who had started the tour in low spirits, confessed that by its end she felt 'fagged to death, my work tires me and I am growing old'. She was then twenty-two.

If her superabundant energy was feeling the strain, her father's health was suffering more. After their return to London he developed disturbing symptoms; once when he started to spit blood Fanny told Harriet that she felt as if she had been turned to stone with dread and fear. Gradually, after a series of partial recoveries and relapses, he regained enough strength to return to Covent Garden where during his illness Fanny had been forced to continue to appear in such plays as did not need her father. Even when Charles Kemble was once again well enough to play, the financial position of the theatre seemed to be slowly getting worse as the political crisis over the Reform Bill grew tenser. By the spring of 1832 the situation seemed so unpromising that Charles Kemble began to consider giving up the management of Covent Garden and going on a tour in the United States. In this he was breaking no new ground. Big cities like New York had a vigorous theatre, and even in the days of sail when the crossing took from three to four weeks or more, well-known actors found it worth while to make the journey. Indeed his sister Elizabeth had spent most of her professional career on the American stage. The idea filled Fanny with dismay but the alternatives looked equally grim. As she told Harriet in a letter dated 1 March, the choice seemed to be 'America, or the provinces or the King's Bench', the latter being an allusion to their desperate financial position. Even more than the money was the question of her father's health. Fanny was terrified that this might break down again under the strain of his worries. 'He seems utterly prostrated in spirit,' she wrote, and she was frightened that he would again 'brood himself ill'. Even America, separation from the rest of her family, Harriet and all her friends would be preferable to that. America might rally her father's spirits, improve his health and restore his finances. If he went there was never any question of her not going with him; they were a team, father and daughter, leading man and leading lady. For Fanny it was to prove the most momentous decision of her life, and the future pattern of all her days was to turn on it.

THREE

The American Venture

The summer of 1832 was an unhappy one for Fanny. Looking back many years later, with the all but impersonal compassion with which the elderly can remember the grief of their younger years, she described her emotions on the eve of her departure for the United States.

'My spirits', she wrote, 'were depressed by my father's troubled fortune, and I had just received the first sharp, smarting shocks in the battle of life, those gashes from which poor "unbruised youth" in its infinite self compassion, fancies its very life blood must all pour away. There is nothing more pathetic than the terrified impatience of youth under its first experience of grief, and its vehement appeals of "Behold and see if any sorrow be like unto my sorrow."'

Fanny was not quite twenty-three, and, whether it was over Augustus Craven or some other member of the Oatlands house-party, she was breaking her heart. Her still almost adolescent woe was poured out in a poem which she wrote shortly after landing in New York. How many of us when young might have written in a similar strain?

> 'Tis all in vain, it may not last,
> The sickly sunlight dies away,
> And the thick clouds that veil the past
> Roll darkly o'er my present day.
>
> Have I not flung them off and striven
> To seek some dawning hope in vain?
> Have I not been for ever driven
> Back to the bitter past again?
>
> What though a brighter sky lord o'er
> Scenes where no former image greets me?
> Though lost in paths untrod before
> Here, even here, pale memory meets me.

Oh life – oh blighted bloomless tree!
Why cling thy fibres to the earth?
Summer can bring no flowers to thee
Autumn no bearing, spring no birth.

Bid me not strive, I'll strive no more
To win from pain my joyless breast;
Sorrow has ploughed too deeply o'er,
Life's Eden – let it take the rest!

Poor Fanny! It was in this waste of deep depression that she faced the grief of being separated for at least two years from her family, her friends, and the country that she loved. By June arrangements had been made with the Frenchman Monsieur Laporte to take over the management of Covent Garden and Fanny was preparing herself for the final break with her first and always favourite audience. Her last performance was on 22 June. It was an emotional occasion on both sides of the curtain. The audience waved hats and handkerchiefs as they shouted their fare-wells. Fanny was almost overcome: the traditional way of acknow-ledging the applause of the audience was to make a deep curtsey but Fanny, with a spontaneous gesture, snatched the little nosegay of flowers from her sash and threw them into the pit with handfuls of kisses. She confessed 'it made my heart ache to leave my kind, good, indulgent audience; my friends as I feel them to be; my countrymen, my English folk'. As she thought 'of the strangers for whom I am now to work in that distant country' her eyes filled with tears. Once off the stage Fanny wept bitterly. It also distressed her to say goodbye to her 'kind, civil, cordial, humble friends' the backstage staff, and in par-ticular to her dresser.

To part with her family was a shattering experience for anyone as affectionate as Fanny, but one member of it beside her father was to go with her. Fanny considered to be still too young to travel without a female companion and Aunt Dall, with her usual willingness to put the family welfare before her own, agreed to accompany Charles and Fanny on their Odyssey. It must have been a considerable sacrifice on her part, for she was no longer a young woman. Travelling by sailing-ship and coach called for physical endurance; there was also the wrench of leaving her sister Maria and young Adelaide, to whom she was devoted. Nor could she expect it to be easy to adjust herself to new ways in a new country. The three voyagers were to sail from Liverpool at the beginning of August but decided to pay a last visit to Edinburgh first. John said his farewell at Greenwich but Mrs Kemble sailed with them to Scotland. Fanny's hero's iron horse had not yet provided a swift and easy route to Edinburgh and to go by ship from Greenwich was much less exhausting than attempting the long journey by coach. Fanny lived to be an old lady in a world where trains were taken for granted, and it is easy to forget how many changes she lived to see. Her letters contain much that is interesting to the social historian, mirroring as they do the way in which the pattern of everyday life of ordinary people was affected thereby. When Fanny said goodbye to Mrs Siddons and to the Combes and their circle America seemed, and indeed was, a far distant land, where only the slow interchange of letters could keep her in touch with the friends and the country she was leaving behind. During the week that the Kembles spent in Edinburgh the shadow of parting lay over them all. Two years' exile seemed an eternity. It was well the sad little party did not know that it would be longer still before Mrs Kemble would see her daughter again, while Dall was never to return. On 7 July Mrs Kemble, accompanied by Sally Siddons, went back to London. The bitter parting over, Fanny sat pretending to read while Charles Kemble struggled to stifle his sobs; neither of them could bring themselves to look out of their window through which they could have seen Mrs Kemble's ship as it sailed down the Firth. It was impossible, thought Fanny, to imagine a sorer, sadder heart than hers.

By 19 July Fanny and her father were in Liverpool. There Fanny had the mixed joy and pain of being again with Harriet, who came over from Ireland and stayed with them until they sailed on the *Pacific* on 1 August. Fanny went on board carrying a bunch of carnations which, in a last gesture of farewell, she had snatched from a vase in the drawing-room as she left it. Like most Victorian ladies of literary pretensions Fanny kept a journal, and that night she wrote in sentimental vein 'dear English flowers, they will be withered long before I see land again, but I will keep them until I once more stand upon the soil in which they grew'. The Kembles had comfortable quarters and Fanny was surprised by the excellence of the dinner that was served to them. Because it was the first day out everything was cold, but both champagne and dessert were provided, luxuries that were sadly wasted on the tearful Fanny. She wept throughout the meal, which must have been a trifle disconcerting for the rest of the party, mostly businessmen travelling to America. Atlantic voyages in 1832 were long and tedious.

There could be no regular schedule while ships under sail were at the mercy of contrary winds and bad weather, and the Kembles did not land until 4 September. The weather varied. One day Fanny described it as 'utter calm, a roasting August sun, a waveless sea, the sails flapping idly against the mast, and our black cradle rocking to and fro without progressing a step'. When their ship ran into a storm life was very different. All day Fanny lay on her berth feeling 'most wretched, the ship heaving like any earthquake. Another horrible night. Oh horror,' she lamented. On one occasion the rolling of the vessel shot Fanny's supper into her lap and, though she gallantly tried to concentrate on the game of speculation she was playing, the sea won; she was forced to retreat to her cabin. It was, she declares, 'a loathsome life'.

Fanny was never a good sailor and bad weather inevitably laid her low, but for Dall the voyage seems to have been an even greater ordeal. Writing to Harriet, Fanny told her that Dall had been 'the greatest wretch on board; she has been perfectly miserable the whole time'. For her niece there had been some alleviations. Like all sea-travellers she had gossiped, played cards, danced and, a more period activity, sung rounds. She had good intentions about learning German, which had hardly time to materialize, and she read *Childe Harold*. She was able to look at Byron more calmly now than four years ago when she had forced herself to forgo the disturbing pleasure that he caused her but she still found his poems full of 'might, majesty and loveliness'. Would he, she wondered, have been so great a poet if he had been less of an egotist? Then followed some interesting reflections on writers and their emotions which, in view of her own experience and aspirations in this direction are worth quoting. 'We must not look', she wrote, 'for the real feelings of writers in their works – or rather, that which they give us, and what we take for heart feelings, is head weaving – a species of emotion engendered behind the bosom and the brain, and bearing the same proportion of resemblance to reality as a picture does; that is – like feeling but not feeling – like sadness but not sadness – like what it appears, but not indeed that very thing; and the greater a man's powers of thus producing *sham realities*, the greater his main qualifications for being a poet.' Finally the voyage came to an end. Their landfall was not auspicious. All that Fanny saw was a wet and dreary coast while contrary winds delayed their disembarking. When the time came to leave the *Pacific* and her late companions Fanny, like so many travellers, felt sad that the people who for a month had made up her little world would now scatter while she and her father had to face an unknown world.

Fanny, like most people visiting the United States for the first time, was jolted by both the similarities and the differences between the British and the American ways of life. That the countries spoke a common language and to a large extent, greater then than now, shared a common culture and a common law, made the differences between them seem more noticeable. This strangeness made Fanny homesick and in the journal, which at that time she had no thought of ever publishing, she commented adversely on much that she found. She was ill equipped both by temperament and by experience to appreciate the America of 1832. Her affections were deep rather than wide. When she loved she loved wholeheartedly and expected her friends to do the same. When she disliked she made no attempt to hide the fact from its object. When she was bored she looked bored. For the world in general, unless some incident called forth her ready compassion and sympathy, usually accompanied by floods of tears, her attitude was one of cool indifference. Her standards were equally clear cut. Black was black, white white and grey outside her spectrum. This, combined with her passionate belief in justice, made her often seem both intolerant and inflexible; the word compromise had no place in her personal dictionary. Later, age and experience were to mellow her somewhat, but in 1832 she had all the arrogance of youth and success. She was fiercely proud of the Kemble name and, adoring her father as she did, was quick to resent anything that could be construed as a slight. Kembles conferred favours; they did not accept them if there were the slightest hint of patronage. Moreover both her previous background and the success of the last two years were a bad preparation for the New World. Among her brother John's friends had been some of the most outstanding literary figures of their generation. In Edinburgh she had enjoyed the friendship of the Combes. After her success at Covent Garden she had had the entree to all that was most sophisticated, urbane and gracious in London society. This combination of temperament, youth and background, allied to a mind naturally lively and curious, made her a critical rather than a tactful observer of the American scene. To some extent this was always to be so, and though later she made dear and deep friends in the country of her adoption it was always in the more intellectual society of Boston and New England that she felt most at home.

Both her attitude and, later, the journal, were to be the source of future trouble. Americans were sensitive to comments which they regarded as condescending, and which Fanny, once she knew the country better, would not have made. As she explained to George Combe some ten months later,

There are differences of customs and manners, which lying on the surface must offend the eye of a hasty observer, who satisfied with a superficial glance – full of the presuppositions and prejudice belonging to habits and education of an opposite nature conclude that because the inhabitants of the United States do not combine the refinements, the arts, the treasures and elegance of an old and wealthy monarchy, with the vigour, energy and political freedom of a young and poor Republic they are a nation of savages and cannot be either too much ridiculed and despised for manners and customs which have grown as naturally out of their institutions and state of society as those of the European nations have grown from the great feudal system which was their root – To speak before one has had leisure to reflect as well as to perceive is a great mistake.

It was one into which she thought most English visitors to the United States fell into headlong; it was one of which in her early months in that country she was often guilty herself. The United States had broken away from Britain little more than fifty years ago; Charles Kemble had been born while the War of Independence was still being fought. Though its resources were growing North America was still cut off by poor communications from the sophistication of Europe, which was the only civilization that Fanny knew. There was a fair amount of coming and going between the businessmen of both nations but probably more wealthy Americans visited Europe than English travellers came to America. The majority in both countries rarely travelled at all.

Fanny's first impressions, gained from a New York hotel, were not favourable. She admitted that the food itself was good but there was too much of it; the wine was drinkable and the fruit lovely to look at but inferior to English hothouse fruit in flavour; there was plenty of ice but everything was put on the table at the same time. Fanny considered this 'a slovenly outlandish fashion, fish, soup and meat all at once, and pudding and tarts and cheese all at another once; no finger glasses and a patched table-cloth – in short a want of style and neatness which is found in every hotel in England'. Lest Fanny should sound too carping a critic and too complaisant about English hotels here is a comment by an American visitor to England, the authoress Catherine

Maria Sedgwick, later to become one of her dearest friends. In *Letters from Abroad to Kindred at Home* Miss Sedgwick wrote, 'The luxury of an English inn, after a day as exhausting as our last on the Isle of Wight, has never been exaggerated and cannot be over praised. We have not been ten days in England, without having certain painful comparisons between our own inns and those of this country forced upon us.' Fanny clearly had some grounds for her strictures. One thing which she much disliked was the general lack of privacy. She was accustomed to stand on her dignity; she was used to the more formal manners of good society and judged by them. Moreover she was Miss Fanny Kemble. She did not expect people to intrude upon her or to claim an acquaintance without an introduction to which she had given her assent. So the less formal, friendly manners of the Americans, and particularly those of the men, came to her as a shock. In her private room in the hotel total strangers who asked to see her would be shown up. One visitor, whom she was afterwards to know well, and to like, called when her father was out. 'In walked an elderly good looking man, who introduced himself as Mr—[Hone] to whom my father had letters of introduction. He sat himself down and pattered a little, and then went away.' As Mr Hone also kept a diary, it is possible to judge of their mutual reactions. Mr Hone, a man of influence and wealth in New York, had come to call on the Kembles, and saw no reason why, if Mr Kemble were out, he should not see the daughter. His first impression was 'She appears deserving of all her reputation – a good figure, easy manners, sprightly and intelligent, self possessed, not very handsome but with features animated and expressive, and calculated for great stage effects.'

American cities Fanny found very different from those with which she had been most familiar in Britain. By the eighteen thirties London and Edinburgh were already, at least for the better-off, gracious places in which to live. Where it has not fallen a victim to the developers Bloomsbury, with its spacious squares and dignified terraces, is typical of the London that Fanny knew and loved when she was living in Great Russell Street, while in Edinburgh the New Town was being built on similar lines. New York, where many of the old frame houses of colonial days still remained, seemed strange to her, though not unattractive. 'The houses', she wrote, ' are almost all painted glaring white or red; the other favourite colours appear to be pale straw and grey. They all have green venetian shutters, which gives an idea of coolness, and almost every house has a tree or trees in its vicinity, which looks pretty and gardenlike.' Broadway she described as the American Oxford Road, 'being of a tolerable width and full of shops, where everyone went to see and be seen'. She was more impressed with Canal Street, which she described as

broader and finer than any I have yet seen in New York; and at one end of it a Christian church, copied from some pagan temple or other, looked extremely well in the full flood of silver light that streamed from heaven. There were many temptations to look around, but the flags were so horribly broken and out of order, that to do so was to run the risk of breaking one's neck.

Though the London she had left was still a frighteningly insanitary place with defective drainage, made worse by the introduction of water closets before the drains had been reconstructed to take the amount of sewerage that flooded them, and impure drinking water, outwardly in the principal areas it was a well kept city. In the late eighteenth century parishes where the wealthy lived had obtained private Acts of Parliament which allowed a board of commissioners, made up of local householders, to levy a special assessment on all houses above a fixed rateable value, in order to improve the lighting, paving and cleansing of the streets. This was an amenity that Fanny had come to expect and she was shocked not to find a similar standard in New York. Three years later, when her journal was published, she added a footnote in which she said that since this description had been written very considerable improvements had already been effected in New York's streets. If critical of their condition, she had been very favourably impressed by the civil and orderly behaviour of the crowds that thronged them. Instead of the jostling and pushing customary in London, young men made room for women to pass and some even took their cigars out of their mouths. To those who know the bustle of modern New York, with its reputation that life there is lived at a quicker pace than in London, Fanny's explanation that 'this crowd was merely abroad for pleasure, sauntering along, which is a thing never seen in London', is historically interesting. She was more critical of the women she saw, observing that they 'dress very much and are like French women gone mad; they all of them seem to me to walk horribly ill, as if they wore tight shoes'. She was fascinated by 'the blacks parading up and down, most of them in the height of fashion, with every colour of the rainbow about them'.

Fanny's favourite place in New York was the Battery, where she and her father loved to walk beneath the trees, enjoying the play of light and shade upon the water. If Mary Anne Thackeray, who loved and admired the more mature Fanny of later years, was correct in thinking that 'the most distinguishing stamp of her character was her great and fervent piety', almost as strong was her love of beauty. Writing to George Combe in the March of 1832 she asserted that 'the soul that loves that which is lovely will never want matter to rejoice in', telling him that in her judgement 'the sense of Beauty, taking that word in its widest sense', was 'the greatest good except revelation that God ever gave to man'. As a counterpoint to the many criticisms that her journal contained of American manners and habits must be set her deep appreciation of the splendour of its countryside. Here is a characteristic passage, written to recapture the magic of a walk that she and her father took one evening along the Battery.

It was between sunset and moon rise, and a lovelier light never lay upon sea, earth and sky. The horizon was bright orange colour, fading as it rose to pale amber, which died away again into the modest violet of twilight; this possessed the main sky wholely, except where two or three masses of soft dark purple clouds floated from behind which the stars presently winked at us with their bright eyes.

Once they made an expedition by steamer across to Hoboken. Here Fanny was enchanted by all the new kinds of trees, the strange flowers and the gorgeous butterflies that they saw. Yet even here the note of criticism made itself felt. When she looked at the rough and ragged grass-covered slopes she thought nostalgically of the lovely lawns of England. In this she was not alone. The English lawn, the product of a long tradition and a favourable climate, had always been one of the glories of English colleges and stately homes; few English travellers even today are impressed by the so-called lawns they find abroad. 'Have you a very definite idea of an English lawn?' Miss Sedgwick asked her friends. 'The grass is shaven every week, this, of course, produces a fresh bright tint, and to your tread it feels like the richest bed of moss you ever set your feet upon.' Considering the standards of Oatlands it is hardly surprising that Fanny was not impressed by the carelessly kept grass at Hoboken; nor had she yet experienced the rigours of an American winter and the heat of the summer that must in any case have made the ritual tending of an English lawn climatically impossible.

One natural phenomenon that Fanny did appreciate, and of which she has left a vivid description, was the tremendous storms that could break over New York. It is characteristic of her dramatic, emotional impulses that storms, like the raging of the sea, when she could view it from the stability of the shore, were matters of delight to her own stormy temperament. Something of the current of delight and excitement that ran through her as she watched a storm raging over the city is conveyed in this description: 'The lightning played without the intermission of a second, in wide sheets of purple glaring flame, that trembled over the earth for two or three seconds at a time; making the whole world, river, sky, trees and buildings look like a ghostly cut out in chalk!' Her description is too long to quote in its entirety but ends with this further dramatic word picture: 'The night was pitchy dark too; so that between each of those ghastly smiles of the devil, the various pale steeples and buildings, which seemed at every moment to leap from nothing into existence, after standing out in fearful relief against a background of fire, were hidden like so many dreams in deep and total darkness.' Some readers may judge this writing to verge on the melodramatic; even so it sheds its own light on the writer's temperament. So is her final reflection that such storms were yet another manifestation of 'God's powerful and beautiful creation.' For Fanny, God and Beauty went hand in hand. Indeed Harriet thought it her duty to warn her against the danger of confusing emotional and imaginative excitement with genuine religious feeling. Against such a charge Fanny defended herself by saying that her wonder at things like the star-paved heavens or the music of great waves was a very different thing from her conception of religion. This for Fanny was the daily and hourly endeavour after righteousness, the humble trust, obedience and thankfulness, which I believe constitutes the vital part of relgous faith'.

It was a faith that Fanny found difficult to carry into her daily life when faced with the need to accommodate herself to the ways and habits of the new society in which she found herself. There was certainly more intolerance than charity in the description of the dinner-party to which Mr Hone, following up the civility of his call, invited Fanny and her father. Here again the biographer is helped by the fact that both Hone and Fanny left descriptions of the evening in their respective diaries. Clearly Fanny was in an edgy, difficult mood, indeed at her most English, when nothing that did not conform to her own standards was acceptable. She described the evening in highly critical terms. 'This is one of the first houses here, so I am to conclude I am to consider what I see a tolerable sample of the ways and manners of being, doing and suffering of the best society in New York.' Almost unconsciously Fanny may have been expecting from such a host something of the style of entertainment provided by her aristocractic English friends, and the contrast drew forth unfavourable comment. 'The dinner', she confided in her journal, 'was plenteous and tolerably well dressed, but ill served; there were not half servants enough, and we had neither water glasses nor finger bowls.' Also to her displeasure, they were served with coffee afterwards instead of the conventional English tea. Fanny was critical too of the way in which the female guests dressed, 'in a sort of French demi-toilette, with bare necks and long sleeves, heads frizzed out after the very latest Petit Courir, and thread net handkerchieves and caps, the whole of which, to my English eyes, appeared a strange marrying of incongruities'. Here again there was a considerable divergence between what was considered good taste in each country. Henry Witkoff, the Philadelphian equivalent of the London 'man about town', was clearly shocked when he went to the London Opera by the way in which society ladies 'make an exposure of their persons, absolutely thrilling to a stranger,' commenting on 'the startling usage of unmasking their loveliness to the extent I witnessed on my advent to the Opera . . . Accustomed to the prudery of my native town, where a nude statue flushed the cheek of innocence, and where the unadorned nymphs of a Rubens or a Titian would have been stigmatized as indecent I considered the spectacle as not only novel but indelicate.' To Fanny, used to the bare bosoms of Regency England, before society had come under the moral delicacy of Queen Victoria, or more properly of Prince Albert, the American attitude was, at best, provincial. Fanny herself was guilty of some lapses of good manners on this occasion. Discovering that one of the guests, Charles Townsend, was secretary at the English Legation, ignoring the other guests, she 'talked over English folk and doings' to what she described as 'my entire satisfaction'. Her manners did not pass unnoticed by her host who, in his account of the evening, wrote 'She certainly has an air of indifference and nonchalance not at all calculated to make her a favourite with the beaux,' adding 'Her fault appears to be an ungracious manner of receiving the advances of those who desire to pay her attention. This may proceed from the novelty of her situation, and may soon be removed. But now is the time to make friends if she wants them.'

Clearly Fanny had not yet taken the measure of American hospitality, with its informality and friendly interest in the affairs of even comparative strangers which she took for a combination of bad manners and impertinence. Moreover, though she approved of the lack of servility among what in English terms she would have described as 'the lower orders', remarking accurately that the term 'working people' was not applicable in a country where everybody worked, in practice she found the cordial friendliness of the shop assistants who served her hard to take after the obsequious London salesman. Once when she went to buy some gauze she had been 'greeted by name, and told how anxious they were to render her stay agreeable'. She confided to her journal that she supposed that a Christian would have expressed great pleasure in return but that,

for my part, though I had the grace to smile and say 'Thank-you' I longed to add 'but be so good as to measure your ribbons and hold your tongue'. I have no idea of holding parley with clerks behind a counter, still less of their doing so with me. So much for my first impression of the courtesy of this land of liberty. I should have been much better pleased if they had called me 'Ma'am' which they did not.

Even long acquaintance with American democracy in action seems to have done nothing to soften Fanny's attitude towards the tradespeople who served her if she thought their manner too familiar. Many years later a Boston lady, Mrs Browne, writing to her daughter, then a pupil at Professor Agassiz's school in Cambridge, told her that 'strange stories are afloat concerning her encounters with clerks at the dry goods stores' adding the hope that 'where ever she displays her tyrannical spirit she will meet with those who will have the courage enough to let her know that the American people know what belongs to good manners.'

English shopkeepers were a more subservient breed and Fanny, who hated shopping, had a sharp tongue on such occasions. Because having to choose bewildered her she never entered a shop until she had a very precise notion of just what she intended to buy, and woe to the assistant who tried to sell her anything else. Mary Anne Thackeray, shopping with Fanny in Regent Street years later, when the purpose of the expedition was to buy muslin window-curtains, recalled vividly how

Fanny's temper mounted on being shown silk and worsted hangings. Finally she snapped

'Young man, perhaps your time is of no value to you – to me my time is of great value. I shall thank you to show me the things I asked for instead of all these things for which I *did not* ask', and she flashed such a glance at him as must have surprised the youth. He looked perfectly scared, seemed to leap over the counter, and the muslin curtains appeared on the spot.

These two episodes provide a neat contrast between English society with it graduations of status and the 'Jack is as good as his master' attitude of the New World. As the modern world moves with increasing rapidity towards the concept of a classless society it becomes increasingly difficult to understand the sense of social shock that Fanny experienced in one which practised at least the outward signs of equality. Yet even in her dealings with American shopkeepers she was capable of a gracious gesture. When Dall was shopping alone in Philadelphia a Quaker storekeeper asked 'And how doth Fanny? I was in hopes she might have wanted something. We should have had great pleasure in attending on her.' Next day she went in person and bought herself a 'lovely silver-coloured gown'.

At least Fanny was consistent. Even in her own country, among her own fashionable friends, when put out she seems to have made little attempt to hide her annoyance and was herself guilty of a display of bad manners of the kind of which Mr Hone complained. She did not even scruple to affront the formidable Lady Holland. The Holland House circle was legendary but until Fanny returned to London as Mrs Butler she had never dined there, her parents having declined Lady Holland's invitation to do so on her behalf, thinking the house of a divorcee no place for their sheltered daughter. As a married woman this taboo no longer applied and the lion-hunting Lady Holland again asked her to dine. Unfortunately Fanny took an instant dislike to her hostess who, she said, 'behaved herself with the fantastic despotic impropriety in which she frequently indulged, and what might have been tolerated in a spoilt beauty of eighteen, but was hardly becoming in a woman of her age and appearance'. So, though Fanny enjoyed the company that she met there, the acquaintance did not prosper. One evening, there being a shortage of gentlemen, she had arranged with a woman friend that they would go in together and enjoy one another's conversation. Unfortunately for this comfortable plan Lady Holland insisted that Fanny sit by her, with the intention of stimulating her guest into entertaining the assembled company by the brilliant talk for which she was well known. Fanny behaved badly. Annoyed at being dragooned into sitting where she had no desire to sit, she sulked in obstinate silence, refusing to utter more than a bare word or so throughout the meal. This display of sheer bad manners towards an older woman, who was also her hostess, illustrates how difficult Fanny could be. She rarely troubled to hide her feelings or opinions, confessing once in a letter to Sam Ward, an American friend, that she was perhaps too indifferent to what the generality of people thought of her.

Fanny Kemble was by no means universally popular. Mrs Lynn Linton was one of her victims. Meeting Fanny, then in her forties, she described the way in which

The deep voice and stage-stateliness of her manner, the assumption of supremacy, and really cruel strength of this lady, crushed me flat. The way in which she levelled her black eyes at me, and calmly put her foot on me, was an experience never to be forgotten. The pitiless brutality of her contradictions, her scathing sarcasm, her contemptuous taunts, knowing that I was unable to answer her, the way in which she used her mature powers to wound and hurt my even then immature nature gave me a shuddering horror for her, such as I fancy a man would feel for one who had flayed him in the market place.

It is an unattractive picture. But at least Fanny's almost aggressive honesty made her no respecter of persons. Her son-in-law James Leigh recounted how once when the famous Dean Stanley was taking her into dinner and made some trivial observation about the weather, Fanny retorted crushingly that she had expected better conversation from him. For the entire meal silence then reigned between the formidable pair.

When Fanny came to America the kind of impression that she created socially seemed less important than that she and her father should make a favourable impact on New York's theatre-going public. It was decided that Fanny should make her debut as Bianca in *Fazio*. Her chances did not seem promising. To her dismay she found that the part of Fazio was to be played by a Mr Keppel, whom she described as 'that washed-out man' who had once played Romeo to her Juliet on tour in England and who, having failed on the English stage, had sought a fresh opening in America. At the rehearsal she found him as nervous and imperfect as ever, so that she wailed 'What on earth will he or shall I do to-night?' Fanny may not have been the easiest of leading ladies with whom to act in so far as people feared her tongue, but she always seems to have tried to help out her incompetent leads. To her the situation on her opening night looked black. 'Mr Keppel,' she reported, 'was frightened to death, and in the very second speech was quite out; it was in vain that I prompted him; he was too nervous to take the word, and made a complete mess of it.' As Fanny left the stage at the end of the first act she told Dall, who always went with her to the theatre, 'It's all up with me, I can't do anything now.' Explaining her despair later, she wrote, 'having to prompt my Fazio, frightened by his fright, utterly unable to work myself into anything like excitement, I thought the whole thing must necessarily go to pieces.' Fortunately death carries off Fazio at the end of the second act and then, unhampered by his distracting presence, Fanny was able to lose herself in the part and work up to her climax. To Hone on the other side of the curtain, unconscious of the difficulties that were facing Fanny, her performance seemed a wonderful exhibition of dramatic art. He wrote

I have never witnessed an audience so moved, astonished and delighted. Her display of the strong feelings which belong to the part was great beyond description, and the expression of her wonderful face would have been a rich treat if her tongue had uttered no sound. The fifth act was such an expression of female powers as we have never before witnessed, and the curtain fell among deafening shouts and plaudits of an astonished audience.

After this eulogy he admitted that,

She has some faults; her low tones are sepulchral and indistinct . . . and she is at times somewhat monotonous, particularly in the unimpassioned passages . . . but on the whole I am quite satisfied that we have never seen her equal on the American stage and England has witnessed none since Miss O'Neill.

Two days later Fanny played Juliet to her father's Romeo, the suggestion of incest having apparently been ignored in the desire to furnish her with an adequate Romeo, and to give Charles Kemble the opportunity to play one of his great parts. Again Hone was there and again he was lyrical over Fanny. He considered Charles was too old for Romeo, but that he overcame this disadvantage by

his perfect conception of the character, the grace of his elocution and the elegance of his deportment. Juliet was something beyond my powers of description. I never saw a female performer at all to compare with her in this part, and I cannot imagine anything to exceed it. She is destined to fill the place of Mrs Siddons, and make the finest performer in the world.

84

Hone thought that the impression that she had made would never be forgotten in New York, and as Fanny and her father were now on sufficiently friendly terms with the Hone family for her to go out driving with his daughter, Mr Hone became more and more fascinated by 'this wonderful girl'. Charles did not always play Romeo, Mercutio being another of his most successful parts; and Fanny's admirers would have had their illusions sadly weakened if they could have heard the conversation on one of these occasions that, *sotto voce*, was taking place between Juliet and her Romeo as the ill-starred lovers died. As Juliet fell distracted over Romeo's corpse she whispered 'Am I smothering you?' to which the corpse replied 'Not at all; could you be so kind, do you think, as to put my wig on again for me? It has fallen off', to which she replied, 'I am afraid I can't but I'll throw my muslin veil over it. You've broken the phial haven't you?' to which the corpse nodded, and Juliet then whispered 'Where's your dagger?' only to receive the disconcerting answer 'Pon my soul I don't know.' There was an even more ridiculous postscript to this conversation. It had been customary in the early nineteenth century to end the play with the spectacle of a magnificent funeral and on this occasion, when the curtain went up on what should have been the corpse of Juliet lying on her bed in her grave clothes, the audience saw instead half a dozen stage hands in patched trousers smoothing down her pillows and arranging the draperies over the dead Juliet. No wonder that Fanny's sensitive imagination exploded in disgust, 'How I do loathe the stage! Those wretched, tawdry, glittering rags flung over the breathing forms of ideal loveliness. What a mass of wretched mumming mimicry acting is. To act this! To act Romeo and Juliet! Horror! Horror!'

Horror or not, the tour was proving most successful. Everywhere the Kembles, but in particular Fanny, were greeted by enthusiastic audiences. From New York they were go to Philadelphia, the state capital of Quaker Pennsylvania. Fanny's description of their journey highlights the difficulties that travellers faced before the completion of the railroads. Because the original states had grown up round the seaboard, and had taken advantage of the rivers to penetrate into the interior, America had developed the river-boat rather than the coach as the easiest means of transport. The best of these boats were very comfortable, though the accommodation varied, as did the food, but there was little privacy. Ladies were expected to share a common cabin and common toilet facilities and Fanny much deprecated the

American habit of spitting into the spittoons provided lavishly, though she had to admit that American men had achieved a high degree of accuracy. When the Kembles left New York on 8 October therefore the first stage of their journey was by steamboat to the New Jersey shore. From there they had to make the journey by land to the Delaware river, where they could again catch a river-steamer up the river to Philadelphia. This overland journey was largely by coach over bad roads, and poor Fanny suffered much physical discomfort. Describing the coach in which the party was condemned to travel, she wrote with loathing,

English eye hath not seen, English ear hath not heard, nor has it entered into the hearts of English men to conceive the surpassing clumsiness and wretchedness of these leather inconveniences. They are shaped something like boats, the sides being merely leather pieces, removable at will, but which in bad weather draw to protect them from the rain. When in place, the unfortunate travellers were all but smothered for lack of fresh air.

Finally the voyagers set off, 'bumping, thumping, jumping, jolting, shaking, tossing and tumbling over the wretchedest road, I do think the cruellest, hard-heartest road that ever wheel rumbled upon'. Inevitably Fanny was making unfavourable comparisons with public transport in England. By the eve of the railway age its road system, by contemporary standards, was excellent. Owing to the pioneering efforts of Macadam, devastating ruts and mud were things of the past. Public coaches had reached a standard of comfort that surprised foreign visitors. Henry Witkoff declared that an English coach 'looked as if it could hardly be meant for public use. If the carriages were so perfect what shall I say of the horses? Never have I seen such beautiful creatures before, with their small heads, slender limbs and perfect shape.' This corroborates Fanny's constant contention that American ones could not be compared to them for excellence. Fanny's passion for riding had not left her. As she told George Combe,

The only habit to which I have resolutely adhered, and with which I suffer nothing to interfere, is that of daily exercise – on horse back or on foot, I am out during some part of almost every day. My health is one of God's best gifts to me and for all possible reasons I endeavour to preserve it at least by these means.

Whenever possible on her tour, Fanny hired a mount and explored the country round her. Any horse was better than no horse at all but Fanny was critical of her hired horses, one difficulty being that they were broken in and schooled to different paces from those of English saddle-horses, which made them uncomfortable for her to ride. In December 1832 she wrote bitterly 'Upon my word, these American horses are most unsafe to ride. I never mount one but I recommend myself to the care of Heaven to have every bone in my body broken before I dismount again.' She was equally scathing about American riders, declaring 'None of these people know how to ride; they just go whatever pace the horse likes sitting as backward as they can in the saddle, and tugging at the reins as hard as ever they can, to the infinite detriment of their own hands and their horses' mouths.' It was comments such as these that infuriated Americans when later unforeseen circumstances led Fanny to publish her journal.

Philadelphia was the second major American city which the Kembles visited. Later Fanny came to know it very well. Her first impressions were favourable. 'The town', she wrote, 'is perfect silence and solitude after New York.' This was a quality that always recommended a place to her; she was particularly susceptible to noise. She continued,

There is a greater air of age about it, too, which pleases me. The houses are not so fiercely red, nor the facings so glaringly white; in short it has not so new and flaunting a look which is a great recommendation to me. The city is regularly built, the streets intersecting each other at right angles. We passed two or three pretty buildings in pure white marble, and the bank in Chestnut Street, which is a beautiful little copy of the Parthenon. The pure clear cold looking marble suits well with the severe and unadorned style of architecture; and is in harmony too, with the extreme brilliancy of the sky and the clearness of the atmosphere of this country.'

Here at least Fanny preferred the New World to the Old; London was notorious for its smoke-laden atmosphere, the product of its multitudinous coal fires. Financially also Fanny had cause to like Philadelphia. Her reputation had preceded her and she was gratified, and a little amused, to hear that there had been 'fighting and rushing and tearing of coats' at the box-office. Even in the eighteen thirties the familiar figure of the tout was to be found; one man, she heard, had made the not inconsiderable sum of forty dollars by reselling the tickets he had managed to purchase. But though the people of Philadelphia were eager to see the Kembles Fanny found them a difficult audience. Her journal was full of complaints. On 12 October she wrote: 'This audience is the most unapplausive I have ever acted to not excepting my *excitable* friends north of the Tweed. They were very attentive certainly, but how they did make me work.' By the 25th, in spite of the rush for tickets and full houses, she was still grumbling, 'I played only so-so; the fact is, it is utterly impossible to this audience at all. They are so immovable, such sticks and stones, that one is fairly exhausted with labouring to excite, before half one's work is done.' Apparently the Philadelphians carried their Quaker sobriety with them into the theatre but Fanny, longing for audience participation, looked for something rather less reminiscent of a Friends' meeting house. Even out of the theatre she found them very different from the outgoing and welcoming New Yorkers. The citizens of Philadelphia prided themselves on their exclusive society and were not prepared readily to ask even distinguished actors and actresses to their houses. So, unlike New York, which had lionized them, in the capital of Pennsylvania invitations were few, and hardly anyone did them the honour of calling at their hotel. They were, Fanny declared, 'about the most inhospitable set of people it was ever my good fortune to fall in with'. It was a relief to return to New York in November. Fanny did not know when she penned her tirades against the inhospitable Philadelphians that one of the few callers who waited on them was the man she was afterwards to marry.

Things went better in New York. *Much Ado About Nothing* was added to their repertoire and Fanny was pleased with her performance, coming to the comforting conclusion that 'I am much improved in my comedy acting.' Experience was beginning to tell; to her natural talent, which at first had been her only asset other than her name and youth, she was adding technique. She was also establishing a rapport with her New York audiences similar to that which she had enjoyed at Covent Garden. On the last night of the Kembles' present season she reported with pleasure, 'The pit rose to us like Christians, and shouted and hallowed, as I have been used to hear. I felt sorry to leave them; they are a pleasant audience to act to, and exceedingly civil to us, and I have got rather attached to them.' It was certainly a more sympathetic audience than the one that had greeted her first appearance in Philadelphia. There, after the performance was over, both Dall and her father had commented on the extremely ungracious way in which she had acknowledged their applause at her final curtain. Fanny's reply is so characteristic of her outlook that it is worth quoting.

I cannot tell; I did not mean to be so; I made them three curtseys, and what could woman do more? Of course I can neither feel nor look so glad to see them as I am to see my own dear London people; neither can I be as profound in my obeisance, as when my audience is civil enough to rise to me: there is a difference look you.

Fanny did not care to please where she had not been pleased. When the Kembles returned to Philadelphia early in the New Year they found the citizens more friendly; invitations became more numerous and, as in London, Fanny was soon the idol of the young men who fell, in large numbers, victim to her charms.

By then the Kembles had seen something more of America. From New York they went to Baltimore, which city failed to impress her. Fanny's comments are interesting in that they underline the patchy development of what was to be one of America's large and prosperous cities in the future. When Fanny visited it was still 'a large rambling red brick village' that reminded her of 'the outskirts of one of our manufacturing towns, Manchester or Birmingham. It covers an immense extent of ground, but there are great gaps and vacancies in the middle of streets, patches of gravelly ground etc.' In 1832 Baltimore bore all the signs of an urban site in the process of development with a corresponding lack of the more cultural amenities which denote the presence of a sophisticated and established society. Fanny was disgusted when she found that she could not procure a side-saddle anywhere in the town.

From Baltimore the Kembles moved on to the Federal capital, Washington. Fanny's comment on it was 'Washington, in fact, is to America what Downing and Parliament Streets are to London, a congregation of government offices, where political characters, secretaries, clerks, place-holders and place-seekers, do most congregate.' Like Baltimore it was very much a city in the making. To Fanny's observant eye it was 'a rambling red brick image of futurity, where nothing *is*, but all things *are to be*'. Going into more detail she declared, 'It is the strangest thing by way of a town that can be fancied. It is laid out to cover. I should think, some ten square miles, but the houses are here, there and nowhere, the streets, conventionally, not properly so called, are roads crooked or straight, where buildings are intended to be.' Even the White House itself had the same half-finished air. Did Fanny's American friends, one wonders, point out that it had been burnt down as recently as 1812 by British soldiers in that short, unhappy war? She thought it 'a comfortless, handsome looking building, with a withered grass plot enclosed in wooden palings in front and a desolate reach of uncultivated ground down to the river behind'. Fanny was still not reconciled to the absence of the traditional English lawn, that even in January would have provided an elegant setting for the white building. The Capitol itself she described as 'A very handsome building, of which the Americans are not a little proud; but it seems placed there by mistake, so little do the miserable, untidy hovels above, and the scattered unfinished red brick town below, accord with its patrician marble and high sounding title'. She did however concede that as she walked up the hill to it that 'the mass of white buildings with its terraces and columns, stood out in fine relief against the cloudless blue sky'.

Not content with an outward view of the Federal capital, Fanny was anxious to see something of the political machine in action, though she did not pretend to have any understanding of American politics. She did however want to hear that great orator Daniel Webster of Massachusetts and accordingly paid a visit to the Senate House. She was surprised to find that, unlike the House of Commons, with its long narrow chamber, where the supporters of the government sat behind the ministers on the Treasury Bench and the Opposition on the benches opposite, 'the senators sat in two semi-circular rows, turned towards the President, in comfortable armchairs'. But what surprised and shocked her more was the behaviour of the female part of the spectators, 'a whole regiment of ladies, whispering, talking, laughing and fidgeting' so that even when Webster was speaking 'a tremendous bustle, and waving of feathers, and rustling of silks would be heard.' Then, by way of a further interruption 'in came streaming a reinforcement of political beauties' with more shaking of hands and how-d'ye-doing so that the senators turned round disapprovingly and even Webster hesitated in his speech. The democratic traditions of the United States made it comparatively easy to meet the President himself. Fanny gave an amusing account of what happened when on certain days the White House was thrown open to the public and receptions were given to which everybody had the right to attend. As on these occasions refreshments were provided, in rushed 'the common people' like a hungry horde and devoured everything that they could find. Finally in self defence the President ceased to provide food and drink for his too numerous guests, whereupon most ordinary people stayed away. In due course Fanny was presented to the President, Andrew Jackson, whose early reputation was due to his successful defence of New Orleans against the British in 1814, and who since 1829 had held the highest office in the State. Though feeling none too kindly disposed to what he called 'scribbling ladies' to whose activities he attributed the trouble he was having with South Carolina, which was claiming the right to nullify any federal law that it conceived to be against its interests, he was pleasant to Fanny. The arguments for and against the authority of the Federal Government to dominate the individual states, which was to become a major issue in the Civil War in the sixties, was a topic which Fanny then neither was interested in nor understood. She did however like Andrew Jackson himself, describing him as 'a good specimen of a fine old battered soldier. His hair is very thick and grey; his manners perfectly simple and quiet, therefore very good.' It was a new experience for Fanny, and indeed all English people, to meet a Head of State who was not a gentleman born. Certainly she found him more approachable than she was to find Queen Victoria when she was presented to her in later years.

There had been some idea of going further south, but the political crisis over Nullification made this seem undesirable and by 30 January the Kembles were once more in Philadelphia, which no longer seemed quite so unfriendly a city. This time they made only a short stay and were back in New York by 15 February. As the winter dragged on Fanny began to think nostalgically of the slow unfolding of an English spring. By the end of February the hawthorn would have been budding, the almond trees blossoming and the primroses beginning to appear. Spring in America was very different; it did not 'stand coaxing and beseeching the shy summer to the woods and fields, as in our own country'. Instead she noticed how the ice seemed to melt by magic, so that 'the whole world breaks out into a halleluia of warmth, beauty, and blossoming like mid-July in our deliberate climate'. In July she paid her first visit to Boston and was enchanted by it, writing 'As a town it bears more resemblance to an English city than any we have yet seen; the houses are built more in our own fashion and there is a beautiful walk called the Common, and the features of which strongly resemble the view over Green Park just by Constitution Hill.' She found this pleasant re-echoing of the old England in New England also in such things as the 'extreme neatness and cleanliness of the houses, the careful cultivation of the land, the tasteful and ornamental arrangement of the grounds immediately surrounding the dwellings', and finally 'that most English of all manifestations above all the church spires, pointing towards heaven from the bosom of each village'. It was not only in outward ways that Fanny found Boston congenial; it was a city full of cultural and intellectual activity. Here she found more 'pictures, sculptures and more books in private houses' than she had seen elsewhere. The inhabitants also met with her approval, an approval that she felt was mutual, writing to Harriet, 'The people take more kindly to us than they have done even elsewhere, and it is delightful to act to audiences who appear as pleasantly pleased with us.' The more Fanny saw of Boston and its people the more she liked them. Writing to George Combe in the April of 1834 she told him,

The New Englanders call themselves a purely English race and in so doing pay us I think a very flattering tribute but one which proves itself true in all the exterior appearance of people, things and manners. I am fond of Boston . . . I prefer it to all the rest of America that I have seen, the lower orders of people are *true* in their speech and *honest* in their hearts.

From this opinion Fanny never varied; throughout her life New England remained very close to her heart. It was from New England that she drew her closest friends and found with them alone the intellectual stimulus that was meat and drink to her.

Foremost among these friends were various members of the Sedgwick family, the best known of whom was Catherine Maria, the novelist. Fanny had first met her in New York, where Catherine Sedgwick had been delighted with the young actress and had made the effort to call upon her. She was some twenty years older than Fanny and was an important literary figure in New England. Although America had long been dependent on Britain in particular and Europe in general for its culture, by the time that Fanny crossed the Atlantic a new and vigorous literature, with its roots in America rather than in Europe, was developing. Between 1830 and 1840 the ranks of those who were to produce the great early classics of American literature including such names as Longfellow, Oliver Wendell Holmes, Edgar Allan Poe, Ralph Emerson, Nathaniel Hawthorne, and Prescott. Catherine Sedgwick has no place among these giants, but she was a novelist of some repute in her day. Like Maria Edgeworth and Charlotte Yonge in England, what she wrote was strictly moral in tone and outlook. Her first novel, published in 1822, *A New England Tale*, had grown out of a tract which her brother Theodore had encouraged her to write. Miss Sedgwick was a person of great charm and integrity and wide human sympathy. Originally she had lived at Stockbridge, but when her beloved youngest brother Charles had become clerk to the court at Lenox in the neighbouring Berkshire hills Catherine had moved there to be near him and his wife Elizabeth. Elizabeth too in her own way was an outstanding woman, who ran a school in Lenox on what were then very progressive lines. Later she, as well as her daughter Kate, were to become two of Fanny's closest friends in America. In the years to come Lenox and the Sedgwicks were her mental and physical refuge. She revelled in the hills and lakes of the Berkshires, and in the intellectual circle that gathered round the Sedgwicks she found the mental refreshment so necessary to her.

The second contact that Fanny made was Dr William Channing, who was to have a great influence over her. Like many of the more intellectual and progressive thinkers in late eighteenth-century England, Dr Channing was a Unitarian. His theology can best be described, though this may seem a contradiction in terms, as 'Enlightened Christianity'. Channing was in revolt against the narrow, dogmatic Puritanism that still dominated much of New England religious thought. Fanny, by some quirk of fate, had run across some of his books in Edinburgh, and writing to George Combe in 1831 had told him,

I admire him more than any writer of the present day with whom I am conversant. There is a magnificence in his view of human nature which raises my soul almost to the level of his exalted estimate of it, there is a grandeur in his reliance on the good of our being that strikes me forcibly and the language in which his thoughts were clothed both becomes them and attracts me, from its power and almost poetic harmony.

Catherine Sedgwick was both a friend and a disciple of Dr Channing and Fanny had looked forward to meeting him with the liveliest anticipation of the spiritual benefit she was to receive. However their first meeting proved a disappointment. Dr Channing seemed intent on meeting Fanny on her own ground, talking about the theatre and expressing views that Fanny found herself unable to accept. Her period of disillusionment was brief and a close relationship developed between them. In April 1834 she told George Combe 'I have seen Dr Channing several times; in spite of a very feeble state of health, he has been kind enough to come and see me once or twice each time we have been in Boston and you will readily believe how much I have valued the intercourse with such a mind. He is indeed very admirable, so enlarged and benevolent in his views, so temperate in all his feelings and opinions, so refined and cultivated in his intellect.'

When Fanny first met Catherine Sedgwick and Dr Channing she cannot have guessed the important parts they were to play in her life. The shadow of the future had not yet fallen across it. She had very little time in any case for reflection as the Kembles moved from engagement to engagement, but both father and daughter had reason to be pleased with their American venture. Financially the tour had been a success and with each month Fanny's technical grasp of her unchosen profession was increasing. By 1833 there was another and more personal reason for her growing liking for America. From his first meeting with Fanny in Philadelphia young Pierce Butler seems to have been bewitched by her and whenever it could be contrived he had followed her from town to town. He was with her in Boston and was riding with her regularly. Their Boston engagement over, the Kembles returned to New York for a last brief appearance before taking a much needed holiday. Their destination was the Niagara Falls and Canada. Their route lay up the noble Hudson river, stopping to give performances en route at such towns as Albany. When they left New York on 30 June by river-steamer they acquired a new travelling companion, the English explorer Edward Trelawny. Fanny at first was inclined to resent what she considered an encroachment on her privacy, but was soon won over by his personal fascination. Also Trelawny had the glamour of having known Byron and, long after their travels came to an end, he and Fanny continued to be friends. Fanny, recording her first impressions of him, wrote,

What a savage he is in some respects. He is a curious being; a description of him would puzzle anyone who had never seen him. A man with the proportions of a giant for strength and agility, stronger, broader than most men; yet with the most listless, indolent carelessness of gait, an uncertain wandering way of dropping his feet to the ground as if he did not know where he was going and didn't much wish to go anywhere. His face as dark as a Moor's with a wild, stray look about the eyes and forehead, and with a mark like a scar upon his cheek; his whole appearance gives one of toil, hardship, peril and wild adventure. The expression of his mouth is remarkably mild and sweet, and his voice is extremely low and gentle.

He was to prove a stimulating travelling companion and when the party was later joined by Pierce Butler Fanny had two very oddly assorted escorts. Judging by the entries in her journal it was a happy expedition, both gentlemen being delightfully attentive. Pierce had even had the forethought to provide the company with silver forks. Sometimes he and Fanny wandered off together but it was Trelawny with whom she shared the great moment of her first sight of Niagara. It was he who, knowing the terrain, urged her on as she made her first implusive dash to the Table Rock. It was he, a kindred spirit in her love for Nature, who stood beside her, safeguarding her from a fatal slip or stumble when the first magnificance of the Falls burst upon her breathless gaze. For once words failed her. All that she could write that night was, 'I saw Niagara. Oh God, who can describe them?'

Her pleasant summer over, Fanny returned to the treadmill of her professional career. In September Mr Hone went to see her in *The Stranger*, reporting that she 'played this evening with the most affecting pathos and tenderness; and so the audience appeared to think, for I never saw persons more attentive and more deeply affected'. Nevertheless Fanny's time on the American stage was coming to an end. Rumours were already flying round. In the same entry in his diary Mr Hone also wrote 'This will probably be her last engagement, if the report is true that she is married already, or about to be, to Mr Pierce Butler of Philadelphia.' Mr Hone's supposition was premature but in substance correct. Fanny was already engaged to Pierce though circumstances were to delay their marriage. Her American journal ends with the laconic statement that in June 1834 she married Pierce Butler. A new and very different chapter in her life was about to begin.

FOUR

Marriage and its Problems

Unlike most Victorian women Fanny had never looked forward to marriage; for her, fulfilment lay in the field of creative writing. With the clear sight of self-knowledge unclouded by emotion, she realized how little fitted she was for the roles of wife and mother as contemporary society understood them. Writing to Harriet in 1828, she told her,

You know that independence of mind and body seems to me the great desideratum of life; I am not patient of restraint or submission to authority and my heart and head are engrossed with the idea of exercising and developing the literary talent which I think I possess. This is meat, drink and sleep to me . . . I do not think I am fit to marry, to make an obedient wife or affectionate mother, my imagination is paramount with me, and would disqualify me, I think, for the everyday matter of fact cares and duties of the mistress of a household and the head of a family. I think I should be unhappy and the cause of unhappiness to others if I were to marry. I cannot swear I shall never fall in love, but if I do I will fall out of it again, for I do not think I shall ever so far lose sight of my best interest and happiness as to enter into a relation for which I feel so unfitted.

Fanny at nineteen was wiser than Fanny at twenty-four. After her successful debut at Covent Garden, as Aunt Dall pointed out to her, there were now other, more mundane considerations which would also lessen her chances of matrimonial happiness:

While you are single and choose to work, your fortune is an independent and ample one; as soon as you marry there is no such thing. Your position in society is both a pleasanter and more distinguished one than your birth and real station entitles you to; but that also is the result of your professional exertions, and might, and probably would, alter for the worse if you left the stage; for after all it is a mere frivolous popularity.

Here Aunt Dall was to prove only too true a prophet. Financial independence and her personal standing meant much to Fanny who, in
response to her aunt's warning, agreed that to marry was 'rather a
solemn consideration; for I lose everything by my marrying and gain
nothing in a worldly point of view'.

Women in love are rarely in a state of mind to weigh 'solemn
considerations'; certainly Fanny was not when she finally agreed to
marry Pierce Butler. An entry in her journal indicates that they first
met in the October of 1832 when the Kembles were playing in
Philadelphia. Young Pierce Butler, more fortunate than some of her
admirers, had been given a letter of introduction by a mutual friend
and she found him sitting with her father when she came down to tea.
It does not seem to have been love at first sight, at least on her part.
She described him as 'a pretty spoken genteel youth enough,' going on
'He is, it seems, a great fortune. Consequently I suppose, (in spite of his
inches) a great man.' With regard to the latter Fanny was misinformed.
Pierce had great expectations but when Fanny met him he was not yet
in possession of the wealth that one day was to be his. The Butlers were
one of the leading Philadelphian families. His grandfather, Major
Butler, was of Irish origin. He had first come to America with the
British army, had married an heiress from South Carolina and in the
War of Independence had espoused the cause of his adopted country.
This change of allegiance had paid him well. Once the war was over he
bought estates in Georgia, made a fortune planting cotton, sat twice in
the American Senate and invested successfully in real estate in Pennsylvania. His estate had passed to two of his daughters, Sarah and Frances.
The former, Pierce's mother, had married a Philadelphian, Dr Mease,
but it had been a condition of his grandfather's will that Pierce and
his brother John should take the family name of Butler. Information
about him as a person is singularly lacking. His detractors, if not more
numerous than his friends, were certainly more articulate, and few
independent and unprejudiced sources on which to base an assessment
seem to have survived. An early daguerreotype portrays him as a young
man with wavy hair, a broad forehead, very level eyebrows, a longish
nose, tightly closed lips and a rather small chin. According to Fanny's
first description of him he lacked inches, but as she was by no means
tall this was unimportant. Such comment as survives suggests that he
was a young man of considerable charm. Sidney Fisher, the Philadelphian diarist, described him as extremely gentlemanlike, and Fanny

had found him 'pretty spoken and genteel'. Both are nineteenth-century terms of approbation, however oddly they ring in twentieth-century ears.

Reputedly wealthy, good looking and by American standards well born, Pierce was undoubtedly a desirable parti: a big fish in the little pond of Philadelphian society. Moreover he was lucky enough to insinuate himself into Fanny's good graces by offering to ride with her. No better method could have been devised of enjoying her company. He began to haunt the riding school from which Fanny hired her mounts and soon she was asking herself, 'I wonder what he'll do for an *interest* by the by, when we are gone.' For this problem Pierce had his own solution; whenever possible he joined the Kembles, wherever they were playing, and often on their journeys. When the Kembles returned to Philadelphia in December Pierce and Fanny were riding together regularly, thereby causing Philadelphian society to gossip, as Fanny was somewhat ruefully aware. On Sunday 30 December, when there was no performance, they had ordered their horses to be brought round at noon with the idea of avoiding the good people of the town as they came out of church. Unfortunately the livery stable was half an hour late and, as Fanny recounted, 'we encountered the pious multitude. I am sure that when we mounted there were not less than a hundred and fifty beholders round the Mansion House.' One can imagine how they stared at the sight of young Mr Butler publicly accompanying the famous actress, even though the young couple were chaperoned by the inevitable Aunt Dall. Coming back they were equally unlucky. Once again they had the misfortune to 'canter down Chestnut Street, just as folk were coming from church, which caused no little staring and turning of heads.'

When they rode together Fanny was gay and in high spirits and Aunt Dall a complaisant chaperon. Pierce had taken the trouble to ingratiate himself with her, presenting her with a cap and a pretty whip with an ivory handle and what Fanny called 'a charming persuading lash', and often Dall seems to have been content to leave the young people very much to their own devices. When they rode out to Laurel Hill, one of their favourite haunts, she rested while they scrambled down to the river below. Whether this was tact or the lethargy of middle age, who can say? On a previous expedition Fanny had discovered a wonderul echo. When they rode there again in an excess of high spirits, standing on the river's edge, Fanny called to the echo, sang scales to it and indulged in what she described as 'every musical discourse' she could think of until her enthusiasm got the better of her balance and she fell into the river, whence she was rescued by Pierce. It was a light-hearted occasion, a lovely day and a lovely scene; in her journal Fanny painted a word picture of 'the still waters in which the shore, the trees and the bridge lay mirrored with beautiful and fairy like distinction'.

When at the end of their engagement the Kembles went on to Baltimore Pierce went with them. He was a gallant and thoughtful escort and for the entire trip her father was well content to leave his daughter and Dall in his charge. Whatever Fanny's feelings at this time it is clear that she was doing nothing to discourage her assiduous admirer, who already seems to have been head over heels in love. By the end of January the Kembles were back in Philadelphia and the rides and meetings went on. In these heady days of success Fanny had many admirers. One of Pierce's friends, Henry Witkoff, confessed in later life that

It would be hard to depict the wild intoxication that overtook me. I forgot everything else, law included. I did nothing but frequent the theatre, and abandon myself to the fascination of this bewitching actress. I went about like one possessed, muttering the favourite passages of her principal roles, till people thought me a fit companion for lunatics. I was not however her only victim. The infection seized on a friend of mine, which took the practical shape of a tender of marriage that after a time was accepted. Pierce Butler, a man of good family and fortune, became desperately enamoured of the marvellous creature, who to the sorcery of the stage added rare charms of person, brilliant accomplishments and high culture. Pierce Butler was envied, and almost detested, by a swarm of rivals for his victory over the Kembles.'

Competition such as this must have made young Pierce even more determined to carry off so desired a prize.

It is not surprising that by the spring of 1833 Fanny's attitude towards America and the Americans was changing. She told George Combe, 'I am quite reconciled to my surroundings, have met nothing but success in public and the utmost kindness and cordiality in private.' She had also found 'many things to like much and a few people to love'. Inevitably her vanity must have been flattered. Americans are traditionally most hospitable to the stranger within their gates. Even today the visitor from overseas is apt to be lionized in a way highly comforting to the ego; Fanny would have been cold-hearted indeed if she had not responded. Moreover the natural beauty in which the eastern states abound would have delighted Fanny even if these beauties had not been enhanced by the presence of Pierce as they explored them. Returning from an expedition up the Hudson, a river as beautiful as any to be found in Europe, in the May of 1833, Fanny summed up her growing liking for both the country and its people in a letter to Harriet, writing,

How you would have rejoiced in the beautiful and noble river scenery! This is a brave new world in more ways than one, and we are in every way bound to like it, for our labour has been most amply rewarded in its most important result, money; and the universal kindness which has everywhere met us since we first came to this country ought to repay us even for the pain and sorrow of leaving England.

Britain, for one must include her deep love for Scotland, still tugged, and was always to tug, at Fanny's heart-strings, but her mind was becoming half conditioned to the realization that she might never live there permanently again, though she declared, 'See it again I will, please God grant me life and eyes.'

During the time that the Kembles spent in Boston, where they stayed for a month, Pierce was slipping into the role of an accepted suitor, though when he first asked Fanny to marry him or when she promised to do so is uncertain. They rode everywhere together and from the entries in her journal it is clear that they now rode unchaperoned. When they went to Roxbury Pierce bought her a nosegay to wear as Lady Teazle, the part she was to play that night. They rode out to Fresh Pond, which Fanny described as a 'beautiful little lake' and back by Bunker's Hill of historic memory. Once they crossed the river by the Chelsea ferry, where the country reminded Fanny of her beloved Scotland – one wonders what she would have thought of it today – and galloped their horses along Nahant's golden sands. But their favourite haunt was the lovely burial ground on the slopes of Mount Auburn beyond the then village of Cambridge. Many years later Fanny recalled that when she was engaged to be married 'Pierce and I used to ride out there and sit together under a group of trees on a very pretty hillside, where the prospect over the countryside was very charming.' Even today it must be one of the most beautiful cemeteries in the world, full of a sense of peace, singing birds and flowers, but it is oddly prophetic that so much of their courting should have been in a graveyard. When the Kembles' theatrical commitments came to an end and they set out on their ill-fated expedition to Niagara and Canada, Pierce went with them as Fanny's accepted fiancé. These were the happy days.

They were not to last. In the next year Fanny was to face both the sorrow of bereavement and the agonizing pull of conflicting loyalties and love. The first was the death of her beloved companion Aunt Dall. The beginning of this tragedy had been on their happy expedition to Canada when the careless driver had overturned the coach in which the party had been travelling. Edward Trelawny was temporarily knocked out, Charles fell on top of Fanny who, with the egotism of which she was supremely unconscious, hastened to assure everybody as she scrambled up that she was all right. Pierce escaped with a few scratches, but poor Dall Fanny described as 'white as a ghost, with her forehead cut open, and an awful stream of blood pouring from it'. However Trelawny came round and was able to administer first aid, and it began to look as if they had all escaped with nothing worse than cuts and bruises. It was not until later that it became obvious that Dall had sustained more serious injuries. Fanny grew increasingly worried, anxious and even guilty as she faced the fact that it was for her sake that Dall had left her home with 'all its accustomed ways, habits and comforts and dear Adelaide, who is her darling, to come wandering to the ends of the earth'. As it became clear that her beloved aunt would never again be able to lead an active life, Fanny cast around desperately to find some way of securing her 'a small independency'. Had her theatrical career continued she could have provided this out of her own earnings, but if she married these would cease. Nor did she feel free to use her savings for this purpose; she was only too well aware of her father's financial position. Indeed when she had told Harriet in February that she might never return to live in England again it was her father's predicament rather than the possibility of marriage that she seems to have had in mind. As she knew that to dissolve the theatrical partnership of father and daughter would seriously affect the former's earning power, Fanny seems to have felt morally bound to hand over her American earnings to him.

In this predicament it was natural that her thoughts should turn to her pen. The sale of *Francis I* had bought a commission in the army for her brother Henry; now she determined that her pen should provide for Aunt Dall. She decided to sell her American journal to a New York publisher. In view of her approaching marriage this was a surprising, and as things turned out, unfortunate decision. When she had scribbled down her day-to-day impressions of America these had been for her personal amusement, and a kind of memory bank on which she could draw when writing to her British friends. Fanny had not wanted to come to the United States; she had not liked much of what she found when she had first got there. This the journal made very clear, and to publish it on the eve of her marriage to an American citizen was bound to cause unfavourable comment. This was something Fanny either failed to realize or disregarded in view of the urgency of her aunt's need. Fanny had always put truth before tact; she could never see that to criticize a friend openly might by some be construed as disloyalty and she credited other people with the same objectivity. In view of Pierce's subsequent reactions it is difficult to believe that Fanny consulted him. It is true that before he inherited his grandfather's wealth his means were limited and this may have been her reason for not doing so but, more probably, it was her sense of pride and fierce love of independence that made her feel that Dall was her responsibility and that she must shoulder it alone. If so it was a pre-marital illustration of her determination to go her own way, a determination that later was to do so much to destroy her own marriage. In the event it proved a useless sacrifice. After the contract had been signed, and there was no going back, Dall died. The last weeks before her death were harrowing for Fanny, who had to leave her each night to go to the theatre; the show must go on. In April, when the Kembles were once again in Boston, it was clear that she was dying. In great distress Fanny wrote to George Combe telling him,

It is now nearly a month since she was first seized with violent spasmodic attacks which have been succeeded by paralysis of the whole lower part of her body. She has not left her bed, I may say she has not stirred, for the last four days, but though free thank God from pain, weakness seems gradually growing on her, and I fear it will extinguish her entirely ere long. The medical gentleman who attends upon her gives us no hope of her recovery and our only consolation in watching the gradual decay of her strength is the certainty that she is free from pain.

A few days later she died, leaving an enormous hole in Fanny's life. For the last two years her aunt had been her constant companion, managing her theatrical wardrobe, travelling with her everywhere, always available. Fanny could not remember a time when Dall had not been part of her life except when she had herself been away at school or in Edinburgh. In some ways the link between aunt and niece had been closer than that between Fanny and her excitable mother. Now there was no Dall to sustain her with the comfort of her love and her robust doses of common sense. Years later Fanny recalled that heart-breaking night when, shaken with tears, she had struggled to pack up the stage costumes which had always been her aunt's especial care, while Dall lay in her coffin in the same room. She was buried in the lovely cemetery at Mount Auburn. This was the first of the sad memories to cast its shadow over the halcyon hours that she and Pierce had spent there.

By April, Fanny was already facing the most agonizing decision that had ever confronted her. She was almost torn apart by her love for Pierce and her devotion to her father. To reconcile them seemed impossible. Pierce could not be expected to follow her round indefinitely while she continued to act with her father. Moreover the time was approaching when the Kembles were due to return to England. What was to be done? Fanny had always been acutely aware of her father's financial embarrassments and had sacrificed her own inclinations because of them. When she had first come to America she had written mournfully to her friend Anna Jameson, saying, 'I do not think that during my father's life I shall ever leave the stage; it is very selfish to feel regret at this, but it sometimes seems to me rather dreary to look along my future years and think that they will be devoted to labour that I dislike and despise.' Then there had been no Pierce to undermine her sense of filial duty. A cottage near Edinburgh with an income of some £200 a year had seemed to her 'the most desirable of earthly possessions'. The situation was very different now, in 1834. First Pierce, then her father, then Pierce again seems to have prevailed. Writing to George Combe on 11 April Fanny told him sadly,

I think in the month of June we shall return to England. Circumstances such as this life is for ever producing to interrupt our plans for the future have very painfully thwarted mine. I did not expect to remain on the stage after the month of May when my marriage was appointed, and I had hoped to be free from a profession which has always been irksome to me, but it is otherwise. I shall return to England with my father in June and continue my labours for another twelve months either there or here.

Charles Kemble had apparently won; the marriage was to be postponed.

This was a few days before Dall died. Whether her death affected Fanny's decision cannot be known. The pressures on her must have been intense. Pierce implored her at least to marry him before she sailed and she found it impossible to resist his pleadings. In a letter written to Kate Sedgwick on 31 May she told her that she was to be married before sailing for New York, where they were to give their final performances, adding that Pierce had behaved most nobly and her father most kindly. By now she must have been so emotionally battered that clear thought was impossible. Apparently Pierce had promised her that after their marriage he would not stand in the way of either her return to England or her duty to her father, and Fanny told her friend, 'I think now that it will be better that he should feel that I am his, fast for life, though at a distance and I shall have reason without appeal for resisting any further claim which might be made on me.' Clearly, too, she felt that his year of devoted attendance had earned at least this reward. Reading between the lines of this letter it is clear that there had been a period of bitter estrangement between the lovers before this compromise and reconciliation. Now Fanny said happily that they were together again nearly the whole day long, writing 'I think seventeen happy days snatched on the very brink of bitterness and parting not to be denied to one who had followed my footsteps for a whole year.' Following this decision they were married on 7 June in Philadelphia. Pierce made his responses in a distinct voice but Fanny, for the first time in any public appearance, was almost inaudible. Under the stress of emotion her tears were always very near the surface and when the bishop who was marrying them had concluded his office Fanny burst into a torrent of tears and collapsed in a faint on her new sister-in-law's shoulder. Poems are always a dangerous source of biographical material but in a volume that Fanny published in 1844 the following lines, which may well express her feelings at this solemn moment, occur:

> She is the daughter of a distant land,
> Her kindred are far off; her maiden hand
> Sought for by many, was obtained by one
> Who owned a different birthland from her own,
> But what reck'd she of that? as low she knelt
> Breathing her marriage vows, her fond heart felt,
> 'For thee I give up country, home and friends
> Thy love for each, for all, shall make amends.'

The day after the ceremony father, daughter and husband sailed for New York to fulfil the Kembles' last engagement in America.

The compromise between the three was short-lived. When Charles Kemble sailed for England he sailed alone. The reason for this dramatic change of plan can only be surmised. In Fanny's *Records of a Later Life* Pierce himself is never mentioned, except by implication when the pronoun 'we' is used. This makes them rather like *Hamlet* with the Prince left out when the biographer searches for clues regarding her marriage. Only a little can be gleaned from between the lines. Even the letters which she wrote to the Sedgwicks, in so far as they dealt with her personal griefs and sorrows, were later destroyed or mutilated at her own request. As a result a veil of almost impenetrable secrecy descends on Fanny's inner private life, a few rents being provided only by the occasional letter that has survived and by Pierce's own account of their marriage which he published to defend his own conduct when it had finally broken down. Certainly when Fanny wrote to Kate Sedgwick barely a week before her marriage she told her that Pierce had given her his word to do nothing to prevent her return and that she trusted him absolutely. Did he break his word, and was that the first cause of dissension between them? In view of Fanny's lifelong determination never to be deflected from any course of conduct that she believed to be right, this seems unlikely. Had Pierce forbidden her to go, and had there been no other reason for her to break her word to her father, she probably would not have done so. It seems more feasible to suppose that what had seemed a solution for the problem of her conflicting emotions before marriage became impossible after marriage. She could not now leave Pierce, either for his sake or for her own.

For months Fanny had been under emotional strain and by the time she married she must have been completely worn out. Pierce and Fanny were deeply in love at the time of their marriage. To quote once again from a poem which mirrored her happy days of courtship, giving vent to her emotions she wrote:

> *The hours are past love,*
> *Oh, fled they not too fast love!*
> *Those sunny hours when from the mid-day heat,*
> *We sought the waterfall with loitering feet,*
> *And o'er the rocks that lock the gleaming pool*
> *Crept down into its depths, so dark and cool.*

The hours are past love
Those blessed hours, when the bright day was past
And in the world we seemed to walk alone,
When heart to heart beat throbbingly and fast,
And love was melting our two souls in one.

Eight years later, when relations between them had become so strained that these were limited to the exchange of letters, Fanny wrote, declaring,

having never loved any human being as I have loved you, you can never be to me like any other human being, and it is utterly impossible that I should ever regard you with indifference. My whole existence having once had you for its sole object . . . it is utterly impossible that I should ever forget this – that I should ever forget that you were once my lover and are my husband and the father of my children. I cannot behold you without emotion, my heart still answers to your voice, my blood in my veins to your footsteps.

Before the clouds of misunderstanding and clashing temperaments and traditions had come between them a woman as much in love as Fanny, newly married and faced with her husband's distress at their imminent parting, would need little persuading to let her father sail alone. Moreover he did not return to England empty handed; Fanny made over to him money that she had saved in America, some £3,000, no inconsiderable sum in contemporary purchasing power. It was a decision which later she had cause to regret; had it been secured to her by a marriage settlement her future would have been easier.

Fanny meanwhile had turned her back on the stage and her past triumphs with genuine relief. On the eve of her marriage she had lamented that 'My studies and the few accomplishments I possessed are alike getting rusty from disuse.' The theatre left no time for the cultivation of her mind; the only reading she could manage had to be done while her hair was being brushed at night and she told George Combe 'I am looking forward with great anxiety to the time when I can improve my poor neglected mind.' In marrying Pierce Fanny had hoped to find both love and leisure. Had she known more of America she might have felt less optimistic. Because the nineteenth century seems only yesterday it is easy to forget how different the England and America of that century were from those countries in the nineteen seventies. To remember this makes it less difficult to realize the depth of ignorance that enveloped Fanny about the country in which she was proposing to live. Even in the England she had left, modern transport was in its infancy and the country in many respects was a bundle of regions rather than an integrated whole. Fanny herself had been a spectator of the railroad's early stages; she had known and hero-worshipped the great Stephenson himself, but when she had travelled to Edinburgh it had been by sea. No railway as yet linked the English and the Scottish capitals. Even in so small a country as England a foreign visitor, penetrating no further than London, could not have had the faintest conception of how the Manchester businessman or the mill-hand 'ticked'. Yet America was infinitely greater. All that Fanny had seen of it were some of the eastern seaboard towns and the inter-vening countryside. How could she know what life outside the cities would be like? How could she even imagine how domestic life, as opposed to her own public life, within them would be when she was no longer a lion at American parties but an American wife, when she was not Fanny Kemble the famous actress but merely Mrs Butler? Still more, how could she even guess what life on a Georgian planta-tion, with its acceptance of slavery, would be like? How could she attempt to fathom the depth of the tradition that would bind a man like Pierce Butler to the old ways of the south? Fanny has been blamed for not realizing this but how in fact could she have been expected to do so? If she had thought about them at all, and there is no evidence that she did, they could have possessed little reality for her. Equally she had failed to understand how superficial American sophistication would prove to be on closer acquaintance, when compared with that of the great English houses where she had been so welcome and so frequent a guest. In committing herself to an American marriage Fanny was building on sand.

External factors would have been less important had there been understanding as well as passion between Pierce and Fanny, but it soon became evident that there was not. They did not run well in double harness and in view of their incompatibility one is driven to ask why Pierce had shown such dogged persistence in persuading Fanny to marry him. Love is reputed to be blind; Fanny when she wanted to be was undoubtedly a most attractive and lovable woman. All her life there is abundant testimony to this. She had tremendous physical energy, vivacity of manner, an amusing, almost comic, streak, was a brilliant conversationalist, and, when the world went well, high spirited. On their expeditions together Pierce saw her only at her best. Moreover she was Miss Fanny Kemble, over whom half the youth of Philadelphia and Boston had lost its head; she was a notable prize to be captured, as Henry Witkoff had pointed out. The more uncertain the outcome of the chase the less time the hunter has to make a cool appraisal of his prospective prey, and it is doubtful if Pierce looked further ahead than the moment of possession. He was young, a year younger than Fanny, and the product of a closed society. Marriage to him represented a certain pattern and a certain relationship. That Fanny might view it differently was unlikely to have crossed his mind. The English aristocracy might occasionally marry actresses; leading Philadelphian families did not, and Pierce's family, though they acquiesced, felt that he had condescended. Once Fanny had become his wife all his subsequent actions indicate that he expected her to sink her individuality in his, and that he could ever have had any such expectations shows how little he can have understood the woman he had married. It would have been as realistic to expect Lake Ontario to sink itself into the Fresh Pond which they had circled on one of their rides. Courtship was one thing, marriage another, as they were soon to find out.

What Fanny had looked forward to in her new life was 'rest, quiet, leisure to study, to think and to work and legitimate channels for the affections of my nature'. At first all seemed well. It had not yet become the accepted convention for the newly married to go away together for that period of ecstatic mutual exploration euphemistically described as a 'honeymoon', and the first weeks of their new life together Pierce and his bride spent at Newport, then a fashionable watering-place, in company with his brother John and sister-in-law Gabrielle. According to young Fanny Appleton, who later married the poet Henry Longfellow, Fanny was in high spirits. Though she rarely appeared during the day, as she was busy preparing her journal for publication, in the evenings she was very lively as she indulged in her passion for dancing. Fanny Appleton was fascinated by her, though she had reservations about her appearance and thought her taste in dress shocking. Unlike most Victorian young ladies Fanny Butler did little to protect her complexion, and her young critic was shocked by the way she allowed her smallpox-coarsened skin to turn bright mahogany under the sun's rays. To make things worse Mrs Butler would appear in the evenings wearing a white muslin dress with a bare neck and gloveless arms. Newport was a happy interlude but, once back in Philadelphia, a note of anti-climax begins to creep into the letters which Fanny wrote to Harriet and Anna Jameson. She and Pierce were living with John and Gabrielle in the Butler family home at the corner of Chestnut and Eighth Streets. In the early nineteenth century it was quite usual for young couples to start their married life in their own quarters under the family roof, and Fanny was in fact lucky that Pierce's aunt Frances was prepared to put Butler Place, a property that she owned some six miles from Philadelphia, at their disposal. They were not however able to move there until the beginning of January 1835 and, without a house of her own to manage, it is clear that Fanny was rapidly becoming extremely bored. Without the stimulus of kindred minds and the cross-fertilization of ideas her own mind became unproductive. To Mrs Jameson she confessed that,

Human companionship indeed, at present I have not much of; but as like will to like, I do not despair of attracting towards me, by and by, some of my own kind with whom I may enjoy pleasant intercourse; but you can have no idea – none – of the intellectual dearth and drought in which I am existing at present.

This was a gap that Pierce was unable to fill. Writing to George Combe, Fanny put as brave a face as possible on her husband's limitations, telling him,

... myself and my husband act as mental moderators to each other ... fact is the end upon which he fastens, and without a most palpable and solid body of fact there is no satisfying him. We are fortunately different in temper. He is cheerful and contented, exceedingly calm and self possessed, and has abundance of patience with my more morbid mental constitution.

Even in Philadelphia there were a few oases in the intellectual desert by which Fanny felt herself surrounded. Edward Trelawny came on a visit and so did that celebrity the English authoress Harriet Martineau whose arrival was the occasion for the giving of various literary parties. There was even a ball when some Philadelphian notable and his wife returned from a trip to Europe, at the prospect of which frivolity Fanny told Harriet 'I have had so long a fast from dissipation, that I find myself quite excited at the idea of going to a dance again.'

It was during their enforced stay at Chestnut Street that the first serious rift between Fanny and her husband took place. In her own letters that she included in her *Records of Later Life* there is no mention of any trouble. All she says is,

I toil on, copying my Journal, and one volume of it is already finished, but now that the object of its publication is gone, I feel rather disgusted at the idea of publishing it at all. You know what my Journal always was and that no word of it was ever written with the fear of the printer's devil before my eyes; and now that I have become careless as to its money value, it seems to me a mere mass of trivial egotism.

Pierce thought it very much worse. One can understand his dismay at the frankness of the criticisms it contained both of American habits and of particular persons, when he read through first the manuscript and then the fair copy that was to go to the printers. It is true that the published version attempted to preserve the anonymity of the individuals she often described so caustically by substituting dashes for names but this device was not always successful when other details could be verified. Her husband had good reason for being perturbed by the inclusion of such entries as '30 November 1832, Sat by that ninny Mr— who uttered inanity the whole of dinner time', or her account of the guests at a dinner-party she had attended six days previously as 'my favourite aversion Mr—; that single fool, Mr—; Miss—, who looked like a hairdresser's wax block'. According to his own account, which is contained in the Statement that he published in his own defence after the breakdown of his marriage, and which is obviously partisan but not necessarily untruthful, he struck out as little as possible, but by November his attempts at toning down the journal had so infuriated Fanny that she told him that rather than submit it to further mutilation she would leave him. The next two days she spent packing her belongings and on the evening of the second day, at about six o'clock, she slipped out, leaving the traditional note behind her. Pierce spent some hours in miserable uncertainty and anxiety until about ten o'clock when she returned. Without even undressing she threw herself on the bed and spent the night in a state of silent misery. Later she told Pierce, after they had made up their quarrel, that she had intended to go to a hotel but, failing to find one that she recognized, she had been forced to return, still with the determination to depart again next day. For Pierce it must have been a shattering experience. Nineteenth-century wives did not walk out on their husbands rather than accept their ruling on matters under dispute.

The future was to show that Pierce had genuine cause for his fears that the journal would give offence. Fanny, writing with the sharp vision of a newcomer, inevitably contrasted the American way of life with that of the literary, aristocratic world she had so recently left, unfair though such a comparison was to the younger, less opulent host country. To those Americans who had feted and lionized both the Kembles, and particularly Fanny, such criticism, with its air of superiority, seemed ungrateful and uncalled for. By many people, whether they recognized themselves or not, it was bitterly resented. Mr Hone, whose standard of entertaining had been so disparagingly described summed up the feelings of many Americans when he wrote,

If she has any good feelings and is at all tenacious of her good name as a lady or an authoress, it must be a very sorry sight to see herself served up to the public gaze. There is all the light gossip, the childish prejudice, the hasty conclusions from erroneous first impressions, in which the diary of an imaginative youthful traveller in a country in which all things are new and untried may be supposed to abound; and the style is sometimes bad; and the remarks that she makes on the private habits of persons who received her and her father kindly are all in bad taste. As a literary production it is unworthy of the character of Fanny Kemble, and its publication, now that she has become the wife of an American citizen, injudicious in the extreme.

Even Fanny's own mother, when the journal was published in England, told Charles Greville that she was divided between 'admiration and disgust', while her father thought it 'full of sublime things and vulgarities'.

Not all the criticism of her readers was so damning. Catherine Sedgwick, admittedly by 1835 a close friend, wrote in her own journal, 'I have read Fanny Butler's book, most of it with intense pleasure. It is like herself, and she is a complex being, made up of glorious facilities, delightful accomplishments, immeasurable sensibility and half a hundred little faults.' Professional reviewers in England were also appreciative of the many good things it contained, vivid word pictures of places visited, intelligent comment on much that she observed, but n the States the sense of outrage tended to prevail. At least two parodies of the journal were produced and one enterprising cartoonist, David Claypole Johnson, supplied eight satirical plates with the title 'Outlines illustrative of the Journal of F–A–K–.' Whatever their appeal to contemporary American readers, the cartoons do not strike one as particularly humorous, though they serve to illustrate the stir that the journal made when it was published in the States. Fanny's oft-expressed contempt for American horses, her use of language, which could be described as 'racy' but which the reviewers thought verged on the coarse and indelicate when used by a lady, and her strictures on American hotels, made the cartoonist surround her with such items as bottles of bug powder, a dictionary of slang and a picture of an emaciated horse. There were also skits on her constant praise of her father's acting and the deference she thought his due, but today the whole production would be considered feeble. This hostile reception of her American journal remained a source of embarrassment not only to Pierce but to Fanny herself. When three years later she ran into Mr Hone while staying at Rockaway with her husband and daughters she was plainly uncertain of her reception. Sensing this Mr Hone took the initiative, telling her how glad he was to see her again and asking her to dance with him. It was a generous gesture and Fanny responded with her usual emotional intensity, saying to him 'Mr Hone, I cannot tell you how happy you have made me by the notice you have taken of me on this occasion. Believe me, I am extremely grateful,' and Mr Hone noticed how her eyes filled with tears.

This however lay in the future. The more immediate significance of its publication was the way in which it foreshadowed the problems that in future were to bedevil the relations between Fanny and Pierce. When the young couple moved to Butler Place in January 1835 Fanny became even more dependent on her husband for companionship. Butler Place was some six miles from Philadelphia. This in itself spelled isolation. In Fanny's words it was separated from that city 'by between five and six miles of hideous and execrable turnpike road, without shade and aridly detestable in the glare, heat and dust of summer and almost impassable in winter'. Fanny had been looking forward to a house of her own, particularly to 'a garden, greenhouse and dairy among my future interests'. Butler Place was a disappointment. Fanny had been betrayed in her expectations by the different values put on the same word by American and English usage. When people had spoken of the Butler estate she had envisaged something not of course as grand as Oatlands, but something more like an American version of her beloved Bannisters. What she found was what to her appeared a glorified farm. Indeed with her tactless honesty she told people that in England such accommodation would only have been considered suitable to house the average farmer's family. Here Fanny in her disillusion was unfair. An extant sketch of Butler Place depicts a pleasant, white-frame building that possessed the dignity of a well-proportioned house. Beside the dwelling the estate consisted of numerous outbuildings and some three hundred acres of land. But to Fanny's great grief 'except the kitchen garden, there is none that deserves the name, no flower beds, no shrubberies, no gravel walks'. There was 'nothing that can call itself a lawn though some coarse grass grows all round the house'. Its only attractive feature was a long avenue of maple trees leading up to the house, and even this was flanked on one side by a field of Indian corn and on the other by an orchard. Used as Fanny was to the trim neatness of the English countryside she mourned that 'the absolute absence of all taste in matters of ornamental cultivation is lamentably evident in the country dwellings of rich and poor alike'. With dogged persistence Fanny strove to impose at least what she considered minimum standards on her own domain and eventually achieved some of the ambience she desired but it was uphill work. As she ruefully observed her gardeners thought only the growing of vegetables worth their labour.

Nor did the management of her household bring to Fanny the satisfaction she had anticipated. In England domestic service was still a respectable way of life; the position of a lady's maid was something that carried status. In the States this was not the case. Even in her premarital days Fanny had been shocked by the free and easy ways of hotel servants. Now she discovered how difficult it was to find suitable domestics for her own establishment. One girl, whom she had engaged as a personal maid, soon left to return to her old occupation as a seamstress, though the close and confined work was slowly killing her. Her reason, she told Fanny, was that she could not endure the idea of being a servant. It was therefore with triumph that Fanny reported to Harriet, 'I have succeeded after many difficulties and disasters manifold, in engaging a tolerably decent staff of servants', though judging by her later letters on this theme 'tolerably' was the operative word. She declared that to manage 'republican servants was a task quite enough to make a "Quaker kick his grandmother", a grotesque illustration of demented desperation of which I have just learned.' Bitterly she regretted the fact that she had received so little domestic training during her own girlhood though, even if she had done so, conditions in America were so different that she would still have found her path strewn with difficulties. This difference between the mores of the old and the new worlds led her into a series of miscalculations and blunders in her early days of housekeeping. At first she interpreted her new responsibilities in terms of those prevailing in England. For instance she attempted to give a party to the people on the estate on the anniversary of Independence Day, only to discover that this was resented as a mark of condescension on her part. In the same spirit the woman who ran the farm dairy made it quite clear that to churn fresh butter for the use of the Butler household every day was quite impracticable. Fanny's well-meaning attempts to play the lady of 'the great house' in the English manner were pathetic failures. One wonders whether Pierce attempted to warn her off, or did she fail to consult him?

When writing to her friends in England Fanny attempted to put a brave face on her future as an American housewife, writing to Mrs Jameson, 'the remainder of my years is lying stretched in front of me, like a level peaceful landscape, to which I shall saunter leisurely towards my grave. This is the pleasant probable future.' This was a picture in flat contradiction to Fanny's love of thunderstorms, tossing waves and mountain peaks; it had little in common with her breathless ecstasy on first beholding Niagara and, according to Pierce, Fanny, far from sauntering peacefully to her grave, was both unhappy and homesick. After four years of hectic living the inevitable reaction had set in. Since her debut at Covent Garden, into each year had been packed enough events and pressures to have filled three of normal living. Now Fanny found herself in a strange environment, cut off from her family and her friends, stranded in an intellectual desert with a pleasant, loving but uncomprehending young man, who at best could satisfy only one side of her complex nature. Later, when the gap between them had widened into a gulf, she wrote him a letter which put the position so clearly that it is worth quoting:

I have renounced all the pleasures of society; this may be condemned by you as frivolous but bear in mind that our tastes are as different as our complexions, and that while you care not in how profound a seclusion you live, I have qualities that adapt me peculiarly for society and the desires that naturally prompt me to seek it, indeed the two go together . . . we are not all made up of affection – we have intellects – and we have passions – and each and all should have their objects and their spheres of action, or the creature is maimed; as for retorting to this, 'What need of intellectual converse, have you not an affectionate husband and two sweet babies?' You might as well say to a man who has no arms, 'Oh! no, but you have two legs.'

When later Pierce opened his heart to Mrs Charles Sedgwick he told her that Fanny was frequently discontented, 'expressing regret at having married me, and a desire for a release from a union that had become distasteful and irksome to her; and she was constantly wishing to return to her native country'. As Fanny was pregnant at this time – her first daughter, Sarah, was born in May 1835 – Pierce said that he had put her state of mind down to this fact and attempted to soothe her by promising her that after the child was born, if she still wanted to go home, he would arrange this. Contrary to these expectations he found that the birth of Sarah did not put an end to his wife's desperate determination, at least in some moods, to escape from what she felt was an impossible situation. Whether because her pen had always been one outlet for her overcharged feelings, or from some deeper psychological impulse, early in their married life Fanny made a practice of bombarding her husband with letters, which he appears to have kept, as later he was able to produce them to substantiate his own case against her. In one of these, written after Sarah's birth, Fanny declared 'I am weary of my useless existence; my superintendence in your house is nominal; you have never allowed it to be otherwise; you will suffer no inconvenience from its cessation,' and once again she demanded to be allowed to return to England. Possibly this deep resentment was part of normal post-natal depression, now a recognized symptom, but the depth of her urge to escape can be measured by the fact that she was even prepared to buy her freedom at the price of abandoning her child, telling Pierce, 'If you will procure a healthy nurse for the baby she will not suffer; and, provided she is fed, she will not fret after me.' For her part Fanny felt that to make the break now 'to me would be far less miserable than at any future time'. In this supposition she was to prove a true prophet. When ten years later their estrangement had become so bitter that Pierce all but forced her to return to England, leaving both daughters in his care, the agony that she suffered was devastating.

Fanny was a creature of moods, swinging from exultation to deep depression. The surviving evidence of their life together, unlike the sundial, records only the unhappy hours. If at times she felt trapped, at others her love for Pierce prevailed, as apparently for some years yet his did for her. Between two such incompatible people marriage could never have been easy. Pierce wanted a conventional Victorian wife and this is the one role that off the stage Fanny could never have played. After their divorce Pierce gave it as his considered opinion that the fundamental reason

for the ill success that attended my marriage will readily be found in the peculiar views which were entertained by Mrs Butler on the subject of marriage, and her unwillingness to abide by the express and inculcated obligations of that contract. She held that marriage should be companionship on equal terms – partnership in which if both parties agree, it is well; but if they do not, neither is bound to yield – and that at no time has one partner a right to control the other.

Pierce had solid contemporary grounds for feeling ill used; today it is Fanny's concept of matrimony that seems right and proper but in the first half of the nineteenth century most English speaking people, women as well as men, would have sided with Pierce. It is hard for modern people to realize how slight were the rights that married women enjoyed (or perhaps 'were allowed' would be more accurate), both by law and by tradition. A wife in the eyes of the law was her husband's chattel, and with her body went her money and estates unless these had been secured to her before marriage in a legal settlement. In English law a husband had the right to exact obedience; he could lock up a recalcitrant wife, administer reasonable physical chastisement and even turn her out of doors. She had no right to continue to reside in the matrimonial home against his wishes. Even her children were his property. He had the sole right to determine their care, their place of residence, their way of life. A wife, however blameless, had not even the right to access. She could be outlawed completely both from the family home and from her children. In England it was not until 1839 that even a woman of irreproachable character was permitted to petition the Lord Chancellor for her case to be heard in a special court. In America the law varied between state and state. Pennsylvania, for example, allowed divorce after two years' wilful separation, as Fanny was to discover to her cost, but in England, though the ecclesiastical courts could order a legal separation for adultery and cruelty, divorce and permission to remarry required a private act of Parliament, which put it out of the reach of all but the very few. Even more persuasive than this reserve of authority, for few husbands pushed their powers to their legal limit, was the contemporary climate of opinion. Men expected their wives to obey them; wives expected to obey. That at least was the theory. The practice was determined by individual relationships. One cannot imagine William Lamb laying down the law to Lady Caroline with any hope of success, or Lord Holland even wishing to govern his beloved but entirely dictatorial wife. Even Fanny was prepared to conform unless a matter of conscience was involved; of that she claimed that she alone could judge.

Her conscience, she declared repeatedly, could never be handed over to the custody of another, not even to her husband.

It was upon this rock that their marriage foundered. Though by temperament Fanny was always impatient of restraint, of which she had had far less experience than most Victorian women, when she married she had been deeply in love; indeed for years she and Pierce continued to declare their love for each other. In spite of jarring personalities and Fanny's moods, had no issue of conscience arisen to divide them irrevocably their marriage might have endured. In the nineteenth century people did not accept divorce as the way out of such difficulties. Unfortunately Fanny, partly because of a very natural reaction and partly because of the humdrum nature of her new life, was hopelessly bored. A month after Sarah's birth she wrote to Harriet describing the pattern of her days. 'I do a little housekeeping, then I do, as the French say, a little music; then I waste a great deal of time in feeding and cleaning a large cageful of canary birds, of which, as the pleasure is mine, I do not chuse to give the rather disgusting trouble to any one else; strolling round the garden, watching my bee hives, which are full of honey just now, every chink and cranny of the day between all this desultoriness is filled up with "the baby" and *study* of any sort seems further off from me than ever.' If she also poured out to Harriet her passionate desire to get away, all such references have been deleted from her published papers. There is no mention of Pierce or of the part that he played in her daily life, though in his Statement he declared that they had never been apart for a single day until her first visit to England in 1837. Meanwhile evidence of boredom, mixed with moods of acceptance, continued to mark her letters home. In the March of 1836 she told Harriet sadly,

I do not give up my music quite but generally after dinner, pass an hour at the piano, not so much for the pleasure it now gives me, as from the conviction that it is wrong to give up even the smallest of our resources ... upon this principle I still continue to play and sing sometimes, but no longer with any great pleasure to myself.

One wonders whether it still gave pleasure to her husband. Pierce was musical; it was one of the few things they enjoyed together, but again there is no mention of him. Instead the letter ends on what is almost a note of desperation, 'dearest Harriet, Oh, I should like to see you once again'.

In between her bouts of homesickness and unhappiness Fanny struggled to achieve some sort of resignation. Both she and Harriet were women in whose lives religion played an important part. Discussions of a semi-religious, semi-philosophical nature had always figured largely in their correspondence. In this they were typical of their day and generation. One has only to pick up such a book as *John Halifax, Gentleman*, or any of Charlotte Yonge's novels, to realize how seriously and how unselfconsciously religious standards and obligations were accepted as part of the warp and weft of everyday life among those members of society who accepted the evangelical outlook. When therefore Fanny heard that Harriet was on the point of setting out on a protracted tour of Italy, a country which Fanny had always longed to visit, contrasting the prospect before her friend with her own restricted existence, she wrote that she realized that her lesson must be 'learnt at present from a page as different as the chapters of Lindley Murray's Grammar are different from those of a glorious, illuminated, old vellum book of legends', declaring bravely 'I not only believe through my intuitive instincts, but also through my rational convictions that my own peculiar task is the wholesomest and best for me, and though I might desire to be with you in Italy, I am content to be without you in America.' Nevertheless her letter ended on a note of unhappy resignation:

How much all separation and disappointment tend to draw us nearer to God. To me upon the earth you seem almost lost – you and those yet nearer and dearer to me than yourself; your very images are becoming dim, and vague and blurred in outline to my memory, like faded pictures or worn out engravings. I think of you all almost as of the dead, and the feverish desire to be once more with you and them, from which I have suffered sometimes, is gradually dying away in my heart; and now when I think of you, my dear distant ones, it is as folded with me in our Heavenly Father's arms, watched over by His care . . . and though my imagination no longer knows where to seek or find you on earth, I meet you under the shadow of His Almighty Wings.

Religious conviction and boredom combined to make Fanny peculiarly vulnerable to the call of a cause. Her ardent nature needed an outlet; as she once told Emily Fitzhugh, 'I absolutely can conceive of no happiness but in the attempt at, and consciousness of progress', just as earlier she had confessed to Mrs Jameson, 'If I were a man in England, I should like to devote my life to the cause of national progress, carried on through party politics and public legislation.' Unfortunately from the point of view of her marriage the cause which Fanny came to espouse was that of the abolition of Negro slavery in the country of her adoption. There is nothing in *Records of a Girlhood* to indicate that the question of slavery had previously entered into her more immediate consciousness. If she had given the matter any thought her views would almost inevitably have been those held by the Evangelicals, whose campaign against slave owning throughout her girlhood had been vigorous and widespread. As far as the British were concerned the slave trade had been made illegal in 1807. After the end of the Napoleonic wars the chasing of the slavers had been one of the occupations of the British navy, as everyone who read Captain Marryat in their youth will remember. The next step in the campaign had been to abolish slavery in the British colonies, particularly in the West Indies. From 1823 the campaign had mounted in intensity and had reached its climax while Fanny was touring in the United States, when, in the year 1833, slavery had been made illegal. The slave owners had been compensated by a parliamentary grant, the adequacy of which was open to question, and there were provisions for a period of transition, which did in practice curtail the freedom of the first generation of slaves. The grounds on which many of the Abolitionists had based this campaign were religious as well as humanitarian and to this approach Fanny was particularly sympathetic.

When she came to America therefore she was already prepossessed to condemn an institution of which she had little knowledge. England had not yet come face to face with a colour problem. The cheap labour that was accused of taking the bread out of Englishmen's mouths and of causing overcrowding and slums was Roman Catholic Irish, not Negro, and Fanny was indignant when the black steward of the ship in which she had crossed, when asking her for a free pass to one of her performances, explained that this must be for the gallery, as that was the only part of the house to which Negroes were admitted. If she was indignant at this evidence of discrimination she was horrified to the state of tears at a description of a flogging inflicted on Negro slaves in the south. It was not however until she discovered, as she told Mrs Jameson, that 'the family into which I have married are large slave owners' that slavery became either an absorbing or a personal issue. By this time the Abolitionist cause was gathering strength in New England. In January 1831 William Lloyd Garrison had published the first number of *The Liberator* and, though there may have been no direct connection between the two events, eight months later a revolt under the leadership of the Negro preacher Nat Turner in Virginia had resulted in the murder of fifty-one white men, women and children. From this point the bitterness between the southerners, only too conscious of their position as a white minority economically dependent on the black majority, and the idealistic northerners, who often knew no more of the practical side of slavery than did Fanny herself, grew. The freeing of the slaves in the West Indies then added impetus to their campaign. By 1835 slavery had become so divisive an issue that the House of Representatives, anxious not to be made an arena for propaganda, in the so-called 'gag acts' resolved to ignore all future petitions on the subject that might be presented to it.

All Fanny's biographers are forced to ask to what extent she was aware of the Butler involvement with slavery before her marriage. She said herself that she 'knew nothing of these dreadful possessions', adding that even if she had realized that the Butler family owned plantations in Georgia this would have conveyed very little to her. Fanny's assertion has been questioned on the ground that her ignorance of her future husband's circumstances could hardly have been so complete. To argue in this way is to ignore both the society in which Fanny had mixed before her marriage and her own limited experience of America. As an actress on tour her travels had been confined to New England and the middle states. Washington was as far south as she went. Though even here the Abolitionist cause was becoming increasingly vocal it was not a topic that her American hosts were likely to favour as a subject for conversation at the parties to which she was invited. Nor was it one likely to intrude its harsh realities into the thoughts of either Pierce or Fanny when they rode together in the carefree days of their courtship, particularly because, though John and Pierce were co-heirs to the Butler plantations, it was not until 1836, after their aunt's death, that they were personally involved. Had Charles Kemble been more of a businessman he might have made fuller inquiries into the financial position of his daughter's future husband, but Fanny brought no dowry to the marriage and there was no settlement. No question therefore arose as to what part of her husband's fortune should be settled on his wife. Today such ignorance on the part of a woman about to marry would be unusual; in 1834, to anyone placed as Fanny was placed, it was not.

Sometime within the first year of her marriage she had come to realize, and to be appalled by, the fact that their present and future fortune depended on extensive plantations in Georgia, and that plantations were synonymous with slave labour. The theme occurs so frequently in her letters that it is clear that it hung over her like a cloud and was never far from her thoughts. Unfortunately for the harmony of her marriage Fanny could never keep her thoughts to herself. An injustice was a cry for action and she was young enough, and enough in love, to believe that, if only she could make Pierce see that slavery was evil and against the laws of God, he too must come to feel the same. As yet she had no personal experience of slavery, which in the northern states was no longer legal. Her reactions were based on Christian belief. As early as June 1835 she told Harriet that she had

just finished writing a long and vehement treatise against Negro slavery, which I wanted to publish with my journal, but was obliged to refrain from doing so lest our fellow citizens should tear our house down, and make a bonfire of our furniture – a favourite mode of remonstrance in the past with those who advocate the rights of the unhappy blacks.

It is not difficult to imagine the horror with which Pierce heard his wife not only express, but also threaten to publish, views so at odds with his own and those held by the society in which he moved, quite apart from the impropriety of Fanny's having views of her own on such matters. In 1836 Fanny received further confirmation of the righteousness of the cause she had so warmly embraced. This was the publication of a treatise against slavery by Dr Channing, whom she had long admired and venerated. His detestation, like Fanny's, was in essence religious; no man had a right of property in any other human being. Dr Channing, much as he abhorred slavery, was not an active Abolitionist. To him emancipation must come through persuasion, not violence; the responsibility rested on the slave owner. Even he, in Channing's eyes, was not in a state of sin through the mere fact of owning slaves; a man might condemn the system and yet genuinely feel that in some circumstances slaves were not ready for emancipation. This was something that only the slave owning States could decide. The north had the right to formulate and publicize its views but must not endanger the tranquillity of the south. Above all anti-slavery propaganda must never attempt to incite the slave to violence; it must concentrate on converting the slave owners. This was a point of view with which Fanny was in full sympathy. She wrote to Harriet in October 1836,

You do not know how profoundly this subject interests me, and engrosses my thoughts; it is not alone the cause of humanity that so powerfully affects my mind; it is, above all, the deep responsibility in which we are all involved, and which makes it a matter of such vital paramount importance to me . . . it seems to me that we are possessed of power and opportunity to do a great work; how can I not feel the keenest anxiety as to the use we make of the talents which God has entrusted to us?

To Fanny it was a terrible thought that she and those she most loved should be supported by unpaid slave labour. Much as she had disliked earning her bread on the stage she would have returned to it 'with unspeakable thankfulness that we had not to answer for what I consider so grievous a sin against humanity'. In a long letter to Harriet, Fanny outlined an elaborate plan by which plantation slaves might be gradually conditioned to take their place as free people in society. This, among other ideas, which included the setting up of savings banks, involved the personal residence on the plantation of the owner and his family during that part of the year when the climate would not be injurious to their health. By so doing she argued that 'the personal character and daily influence of a few Christian men and women living among them would put an end to slavery more speedily and effectually than by any other method . . . Oh how I wish we could make the experiment.'

Looking back in her old age, with a considerable knowledge of America behind her, and the slaves all freed at the end of the Civil War, Fanny was able to understand the 'amazement and dismay, the terror and disgust, with which the theories I have expressed must have filled every member of the American family with which my marriage had connected me'. But in 1836 it seemed to her that her overriding duty to her husband was to rescue him from the sin of slave owning. As she retorted to Harriet, who had been trying to preach a little moderation to her embattled friend, 'You must remember that *we are slave owners*, and live by slave labour, and if the question of slavery does not concern us, in God's name whom does it concern?' Inevitably by the very intensity of her conviction Fanny put an additional strain on the fabric of her marriage. One cannot but have some sympathy with Pierce, who had married a vivacious, charming, popular actress and found himself living with a dedicated crusader in a cause that ran counter to all his convictions and interests. It was enough to put the most promising of marriages in jeopardy.

With the death of aunt Frances Butler, John and Pierce became directly responsible for the running of the Georgian plantation, which for some years had been left in the hands of an overseer. Accordingly the brothers decided to visit their new possessions that autumn. Fanny was passionately anxious to go with them so that she could study slavery at first hand, but neither man felt this was feasible. It was not that Pierce was reluctant to have Fanny with him; he seems to have been convinced that once she was acquainted with life on a well-run plantation she would drop what to him were her wild notions. The difficulties were practical; there was no suitable accommodation for a gentlewoman accompanied by a nurse and small child.

Ever since her marriage Fanny had been clamouring to go home, entreating, imploring, threatening to run away. Now the absence of Pierce in the south seemed a good opportunity and she set off, though viewing the plan with very mixed feelings. Had she been with him she felt that she could have done much to open his eyes to the evils of slavery. She had also confessed in a letter to an American friend that half her pleasure in returning to England would be lost if she could not share it with her husband. However strong her longing had been to get back to England when the time for separation came, Fanny realized how much she would miss Pierce's companionship, which indicates that the past two years had held happiness as well as tears. During the two years of her marriage her friendship with the Sedgwicks had deepened to the extent that both she and Pierce had spent the autumn of 1835 with them at Lenox in the Berkshires, which Fanny described as 'this secluded Paradise, full of crystal springs'. Fanny, a creature of moods, remembered both good and bad moments with intensity, but never at the same time. No wonder that the more pragmatic, conventional Pierce found her inconsistencies hard to understand. There were times during the crossing when she must have wondered whether she would ever see either her husband or her family again. Tempestuous seas and gale-force winds damaged the main mast and for three days their vessel, driven before the storm, could carry no canvas. Such were the hazards of crossing the Atlantic in the old sailing-ships. But once safely on shore to be back in England was a great refreshment to Fanny's spirit, so long starved, except for the Sedgwicks, of congenial company. Yet even here there was disappointment. Harriet had left on her Italian tour and Mrs Jameson, involved in her own matrimonial troubles, had already sailed for Canada to see her husband. There was however the great joy of being united with her family, now living at 10 Park Place, St James's, and also of renewing other close friendships. Lady Dacre and the Egertons received her with open arms, and once again Fanny plunged into the whirl of London society. As well as old friends she made some stimulating, exciting new ones. These included Sydney Smith, whose puckish humour delighted her, though after the unworldliness of Dr Channing she was not sure that it was entirely suitable when coming from a clergyman. Another new acquaintance was the poet Rogers, of whom she wrote that his 'keen edged wit seemed to cut his lips as he uttered it; Sydney Smith's was without sting or edge or venomous point of malice, and his general humour was really the overflowing of a kindly heart'. Once again Fanny found herself revelling in a 'brilliant society, full of every element of wit, wisdom, experience, refined taste, high culture, good breeding, good sense and distinction of every sort that can make human intercourse valuable and delightful'. But greater than her enjoyment of all these delights was her happiness at being again united with her beloved father. She felt too that this was one of the moments in his life when he needed her. Charles Kemble had decided to retire in December and Fanny dreaded the inevitable flatness that must follow after so many years in the limelight. In supposing that he would miss the life of the theatre and the nightly applause she was right, but in supposing that his final farewell would indeed prove to be final she was a less good prophet. Like many famous actors both before and after him his fare-wells were to prove protracted.

It was a great joy, too, to be with Adelaide. When Fanny had seen her last, her sister had still been a teenager; now she was just embarking on her career as a professional singer. Fanny dreaded for her those pressures of a public life that she had herself found so distasteful. Her anxiety was needless; Adelaide possessed a very different temperament from that of her storm-tossed sister, and in the future was to be a great help and stay to Fanny herself. Over the years the link between the two sisters grew and deepened until it bound them very close together.

English society and the world of politics in the eighteen thirties were still inseparably intertwined, and the great aristocratic families still dominated Parliament in spite of the modest changes of the

Reform Act. Fanny, moving among her friends, was interested to notice the subtle difference that had taken place since she had left England in 1832. Writing to Mrs Jameson, little more than a month before the death of William IV gave a new Queen to Britain, she told her that

Liberalism appears to me to have gained a much stronger and wider influence than it had before I went away; liberal opinions have clearly spread, and I suppose will spread indefinitely. Toryism, on the other hand, seems as steadfast in the old strongholds as ever; the Tories, I see, are quite as wedded as formerly to their political faiths, but at the same time more afraid of all that is not themselves, more on the defensive, more socially exclusive; I think they mix less with the other side' than formerly, and they are less tolerant of differences of opinion.

After this interesting comment on the political alignments of the day, Fanny went on to discuss the more general state of the country, writing 'I find London more beautiful, more rich and royal than ever; the latter epithet, by the bye, applies to external things alone, for I do not think the spirit of the people as royal, i.e. loyal, as I used to fancy it was.' This was hardly surprising. In the year that Victoria came to the throne Britain was in the grip of an economic depression; there was much unemployment and life was hard for working people. After the euphoria with which they had greeted the great Reform Act the collapse of grandiose schemes for national trades unions and the realization that it was only the middle classes whose political power had benefited from parliamentary reform had left a bitter taste in the mouths of the mass of the people. Young Victoria was succeeding to a difficult heritage with the reputation of the monarchy at an all-time low ebb, and Fanny pitied her. This pity was misplaced; from the first moments of her succession Victoria enjoyed being Queen, regarding her difficulties and responsibilities as a challenge under God. Fanny, who through the courtesy of the Lansdownes – Lady Lansdowne was First Lady of the Bedchamber – was present at the opening of Victoria's first Parliament, found it a moving experience:

The severe serious sweetness of her candid brow and clear soft eyes gave dignity to the girlish countenance, while the want of height only added to the effect of extreme youth of the round but slender person, and gracefully moulded hands and arms. The Queen's voice was exquisite; nor have I ever heard any spoken words more musical in their gentle distinctness than the 'My Lords and

Gentlemen' which broke the breathless silence of the illustrious assembly, whose gaze was riveted upon the fair flower of royalty.

From an actress this was no mean tribute, and Fanny was disappointed that she had to leave England before the Coronation.

At first Fanny had thrown herself with enormous enthusiasm into the whirl of London's social life and it had been, and continued to be, an abiding joy to her to be once more with her family but, once the first glitter and excitement had worn off, she discovered, to her own considerable surprise, that 'the turmoil and dissipation of a London life, amusing as they are for a time, soon pall upon one, and I already feel in my diminished relish for them, that I am growing old.' Perhaps she was missing Pierce because she confessed to thinking more kindly of her American life 'comparatively remote as it is from the best refinement of civilization and all the enjoyments of society'. Any biographer must ask how much weight can be given to such statements. Few people are totally consistent, and Fanny had in fact been described as a bundle of inconsistencies. Was distance lending enchantment to the view? Once she had returned to Butler Place there is little to suggest that she was happier there after her visit to London than she had been before she left America. Even at this moment of apparent satiety it was only of London that she was tiring. For Fanny, 'To live in the country in England – that indeed would be happiness and pleasure' – was, as she knew, an impossible dream. 'We shall never desert America and its duties,' she wrote, adding, 'I should be the last person to desire that we should do so, and so I think that henceforth England and I are "Paradise Lost" to each other.'

Fanny was uncertain how long her stay would be. The arrangement was that her husband should come over to fetch his wife and daughter and she had hoped that they would be able to spend some time together in England. Politics shattered this plan. Pierce Butler was a member of the Convention that was sitting to revise the constitution of Pennsylvania, which, instead of having finished its business, had merely been adjourned to 17 October. As her father and Adelaide had already left for Germany, where the latter was to give a concert in Carlsbad, Fanny went to stay with her friend Emily Fitzhugh at her beloved Bannisters. There she revelled in long rides and developed an enormous appetite before leaving with young Sarah and her nurse Margery O'Brien for Liverpool to wait for Pierce's arrival. There they had to wait for a fortnight because his ship was delayed by contrary winds, which in

view of the fact that his visit had already been curtailed, was particularly frustrating. Though this shortening of her husband's stay in
England meant that she had less time to introduce him to her aristocratic English friends or to take him to Bowood, where they had been
invited by the Lansdownes, and though they would be forced to sail
before her father and Adelaide returned from abroad, Fanny had at
least the very great happiness of seeing Harriet again. She had just
returned from Italy, and stayed with them until they sailed. Pierce's
visit, though short, seems to have been happy. He was made very
welcome by those of her friends whom he had time to meet. Once
again he saw Fanny in a world that valued her, her world in which her
husband had an accepted place, so that she was happy to write 'that *we*
are leaving England with the desire and determination to return as soon
as possible'. An additional proof of their happiness at being together
again is the fact that Frances, their second daughter, was born nine
months after they were reunited.

Yet even before they sailed signs of friction began to appear. Pierce
was anxious to get away as soon as possible; the villain of the piece, as
usual, was contrary winds. Though, because they were due to sail on
Sunday, the captain assured his passengers that it was most unlikely
that he could procure a steam tug to take them out, Pierce insisted on
going on board, in spite of Fanny's remonstrances. The ship was
crowded with emigrants and their own quarters were confined and
airless. All the hope that the captain could hold out was that they 'might
perhaps' sail in the afternoon, but when the wind veered dead ahead,
he went ashore himself. All day Fanny lay in her berth with a blazing
headache and that night a gale blew up, so that the ship dragged her
anchor and her passengers suffered accordingly. Next day they were
forced to go ashore once more to wait for better weather. Fanny was
justifiably bitter. If Pierce had listened to her in the first place they
would never have embarked until it was clear that the ship would get
away or, even if they had done so in a mood of hopefulness, they would
certainly have come ashore again when the captain did. She would not
only have been spared twenty-four hours of physical distress, she would
have been able to enjoy two more days of Harriet's precious company
as her friend had accompanied them to Liverpool but had left once
they had gone on board. Whether his decision was due to a lack of
judgement or an obstinate determination not to be dominated by his
wife, there is no way of knowing. It was not an auspicious beginning

to a voyage that lasted thirty-seven days and was so stormy that Fanny was hardly able to leave her berth more than six times during the whole voyage. When she reached New York she was so weak that she could hardly stand, and had to stay there for a few days before she felt fit to travel back to Philadelphia. Meanwhile Pierce had been forced to hurry on to Harrisburg where the Convention was sitting. Her own journey back was an uncomfortable one. The train was overcrowded and overheated and as the track itself was not yet completed the passengers had to walk a quarter of a mile through woods until they reached the new section. As a result little Sarah developed a worrying cough. Even when she reached Philadelphia Fanny was faced with the irritating uncertainty of not knowing whether she and Sarah were to join Pierce in Harrisburg or wait until the Convention was reconvened at Philadelphia. One of the obvious strains between this ill-assorted pair was that Fanny liked to plan ahead and had an almost obsessive need of a steady routine while Pierce either could not make up his mind, or was apt to exercise his authority by only making his decisions known at the last possible minute. Fanny found this utterly maddening; her letters are full of complaints of rushed departures and hurried packings. When the Butlers returned to America the omens for their future were not good.

FIVE

Georgia and Slavery

The story of Fanny's residence on her husband's Georgian plantations has a double interest. For the social historian it provides a vivid picture of both the difficulties that faced any traveller between the north and the south on the eve of the railway age, and of life on a slave plantation in the decades before the Civil War. For Fanny herself it was an experience which was to have a profound effect on the rest of her life. She had long been anxious to study slavery at first hand and had seized the first opportunity to do so, though the prospect of travelling with a three-year-old daughter and a baby of eight months, even with the help of her nursemaid, Margery O'Brien, on a journey that must take several days and involved a mixture of railroad, river boat and coach might have daunted a less determined woman. Once safely arrived at Butler Island Fanny sent a graphic description of the trials and tribulations of the journey to Harriet. The Butlers had left Philadelphia on Friday 21 December 1838. The first part of the journey was by rail. Fanny had rarely a good word to say for the American railways. She hated the long coaches which, unlike the contemporary English individual carriages with which she was familiar, resembled the modern Inter-City coach, the passengers being seated on either side of a central aisle. In winter these were heated by an anthracite stove which made the atmosphere almost unbearable, while any attempt to open a window was greeted with a 'universal scowl and shudder'. Fanny, with her robust notions, could never understand why travellers could not wear warmer clothing instead of submitting to overheated carriages. When possible she retreated to a special compartment for women where there was no stove and there were no men spitting in the aisle. This was a habit she never ceased to deplore, though in general spittoons were provided, but later, when travelling in Europe on a river-boat, she wrote

Oh, my poor dear American fellow citizens! how humbly, on my knees, do I beg your pardon for all the reproaches I have levelled against your national diversion of spitting and the consequent filth which you create around you. Here I sat in the cabin of the boat, surrounded with men hawking and spitting, and, whereas spittoons have hitherto been the bane of my life in the United States, a spittoon here to-day would have been the joy of my heart and the delight of my eyes.

In many ways Fanny was equally critical of the female travelling public when these consisted of mothers and their children whom they stuffed from morning to night in an effort to keep them quiet. It was difficult to confine little Sally to a diet of bread, milk and meat when strangers kept offering her pound cake and other unsuitable fare.

In addition to these discomforts the railroad offered other hazards. In places the track itself was still incomplete. When for instance the train crossed the Schuylkill river, hardly a mile from Philadelphia, men were still working on the bridge, one of the piers of which was still incomplete, while some of the inlets of the Chesapeake had to be negotiated on bridges which consisted of piles driven into the river over over which iron rails had been placed that raised them just above the level of the water. Even Fanny confessed that she felt considerable relief when the train once again reached firm land. At Harve de Grace where they had to board a river-steamer in order to cross the Susquehanna, before joining another train for Baltimore, the ice was over an inch thick. This completed the first stage of the journey. From Baltimore they went by steamer, on which they passed what Fanny described as 'a very wretched night', to Portsmouth, arriving about nine o'clock next morning. All that day the Butlers travelled by train through Virginia, where Fanny saw her first slaves, and North Carolina, reaching Weldon, a kind of staging post, in the late afternoon. There they were condemned to wait until the arrival of another train to take them on their next stage. The purpose of the break was rest and refreshment, but this was a miserable place. The women passengers were shown up to a dilapidated room, the walls smeared and discoloured, the windows begrimed and the main furniture being three beds, half covered with tattered and dirty clothing. The only alleviation for the weary party was a blazing fire of pinewood around which they thankfully gathered. The dinner, when they were summoned to it, proved uneatable, consisting as it did of unbelievably tough chicken swimming in black grease with, instead of bread, lumps of hot dough. Once the meal was ended Fanny and the other women were forced once again to await the arrival of the branch line train in the 'horrible hole' upstairs because rigid American convention prevented men and women, even husbands and wives, from sharing the same quarters. Between eight and nine the train arrived and for once the Butlers secured a compartment to themselves. Their comparative comfort was short-lived. In the early hours of Sunday the 23rd the railway line petered out, incomplete; the rest of the journey had to be made by coach. It was a terrible experience. The road, which lay through dismal swamps, consisted merely of logs, the so-called corduroy road, which jolted the passengers intolerably. Again their so-called 'rest-house' provided inedible food. Breakfast consisted of eggs, begrimed with smoke and powdered with cinders, undrinkable tea and unbaked dough. To Fanny's dismay the only toilet facilities were a basin, a ewer, a relic of soap; it took all her determination to procure even a clean towel. The lack of such facilities was a constant annoyance to the fastidious Fanny. Travelling in France years later, she was forced to admit that this inadequacy was not confined to America, any more than the objectionable habit of spitting. In 1847 she confessed 'after raving at every inn I put up in in America for the insufficient ablution-ary privileges, I find myself now in one of the best hotels in Paris with a thing like a small cream jug for a water vessel in my bedroom, and a basin as big as a little pudding basin'.

It was nearly sunset when the travellers reached the place where they were to take the train but when they arrived there was no train; nor was there house or village. There was nothing to do but sit in the coach and wait. Finally one passenger remembered that there was a colonel, a veteran of the revolutionary wars, who had a farm a mile away and to it the party repaired in search of food and warmth. There some milk was provided for the children but the adults had to make do with dirty water masquerading as tea, old cheese, bad butter and dry bis-cuits. At last the train appeared but it was five o'clock on Monday morning before the Butlers reached Wilmington. Even then their tribulations were not over. When Fanny, dropping with fatigue, not having been to bed for two nights, asked to be shown their rooms, she found to her dismay that she, Pierce's aunt, who was travelling with them to Charleston, Margery and the children were to share one which contained a large bed, a curtainless cot and a mattress on the floor. Remonstrance was useless but at least they were able to enjoy what Fanny called 'the supreme convenience of sleep'. In the afternoon, somewhat refreshed, though once more Fanny was so disgusted by the dinner provided at the public table that she could not bring herself to eat it, they boarded the *Governor Dudley* for Charleston. It was a clean and comfortable boat, on which Fanny was able to indulge in a good night's sleep. They arrived at Charleston on the morning of Christmas Day. Charleston, with its old houses and English air, was a balm to Fanny's senses, 'oppressed with newness'. Moreover the hotel was comfortable, which made having to wait for two days for the boat to take them to Savannah a pleasant interlude in their exhausting journeying. Having left Pierce's aunt with friends they went on board the *William Seabrook* which, because it was old and small, had to take the inner passage so that another two nights and a day passed before the Butlers reached Savannah. Even this was not the end of their odyssey. After a brief rest at the hotel yet another boat took them to the small port of Darien. That was nearly the end of their ordeal. Here their own boats were waiting and, greeted by the joyful salutations of Pierce's slaves, their craft made its slow and devious way until it reached the low, reedy banks of Butler Island. Fanny had reached her new home.

If Fanny had been somewhat scornful of Butler Place, which she had likened to an English farmhouse, she found her new quarters 'more devoid of the conveniences and adornments of modern existence than anything I ever took up my abode in before'. Normally the house would be occupied by the overseer but now he was relegated to two small rooms. The main living-room used by the Butlers was some fifteen by sixteen feet, its plastered walls without paint or paper and its furniture of white wood, made by the slaves on the estate. A similar room, divided from their combined sitting and dining-room by a wooden partition, provided their bedroom. In addition Pierce had a small closet for a dressing-room and an equally small one for his office and place of business. A sort of loft over the sitting-room furnished quarters for Margery and the two children. In these circumstances Fanny declared that she was hardly likely to be dazzled 'by the luxurious splendour of a Southern slave residence'. Indeed throughout her stay at Butler Island and later, when they moved to St Simon's

Island, she constantly commented on the dilapidated, run-down houses of the southern planters, and the general air of lack of funds. The Butler estates consisted of two major plantations: Butler Island, a low and swampy area of some 1,800 acres, and Hampton Point, on the higher and healthier St Simon's Island, communication between them and also to the port of Darien being by way of the winding channels of the Altamaha river. Geography dictated a specialization of crops. Butler Island was ideal for the cultivation of rice, Hampton Point was given over to growing long-staple cotton. Originally the latter had been the more profitable crop. In the time of Major Butler, Pierce's grandfather, its reputation had been so high that it had been quoted separately on the Liverpool exchange, where Fanny recorded that it had brought half a guinea a pound; now it was hardly worth a shilling. With this decline in the value of a major crop the luxury of the Georgian planters had also declined, hence the run-down appearance of so many of their dwellings and life style. The Butlers were lucky in that they had an alternative crop in rice. The very different demands of the two crops, cotton and rice, brought with them the further advantage of making some division of labour between their places possible. Of the two the cultivation of rice was the more arduous, with the result that the younger and physically stronger slaves were concentrated on Butler Island, while the older members of the slave force and those less physically fit were kept on the estate at Hampton Point.

Fanny's views on slavery were already well known to her husband, but he seems to have had few misgivings over the wisdom of taking her with him to Georgia; his expectation was that, Fanny's having seen at first hand life on a well-run plantation, a 'total change' in these views would take place, a statement which Fanny told her friend Emily Fitzhugh 'only convinces me that one may live in the most intimate relations with one's fellow creatures, and really know nothing about them after all'. Fanny herself seemed to hope that she might find the practice of slavery on her husband's plantation less abhorrent than the theory. As she wrote to Elizabeth Sedgwick, 'Assuredly I *am* going prejudiced against slavery, for I am an Englishwoman in whom the absence of such a prejudice would be disgraceful. Nevertheless I go prepared to find many mitigations in the practice to the general injustice and cruelty of the system – much kindness on the part of the masters, much content on that of the slaves.' When she wrote to Harriet on 8 January she admitted that, 'The people are, I believe, regularly and sufficiently fed and clothed, and they have tolerably good habitations provided for them, nor are they without various small indulgences.' Moreover she had not yet seen 'anything to shock me in the way of positive cruelty'. Nevertheless her deep conviction that slavery was a moral evil remained unshaken. As she wrote in the same letter to Harriet,

When I remember, too, that I have seen none of the worst features of this system; that the slaves on this estate are not bought or sold, nor let out to hire to other masters, that they are not cruelly starved or barbarously beaten, and that members of one family are not parted from each other for life, and sent to distant plantations in other states . . . I remain appalled at the state of things in which human beings are considered fortunate who are only condemned to dirt, ignorance, unrequited labour, and, what seems to me worst of all, a dead level of general degradation.

All too soon she was to find much to distress her on Butler Island, and even more in the tales that were poured into her ears when she moved to St Simon's, so that she wrote 'How new and how sad a chapter of my life this winter has been.' It was a winter that brought her great anguish of spirit, an anguish revealed in page after page of her Georgian journal.

Even before Fanny had had time to explore Butler Island, or to understand the way in which the plantation was run, the lack of personal hygiene on the part of the house slaves demonstrated to her the evils of the system. Mary, her housemaid, was so offensive in her person that Fanny could not bear her near her, while the two boys who were supposed to wait at table were 'perfectly filthy in their persons and clothes'. Their faces, hands and feet, Fanny declared, were encrusted with dirt, so that she wrote to Harriet 'How I have wished for a decent, tidy English servant of all work, instead of these begrimed, ignorant, incapable poor creatures, who stumble about round us in zealous hindrance of each other, which they intend for help for us.' Yet one of these boys, Aleck, she described as uncommonly bright and intelligent, quite capable, had he not been a slave, of earning fourteen or fifteen dollars a month as a waiter. Much as Fanny disliked its practical manifestations she refused to accept the southerners' contention that this malodorousness was inherent in the Negro race, arguing that the stench in an Irish, Italian or French hovel would be quite as intolerable and that if the southern Negro stank it was due to the fact that he was a slave. Her argument was that

A total absence of self respect begets these hateful physical results, and in proportion as moral influences are remote, physical evils will abound. Well being, freedom and industry induce self respect, self respect induces cleanliness and personal attention, so that slavery is answerable for all the evils that exhibit themselves where it exists – from lying, thieving and adultery, to dirty houses, ragged clothes and foul smells.

In her vehement detestation of slavery Fanny did not stop to explain why, if slavery were the sole cause of so much evil, the Irish and Italian peasant, who was legally a free man and whose moral life was the concern of an active priesthood, lived in the same filth.

Fanny's growing familiarity with the running of the plantation did nothing to reconcile her to the south's 'peculiar institution' and the fact that Mr Butler was generally considered to be a humane master only threw the system into darker relief. She was appalled by the power to inflict punishment through the lash and the resulting physical exploitation, the only defence against which was a combination of lying, flattery and deceit. Mr Butler owned between seven and eight hundred slaves divided between the two plantations and in each the general pattern of management was the same. Slaves were divided into two categories. On the one hand were the household slaves and craftsmen; plantations, like medieval manors, had to be self-sufficient: they had their own bricklayers, carpenters, blacksmiths, and so on. These were the elite. On the other hand were the mass of field-hands, usually most of the able-bodied women and the less intelligent of the male slaves. All slaves had an assigned task which had to be performed every day under the supervision of a driver, himself a slave, entrusted with the power to inflict up to twelve lashes for non-performance of the allotted task. The work of the field-hands was infinitely the more laborious of the two. At the end of the day each gang-driver reported to the head driver, also a Negro but a responsible and trusted slave, and he in turn had the power to inflict up to three dozen lashes on any troublesome member of a gang deemed in need of correction. The only white man on the estate in the absence of the owner was the overseer, who could inflict up to fifty lashes, though, as Fanny was quick to point out, in the absence of the owner there could be no effective check on the overseer's power. There was nobody to whom a slave could complain and no one would take his word against that of a white man. Fanny herself came very little into contact with the male slaves. What shocked and horrified her were the lashes inflicted on the female field-hands. On one occasion a slave called Harriet had excused the filthy state of her small child as being caused by her own excessive weariness after a day in the rice-fields when she, herself, was unwell. She came to Fanny next day, crying bitterly and declaring that she had been flogged that very morning for having complained to her. Burning with indignation and protesting that if people were to be flogged for what they said to her, she must leave, Fanny poured out her anger and distress to Pierce. He, while assuring her that she should not believe a word these people said, promised to ask the overseer for more information. His explanation was that Harriet had been beaten not for complaining to Fanny but because, when told to resume her work in the rice-field, she had been insolent. To Fanny it was no mitigation that a woman should be beaten for protesting that she was too ill to work, though in Harriet's case it is at least possible that feeling that the sympathy of the master's wife was with her, she had been both truculent and insolent.

Fanny's first knowledge of the plight of the women slaves was derived from her visit to the infirmary. This was a two-storey building, made of whitewashed wood, which contained four large rooms, two up and two down. Its exterior failed to prepare Fanny for the total lack of comfort, and even decency, which she found within its walls. Contemporary English hospitals, inadequate as they were, in modern eyes, both in convenience and in cleanliness, were at least furnished with beds and bedding. Here the patients lay without mattress or pillow on the bare floor, covered only with a tattered blanket. Around a miserable fire, some on settles, some on the ground, the less ill were cowering and crouching in the half dark, such windows as were glazed being utterly begrimed and the rest shuttered to keep out the draughts. Everything was filthy and in this squalor women were waiting for their confinements, or nursing their newly born babies, or grieving over a still birth. Fanny stood in horror, tears pouring down her cheeks at the sight of such misery. Then she bestirred herself and turned to make up the fire, an act that brought forth cries of protest both from Rose, the old Negro midwife, and from her patients, all exclaiming 'Let alone, missis, let be; what for you lift wood? you have nigger enough missis to do it!' Under Fanny's energetic direction some slight appearance of decency was achieved, tattered blankets neatly piled, filth swept from the floor, the windows opened to let in some light. Fanny burned with pity, compassion and indignation and from her first sight of the infirmary threw herself heart and soul into a determined campaign to improve the conditions at least of the female slaves on the Butler plantation. For the next four months it was to absorb all her energies and command all her sympathies.

The evils which these women suffered were, in Fanny's eyes, two-fold; physical and moral. Both were the result of their servile status, in that both were the consequence of the heavy labour of hoeing exacted from women working in the rice-fields. Their physical ills were largely caused by too frequent pregnancies, miscarriages, and a too early return to work – four weeks after their confinement was the plantation rule at Butler Island, three at St Simon's, and by the heavy and exhausting work done in the damp atmosphere of the paddy-fields which resulted in rheumatism and kindred aches and pains. Fanny, who forced herself to look at filthy, pain-racked limbs and revolting sores, and to listen to the pitiful tales poured into her sympathetic ears, was shaken to the depth of her emotions. She was horrified to learn that a woman of thirty had already borne ten children, With a perhaps some-what too limited vision she attributed these all-too-frequent preg-nancies to the fact that less labour was expected from pregnant women. There was also a common belief among them that to produce 'more little niggers for massa' was one way of enhancing their value in his eyes. In Fanny's, the moral consequences of so speedy a return to work were also disastrous in that it curtailed the role that the mother could play in the life of her children. After four weeks the infant was left in the care of an older child, who carried it to be suckled by its mother while she fulfilled her appointed task in the fields, and who, when she returned to her cabin, still weak from her confinement, was often too weary herself to give it needful care. These conditions applied both in what today would be called 'one-parent families' and where the mother enjoyed a more stable union, which might or might not have been solemnized by a minister. Fanny's first visit to the slave quarters, cabins which consisted of one large room and two small sleeping-closets, was enough to convince her that the long hours of exhausting field work were such as to discourage wives and mothers from making the slightest effort to keep their houses and their children clean. Every-where there was a careless acceptance of filth. Hens and ducks, which the slaves were allowed to keep, wandered in and out, adding to the stench and dirt; small children sprawled everywhere, looking after still smaller babies. Nor did she believe that the only evil effect of slavery on family life was domestic squalor. The mere fact that the slaves had no need to take thought for the morrow, no incentive to plan for their children's future, seemed to her to deprive parenthood of half of its most sacred responsibilities. All that remained were the animal functions of breeding, bearing and suckling.

Fanny's horror and revulsion became the driving force of her days. How far she lacked a sense of proportion in being so possessed is less easy to determine. Nothing is more difficult than to judge the abuses of past ages in their own contemporary framework. Cruelty and exploitation remain cruelty and exploitation whether they are accepted as part of the normal pattern of society or not and, by the time that Fanny experienced her first-hand contact with slavery, revulsion against it was growing. In Britain public opinion had been such that first the slave trade and then slavery had been abolished throughout the British colonies. Nevertheless, as Fanny acknowledged herself, she did not see slavery at its most horrific. The conditions which she found intolerable on her husband's plantations were no worse than those which English society, apart from a small band of social reformers, was prepared to countenance for their own working people. Fanny spoke of 'the brutal inhumanity of allowing a man to strip and lash a woman'. In England female vagrants were no longer stripped to the waist and lashed until their backs were bloody, but these things had happened in living memory. Mr Butler did not exact labour from slaves under the age of twelve but in 1830 Ostler sent his famous letter to the *Leeds Mercury* in which he wrote 'Thousands of our fellow creatures and fellow subjects, the inhabitants of a Yorkshire town, are at this moment existing in a state of slavery *more horrid* than are the victims of that hellish system – "*Colonial Slavery*" . . . The very streets which receive the droppings of an "*Anti-Slavery Society*" are every morning wet with the tears of innocent victims at the accursed shrine of avarice, who are compelled (not by the cart-whip of the Negro slavedriver but by the dread of the equally appalling thong or strap of the overseer), to hasten half dressed *but not half fed* to those mazagines of British Infantile Slavery – the *Worsted Mills* in the town and neighbourhood of Bradford!!!' Even the first serious attempt to limit child labour in the textile-mills, the Factory Act of 1833, merely forbade the employment of children under the age of nine and limited the hours of those between nine and thirteen to a forty-eight-hour week, prohibiting young persons under the age of eighteen from working for more than twelve hours a day or at night. Above this age there was no protection for women, any more than there was for men. It was not until 1844, five years after Fanny's sojourn in Georgia, that women were prevented from working underground in the mines in appalling conditions, and even that boys were not allowed underground before they had reached the age of ten. Men like Pierce Butler had some grounds for arguing that the Negro children, rolling and playing in the dust, were better off than this.

Economic slavery in nineteenth-century England was in fact producing in other spheres very similar results to those which Fanny argued were the results of legal slavery. There was the same reckless, improvident attitude towards childbearing; in the days of child labour children, if they lived, helped to supplement the family income. But, because mothers were forced by economic necessity to return to the mills too soon after their confinement, leaving their babies not to elder brothers and sisters, because they, like their parents, were at the mill, but to child minders (who dosed their small charges with medicines such as 'Quietness', containing opium), the rate of mortality among them was appallingly high. In Manchester in 1840 out of 4,620 persons of the labouring classes who died, 2,649 were under the age of five. The average expectation of life among the labourers in Liverpool, admittedly a city with perhaps the worst health record, was fifteen years. No such statistics are available for the mortality among Mr Butler's slaves but it may be doubted whether their expectation of life was so short, though according to Fanny the death rate among the children was high. Other domestic evils, overcrowded, squalid dwellings in Lancashire, as in Georgia, were the result of wives and mothers working long hours. Indeed the overcrowded industrial towns in the thirties were probably less sanitary and more of a hazard to health than the slatternly cabins of the Negroes which had seemed to Fanny so lacking in even the common decencies of life. Moreover the system of giving each slave a task to perform and allowing them the rest of the daylight hours in which to occupy themselves as they would, must often have left Mr Butler's female slaves with more leisure and more opportunity to devote to domestic chores and to their children than the female mill-hands working a minimum twelve-hour day amid clattering machinery in the fluff-filled atmosphere of the cotton-mill.

Even in the English countryside the standard of living among rural labourers was so low that they, traditionally the most patient of men, had broken out in riot and revolt, for which their leaders had been hanged or transported, barely nine years before Fanny wrote her journal. Yet though in her detestation of slavery Fanny saw it as the root cause of evils that could in fact be paralleled in her own country, she was justified in her belief that between legal slavery and economic slavery there was a vital difference. Pierce Butler and other slave owners could argue, with some justification, that their slaves were better off than the wage slaves of a capitalist society in that they had security and their living conditions were often more bearable; but to Fanny 'the bare name of freedom – the lordship over his own person, the power to choose and will – are blessings beyond food, raiment or shelter'. From among the ruck of mill-hands in Lancashire some emerged as masters; there was always hope. The plantation slave had very little hope of ever being able to better his status. It is true that a slave who had been trained as a craftsman, by working for years at his craft after his day's task had been completed, might earn enough to buy his freedom, but such thrift could rarely purchase that of his wife and family. For the field-hand there was not even this remote possibility, whereas there was always the dread that if the estate were broken up, or even at the whim of the master, a slave, male or female, might be sold or given away and so be separated for ever from his or her family. Humane owners generally tried not to do this, but even Pierce on one occasion, to Fanny's horror and dismay, in a fit of careless generosity towards a friend, did just this. The wage slave might starve when times were bad, but in the bustling days of the new industrialism he might also make a modest fortune. In the last analysis freedom provided a hope which slavery could never do, little though in practice that hope might be fulfilled.

Fanny found it difficult to keep a balance between the dictates of her conscience and her wifely duties and loyalty to her husband. So great was her own revulsion from slavery that she told Elizabeth that she would cheerfully go to the slave block in Charleston to be sold there if the only alternative were to go there to buy. At the same time she realized her husband's difficulties, asking, 'But, after all, what can he do? How can he help it all? Moreover, born and bred in America, how should he wish or care to help it? And of course he does not', adding as a sad postscript, 'and I am in despair that he does not; and voilà, it is a happy and hopeful plight for us both.' In general Fanny behaved with discretion, being careful not to condemn verbally the institution she was coming more and more to detest. As she told Elizabeth, 'whatever I may do to the master I hold my tongue to the slaves', though she doubted whether Pierce gave her the credit for so much prudence and self-control. Indeed she confessed that at times she hardly knew how to contain herself. But within these self-enforced limits Fanny was determined by her whole attitude towards her slaves, or rather, as she thought of them, of Mr Butler's slaves, to give a wordless demonstration of the equality of all human beings, black and white, slave and free. From her actions she hoped that they might learn 'a thousand things of deepest import' about human relationships. At first she even tried to prevent them from addressing her as 'missis', exclaiming 'For God's sake do not call me that', trying to make them understand that though she was the wife of the man who claimed to own them, she was no more their mistress than they were hers. The stupid amazement on their faces soon made her desist. In their eyes, 'missis' she was and 'missis' she would remain; it was useless to expect them not to address her in this way, though she comforted herself with the thought that perhaps a few of them had grasped the idea that lay behind her protest. Passionately devoted as Fanny was to the concept of freedom, she may have been over-ready to credit her black dependants with the same deep longing.

When the Butlers had first come to Butler Island Pierce had given to Fanny, as her personal slave and attendant, an intelligent young Negro called Jack. Because of the swampy nature of the terrain, riding was an impossibility, only the dykes providing solid ground. If Fanny wished to explore further than the immediate vicinity of the house, the Negro cabins and the workshops, such expeditions had to be by boat, and it was Jack's function to row the small craft. Accordingly they were much together. Once she asked him whether he would like to be free. After a moment's hesitation and confusion, he replied, 'Free, missis? What for me wish to be free? Oh, no, missis, me no want to be free, if massa only let me keep pig,' repeating, 'No, missis, me no want to be free – me work till me die for missis and massa.' But Fanny, who described the gleam of light that had illuminated his face 'like vivid and instantaneous lightning' was convinced that it was only his fear of offending that made him deny his instinctive wish to be free. Whether she was correct in so thinking, who can say? It could be that freedom was so far outside the range of young Jack's thoughts that his aspirations did in fact go no further than permission to keep a pig. This had formerly been allowed, but the privilege had been withdrawn, partly because of the stench of ill-managed styes, partly because, as Pierce explained to Fanny, the allowance of food issued to the slaves was only sufficient for their own needs and could not be stretched far enough to feed a pig as well. Fanny, on the contrary, thought that this objection could have been met by the cultivation of the small patches of land attached to every cabin and now largely neglected by the improvident Negroes. Perhaps Pierce, in refusing her request, was showing a greater knowledge of Negro mentality.

The problem of the slaves' reaction to the concept of freedom lies outside this biography except in so far as it concerned Fanny. Because she found it impossible not to believe that the longing to be free was an inherent quality in every human soul, she was forced to find explanations for the obvious affection shown to 'missis' and 'massa' by their slaves. It was not difficult to understand why an ancient household slave like 'Old House Molly', one of the oldest and most respected slaves on the plantation, went into ecstasies when greeting Pierce after his return, but her enthusiastic reaction seems to have been shared by the rest of 'his people'. One old crone, when Fanny and Pierce were visiting an outlying part of the plantation, clapping her hands in glee, gave thanks that once more 'we have seen massa before we die', and everywhere on the island Pierce on his return was greeted with the same show of delight. When soon after their arrival a contingent came over from Hampton Point to greet their master and inspect their new 'missis', the same jubilant scenes took place. The slaves clustered in crowds round the house door where not only Fanny but the children too had to show themselves amid endless handshaking. Even Fanny had to admit that 'the expressions of devotion and delight of those poor people are the most fervent you can imagine. One of them, speaking to me of Mr Butler, and saying that they had heard that he had not been well, added "Oh, we hear so, missis, and we know not what to do. Oh! missis, massa sick, all his people *broken*." ' Fanny had her own explanation for this apparent devotion, and in particular for the enthusiasm shown towards the new 'missis' and her children. A wife and family meant heirs, and heirs meant continuity. They were a security against the estate's being broken up and the slaves sold, and all the separation of families that this would entail. Moreover the owner was a little god, to be propitiated in the hope of all the small favours that he might bestow on them; whereas the overseer, who had to show a profit on his handling of the estate, was likely to be a stricter taskmaster. The more Fanny heard of the often brutal conduct of the late overseers, a father and son named King, the more feasible did this explanation seem. It may however have been a little too rational in that Fanny did not allow enough for tradition, for the memory of the first Major Butler, and for Pierce's own place in their affections. Fanny, loathing the whole system, saw only its evils, the discipline, the lashings, the exploitation of unpaid labour, and was repeatedly shaken by her husband's acquiescence in them. But by his own standards, and probably by those of his slaves, born and bred in the system, Pierce was a good master. His relations with his slaves resembled that of a man with his dogs. For infringement of the rules, rules well known to each party, slaves, like dogs, would be thrashed but there was no unnecessary cruelty. Food and clothing were adequate by his standards, though not by Fanny's, and the labour exacted not unreasonable. When he and his brother John had first taken over the management of the plantation from Mr King they found that he, in contradiction to the practice of old Major Butler, had forced the women to perform the same tasks as the men. This the brothers had promptly reduced, though Fanny still thought the women's work excessive, particularly after a confinement. Once the allotted task for the day had been completed slaves could use their leisure as they pleased, the men either in idleness or in following their crafts, or in gathering the moss that garlanded the trees, which could be used for stuffing mattresses and similar purposes. A storekeeper in Darien told Mr Butler that in the course of a few years he had paid out to Negroes on the estate several thousand dollars for this moss. In addition to such natural resources each cabin had its patch of land, which the industrious could cultivate, and they were allowed to keep hens and ducks and sell the eggs. On Saturdays, with permission, they were allowed to paddle their own home-built canoes to Darien, where they could sell anything they had procured or produced and buy whatever small luxuries they could afford. Much of their gains must have gone on clothes, for Fanny commented on their Sunday attire. She also commented with disgust at the way in which these slave customers were exploited by the storekeepers of Darien.

On a rowing expedition with Jack one Saturday, Fanny saw groups of slaves all singing, laughing and talking. As they passed they hailed her boat with calls to Jack to 'mind and take good care of missis'.

Briefly at least they seemed happy and carefree. Judged by the conditions on the sugar plantations and on the newer estates in the west,
states like Alabama, Butler's people were fortunate indeed. Within the
framework of the 'peculiar institution' Pierce cared for his people;
though the field-workers must have been an anonymous mass, the
slaves with whom he came in personal contact were individuals in his
eyes. For instance, when a young slave to whom he was attached fell
ill, both Pierce and his overseer spent the night beside his bed and a
doctor was sent for from Darien. Nor was this an isolated instance;
Fanny records other similar ones.

But however kindly a slave owner might be towards his own
'people' he still remained anxious that they should never be exposed
to any influence that might make them discontented with their lot.
All ideas that might incite them to demand their freedom were rigidly
suppressed. Half the population of Georgia was black; in the areas
where the Butler plantations were situated the percentage was as high
as eighty. Clearly the white population faced with apprehension anything that might incite the majority to violence. They were living on
the slopes of a dormant volcano and they knew it. By the laws of
Georgia it was an offence to teach a slave to read, and though some
few did acquire the art, their reading was perforce largely confined to
the Bible, almost the only book available to them. When Fanny asked
the overseer whether any of Mr Butler's slaves could read, the answer
was 'No, very few, he was happy to say, but those few were just so many
too many.' One slave, their headman Frank London, had attracted
Fanny's attention by the way in which he had conducted the burial
service for Shadrach, a trusted slave, a ceremony that both she and her
husband had attended. London was the leading Methodist preacher
in the Negro community and Fanny had been much impressed by the
quiet dignity with which he had led his congregation in hymn-singing
and in prayer, and finally by his reading of some portion of the burial
service and giving an address on Lazarus and the resurrection of the
dead. When however she tried to find out how he had learnt to read
he was most evasive. The first time she tackled him he was clearly
determined to say nothing, but later, when the Butlers were on the
point of leaving Butler Island for Hampton Point, he told her 'Well,
missis, me learn'; 'well missis, me try', and finally, 'well, missis, me
spose Heaven help me', which drove Fanny to the comment that 'I
knew Heaven was helpful, but hardly to the tune of teaching folk their

letters'. As Fanny realized, London was clearly determined to give no information that could bring whoever had taught him into the grip of the law. Had Fanny ever read an early eighteenth-century English pamphlet, Mandeville's *Fable of the Bees*, she would have found the same fears expressed in it, that education would make the poor rebellious with their place in society, that now haunted the southern planter. If there were no poor, asked Mandeville, who would be content to do the hard and disagreeable work?

To Fanny this was a challenge, not a deterrent. If knowledge was the way to freedom she would do what she could to disseminate it whatever the law might say. When therefore almost at the end of her time on Butler Island young Aleck, the house slave whose intelligence had earlier impressed her, plucked up enough courage to ask her to teach him to read, she willingly consented. Her only regret was that as a woman she could not herself pay the full penalty for so breaking the law. The first two offences were punishable by fine, which her husband would have to pay. Only the third carried with it the penalty of imprisonment which made Fanny regret that she could not begin with the third lesson 'because going to prison can't be done by proxy'. However she had no intention of telling her husband, declaring 'I'll leave him to find out, as slave and servants and children and all oppressed, and ignorant, and uneducated and unprincipled people do.' Even so Fanny was not prepared to disobey his definite commands, adding 'if he forbids me I can stop – perhaps before then the lad may have learnt his letters'. Aleck proved an apt pupil and, short though the time of tuition was, seems to have achieved this modest aim; apparently Pierce did not discover Fanny's subversive action. Nevertheless for her it was tragic that she should be reduced to resort to subterfuges so alien to her open and independent nature. Slave owners might prevent their slaves from acquiring the art of reading; it was more difficult to deny them the knowledge of the truths of the Christian religion. It was this that Fanny thought most likely to provide a chink in the screen of deliberate ignorance which they were struggling to maintain between 'their people' and disruptive ideas. On this subject there was less agreement. It was difficult to forbid all exercise of religion and the more humane and practising Christian owners did make some religious provision for their black dependants, but on the newer and more distant plantations religious gatherings, like fire-arms and pigs, were forbidden as being too dangerous to the status quo. Mr

Butler's slaves were allowed to go to the native church at Darien once a month; on the remaining Sundays on Butler Island men like the Methodist preacher conducted the service. Hampton Point was less well served until Fanny moved there and got Pierce's permission to hold services in her own house for such as liked to come.

For the slave owning south the problem as a whole was a difficult one. The pressure from the north by the thirties was such that it could no longer be ignored and this raised the question of how much Christian doctrine could safely be taught to the slave population. Would it make them more honest, more loyal in the service of their masters, or would it incite them to revolt? Mr Butler's overseer was forced to admit to Fanny that so far he had no complaints to make against such men as London but, he argued, 'every step they take towards intelligence and enlightenment lessens the probability of their acquiescing in their condition'. For this reason he condemned every sort of teaching, preaching and moral instruction of a religious kind because of its unsettling effect. Fanny agreed with him that the northern pressure on the southern slave owner to allow what they hoped would be 'a little harmless religious enlightenment' might have disastrous conseqences. As she put it, 'The letting out of water, or the letting in of light, in infinitesimal quantities, is not always easy. The half wicked of the earth are the leaks through which wickedness is eventually swamped; compromises forerun absolute surrender in most matters, and fools and cowards are, in such cases, the instruments of Providence for their own defeat.' She had also caustic comments to make on those whom she described as 'uncomfortable Christians', men who were trying to reconcile God and Mammon. Eventually she declared they would be driven to draw up a slave Christian catechism and to produce a slave Bible, otherwise they would end up by cutting their own throats with the 'two-edged sword of truth'. Fanny herself did all she could to foster the spread of religion on the Butler plantations and Pierce, though Fanny thought it unlikely that he would build for his slaves the church for which they had petitioned him, did nothing to prevent his wife's activities in this direction.

Whatever hope for the future there might be in the gradual dissemination of ideas of equality before God, Fanny realized that any dream she might cherish that Pierce would free his own slaves and run the plantation with free labour would remain dreams. All that she could hope to do was to try to deal with individual cases of hardship and to improve the material conditions in which 'his people' lived. She therefore turned her attention to the state of the infirmary, the condition of which had so filled her with horror on her first visit. Here at least she met with no opposition. Indeed the overseer told her that when he had taken over from Mr King he too had thought conditions there should be improved but that, receiving no encouragement either from the retiring overseer or from John Butler, he had taken no further steps. On this subject Pierce, far from discouraging her, seems to have cooperated actively because by February Fanny was able to tell Elizabeth that the infirmary had been furnished with bedsteads, mattresses, pillows and blankets, and that in addition a third story was to be added to the building to accommodate the less serious cases. Improvements on this scale could only have been carried out with his consent and under his orders, and indeed it is only fair to record that unless Fanny's pleas and plans seemed to threaten the discipline he thought necessary to run the estate he was anxious to do the best that he could for his black dependants. Even without his help there was much that Fanny could do herself. If she could not inculcate ideas of equality at least she could campaign for cleanliness among the women and children. Here she confessed to descending to bribery and corruption, fearing that appeals to the 'abstract loveliness of cleanliness' were unlikely to be effective. Instead she promised a cent to each small baby-minder whose tiny charges had clean hands and faces, and another if their own hands and faces were likewise clean. The result was immediate; on her next appearance she was surrounded with children, carrying babies on their backs, and all with wet, shining faces.

In the infirmary, or rather in that part of it which functioned as a maternity ward, Fanny assumed a more active role, superintending in person the washing of small babies. The mothers were in no position to resist these ministrations but it was with unutterable dismay that they looked on when Rose, the old midwife, got a tub of warm water and prepared to immerse their babies in it. So desperate was one mother that she flung the clothes which had just been taken off her infant into the water, 'to break the shock'. Fanny promptly pulled them out, only to find they were its only garments, which had then to be wrung out and dried. So strange was the whole proceeding that the poor bewildered mothers seemed utterly incapable of either drying or dressing their offspring, a task which Fanny had to finish herself. Not content with imposing her standards of hygiene on the captive mothers in the infirmary, Fanny carried her crusade for cleanliness into the cabins of the slaves, lecturing a group of teenage girls, who were romping about outside their hovels, for idling away the time which could have been spent cleaning up the filthy disorder within, telling them sternly that it was a disgrace for any woman to live in such conditions of dirt. Her fetish about cleanliness seems to have had some effect. Moreover it preceded her to Hampton Point where she found the babies' heads no longer covered by filthy woollen caps, and the adults looking remarkably clean and tidy, though, as she admitted, this may have been due in part to the fact that their arrival coincided with Sunday, when the Negroes appeared in any finery that they might possess. Even so, she did notice a distinct improvement in many of her black dependants, though rather sadly she had doubts as to its continuance after her departure.

The desire to win 'missis' approval was certainly there; the motives behind it are less certain. Mr Butler's female slaves had, for the first time in their lives, found a white woman, and what is more the wife of that all powerful figure, 'massa', who listened to their grievances, who treated them as human beings like herself, and who was also in a position to provide the little luxuries, such as sugar, which were so highly appreciated. If she attached so much importance to cleanliness of person and cabin, that was a small price to pay for the comfort, both emotional and material, that she brought. Driven by her conscience and an almost overwhelming shame that she and her children should live in comfort, even luxury, at the expense of unpaid, exploited slave labour, Fanny soon became a vulnerable target for all their petitions, all their tales of ill usage, all their complaints. Writing in January, not long after her arrival, she told Elizabeth,

no time, no place, affords me a respite from my innumerable petitioners, and whether I be asleep or awake, reading, eating or walking; in the kitchen, my bedroom or the parlour, they flock in with their urgent entreaties, and pitiful stories, and my conscience forbids me ever postponing their business for any other matter; for, with shame and grief of heart I say it, by their unpaid labour I live – their nakedness clothes me, and their heavy toil maintains me in luxurious idleness. Surely the least I can do is to hear these, my most injured benefactors; and, indeed so intense in me is the sense of injury they receive from me and mine, that I should scarcely dare refuse them the very clothes from my back, or food from my plate, if they asked for it.

The journal is full of the stories that the Negro women poured into her sympathetic ears, giving the impression that her mind was almost obsessed by their sufferings. Twice she told Elizabeth that slaves had been flogged for appealing to her, though both Pierce and the overseer assured her that the lashes had been inflicted because they had failed to complete their daily task. But the mass of the complaints arose out of the ordinary routine of plantation life, in particular the hardships imposed on the women by constant physical labour. It was with them that Fanny came most into contact through the infirmary and in her eyes they were the main victims of the detested system. She did not think that the adult males were excessively overworked and that at the level of an animal existence they were not 'very ill-off brutes' though the young of both sexes she considered idle and the old neglected once their usefulness was passed.

But for the women, if Fanny's complaints are to be believed, ill health was an all but inescapable part of life. Apart from some diseases caused by filth or the damp atmosphere of the rice-fields most female ill health came from a combination of too frequent childbearing and too early a return to labour in the fields. In the rice-growing plantation this was four weeks and in the cotton fields three weeks after the delivery, and the result was what one slave described as 'falling of the womb and weakness in the back'. Again and again the women came, sometimes as individuals and sometimes in groups, to beg Fanny to ask 'massa' to lighten their tasks during pregnancy still further, and to allow them more time after a confinement. Rheumatism was another great scourge, which in view of the long hours worked in the swamps of Butler Island was not surprising. Even Pierce seems to have suffered from some rheumatic complaint in spite of which Fanny attributed the aches and pains of her black clients exclusively to excessive toil, writing that 'this climate is the last that ought to engender rheumatism'. One case which aroused her indignation was that of the wife of Ned, the engineer at the rice-mills, who asked Fanny to intercede with 'massa' for his wife on the ground that she was 'most broke in two'. Ned himself was in a privileged position in that he was a craftsman, but this did not prevent his wife from being forced to work as a field-hand. To Fanny it was monstrous, and a further indictment of the whole system, that a man whose skill as an engineer would have enabled him to earn a good wage and keep his wife in comfort, had he been free, was forced to stand by while she,

covered with one filthy garment of ragged texture and dingy colour, barefooted and bare headed, is daily driven afield to labour with aching, pain-racked joints, under the lash of a driver, or lie languishing on the earthen floor of a dismal plantation hospital in a condition of utter physical destitution and degradation such as the most miserable dwelling of the poorest inhabitant of your free Northern villages never beheld the like of.

During the first month of her stay on Butler Island Fanny was to receive another illustration of the complete power of the master over his slaves. It was a case that touched her nearly in that it concerned the girl, Psyche, who was acting as under-nurse to Margery and whose sad expression had attracted Fanny's attention. When Mr King, the ex-overseer, came on a visit to Butler Island the cause of this became apparent. Apparently Psyche had reason to believe that she was Mr King's, not Mr Butler's, property, and was therefore filled with fear lest he should claim her and take her back to his new plantation in Alabama, thus separating her and her two small children from her husband and from all her own family. Fanny promptly made inquiries and was able to assure Psyche that as Mr King thought she and her two small children would be more trouble than would repay him, he had sold them to the present overseer. But no sooner had Fanny, and through her Psyche received this reassuring news than a fresh tragedy threatened. In a fit of careless generosity Pierce gave her husband Joe, an intelligent and valuable slave, to Mr King as a parting gift and, when faced with his despair merely told him not to make a fuss over something that could not now be helped. Hardly able to contain herself, Fanny pleaded desperately with her husband, for the sake of his own soul, not to commit this bitter piece of inhumanity. To all her torrent of words and tears he gave no answer and later, recalling the 'intemperate vehemence of my entreaties and expostulations' she conceded that perhaps she had deserved none. For all her claims to independence Fanny remained a Victorian wife in whose eyes her husband was still the final authority. The sad story had a happy ending. Mr King, finding that Joe had 'kicked up a fuss about it', decided that he did not want to be bothered with a 'nigger who might be troublesome' and, with a generosity that delighted Fanny, Pierce bought Psyche from the overseer. Now husband, wife and children were all Mr Butler's slaves and the fear of separation was lifted from them. This story is worth recounting for two reasons. In the first place it illustrates how even on a well-run plantation with a good owner the personal lives of the slaves could be utterly destroyed by a chance whim. The second reason is the effect of the incident on Fanny. It was this episode that created in her what she described as 'for the first time almost a sense of horrible personal responsibility and implication' that took hold of her mind so that she wrote,

I felt the weight of an unimagined guilt upon my conscience; and yet God knows this feeling of self condemnation is very gratuitous on my part since when I married Mr Butler I knew nothing of these dreadful possessions of his, and even if I had, should have been much puzzled to have formed any idea of the state of things in which I now find myself plunged, together with those whose well doing is as vital to me almost as my own.

The intensity of Fanny's feelings put an additional strain on her relations with her husband. Though she was capable of realizing intellectually the strength of the ties that bound him to the old traditions, emotionally his attitude continued to cause her deep distress. When during her first month at Butler Island she heard Pierce lecturing a group of pregnant women, who were complaining to him of being overworked, on the need for them to perform their appointed tasks, Fanny could hardly contain herself, exclaiming,

How honourable he would have appeared to me begrimed with the sweat and soil of the coarsest manual labour, to what he then seemed, setting forth to these wretched, ignorant women, as a duty, their unpaid exacted labour! I turned away in bitter disgust. I hope this sojourn among Mr Butler's slaves may not lessen my respect for him, but I fear it; for the details of slave holding are so unmanly, letting alone every other consideration, that I know not how anyone with the spirit of a man can condescend to them.

Again and again Fanny found herself criticizing Pierce. When for instance at Shadrach's funeral all the congregation knelt on the sand, Fanny knelt with them,

Mr Butler alone standing in the presence of the dead man, and of the living God to whom his slaves were now appealing . . . there was something painful to me in Pierce's standing while we all knelt on the earth, for though in any church in Philadelphia he would have stood during the praying of any minister, here I wished he would have knelt, to have given his slaves some token of his belief that at least in the sight of the Master to whom we were addressing our worship – all men are equal.

Silent criticism he could have ignored, or even been unaware of, but when faced with some instance, as for example the flogging of one of the women who had appealed to her, Fanny was far from silent. On hearing of a flogging inflicted on the slave Teresa, Fanny recorded 'a long and painful conversation with Mr Butler'. To her husband's assertion that the punishment was just, Fanny spoke out on

the manifest injustice of unpaid and enforced labour; the brutal inhumanity of allowing a man to strip and lash a woman, the mother of ten children, to exact from her toil which was to maintain in luxury two idle young men, the owners of the plantation.

When, over individual cases, Pierce produced what to him seemed an adequate explanation, Fanny had no difficulty in shifting her ground to an attack based on general principles and it seems legitimate to suppose that Pierce found her attitude incomprehensible and her combination of tears, scorn and indignation irritating.

When the Butlers moved to Hampton Point in mid February the situation grew worse, though in many ways life for Fanny was both easier and pleasanter. Their new house was an improvement on that on Butler Island, the climate was better and once more Fanny could indulge her passion for riding. At last she had a garden, which though neglected could boast a couple of peach-trees in full bloom, narcissi, jonquils and violets while all around were thickets of beautiful evergreens. Her joy in the latter was somewhat damped when Pierce warned her that these woods were infested with rattlesnakes, but even so to be away from Butler Island and its dykes and swamps was a great refreshment to her spirit. There was, alas, a darker side to the picture. There were far more older people on the plantation on St Simon's Island, people who had longer memories and could tell her of the conditions which they had been forced to endure when the Kings, father and son, had been masters in the absence of the owners. The task work demanded from them had been excessive, so had the discipline imposed when this could not be completed. Women were tied up, stripped and flogged with such severity that some, desperate at the prospect of another beating, fled into the swamps and thickets, braving rattlesnakes and the threat of starvation. It was not only a beating that the women had to fear. If Mr King took a fancy to one, be she married or single, he took her and there was no redress. Indeed Fanny, when she first came to Hampton Point, remarked on the striking resemblance that some of the young slaves bore to Mr King. It is true that excessive labour, brutality and lust on Mr Butler's plantations were things of the past, but to Fanny they were all part of the system, revealing all its

Fanny Kemble as Bianca (Thomas Sully)

Charles Kemble as Pierre in Otway's
Venice Preserv'd

Mrs Charles Kemble, née Maria Theresa
De Camp

Sarah Siddons, Fanny's aunt, as Euphrasia in *The Grecian Daughter*

Fanny in her dressing room at Covent Garden Theatre before her first performance as Juliet, with her mother and father as Lady Capulet and Mercutio and Mary Davenport as the nurse. From a lost painting by Henry Perronet Briggs R.A., at one time in the Shakespeare Memorial Theatre picture gallery

'The attitudes' adopted by Fanny Kemble in her first major role of Juliet in 1829 with Mary Davenport as the nurse and William Abott as Romeo

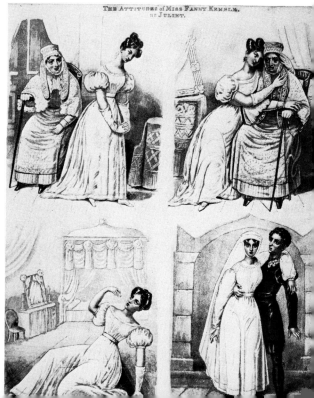

THE ATTITUDES OF MISS FANNY KEMBLE, as JULIET.

Covent Garden Market in the 1820s

Butler Place

Fanny in America

ABOVE Fanny's daughters, Sarah and Frances

RIGHT Pierce Butler

LEFT Catherine Maria
Sedgwick, authoress and
life-long friend to Fanny

BELOW Monument
Mountain, The Berkshires

George Coombe, the
phrenologist, and Fanny's
mentor and friend

Henry James, to whom Fanny
was 'My sublime Fanny – one
of the consolations of my life'

ABOVE Fanny reading Shakespeare
at the St James's Theatre in 1850

LEFT Fanny as an elderly lady

potentiality for evil and for helpless suffering, so that she lent an ever more credulous ear to the complaints of the present.

Towards the end of February Pierce apparently found his patience exhausted. On 26 February Fanny wrote to Elizabeth in great depression and distress to tell her that she had had

a most painful conversation with Mr Butler, who has declined receiving any of the people's petitions through me. Whether he is wearied with the number of these prayers and supplications which he would escape but for me, as they probably would not venture to come so incessantly to him . . . or whether he has been annoyed at the number of pitiful and horrible stories of misery and oppression under the former rule of Mr King, which have come to my knowledge since I have been here, and the grief and indignation caused, but which cannot, by any means, always be done away with, though their expression may be silenced by his angry exclamations of 'Why do you believe such trash; don't you know the niggers are all d—d liars?' etc., I do not know; but he desired me this morning to bring him no more complaints or requests of any sort, as hitherto the people had no such advocate and had done very well without, and I was only kept in a state of incessant excitement with all the falsehoods 'they found they could make me believe'.

For Fanny this was the bitterest of blows. Though she was prepared to concede that

Pierce is weary of hearing what he has never heard before, the voice of passionate expostulation, and importunate pleading against wrongs he will not even acknowledge, and for creatures whose common humanity with his own I half think he does not believe,

yet she declared that she would have to return north, arguing that if she remained her condition

would be almost worse than theirs – condemned to hear and see so much wretchedness, not only without any means of alleviating it, without permission even to represent it for alleviation–this is no place for me, since I was not born among slaves and cannot bear to live among them.

According to Pierce's Statement, made later, Fanny carried out her threat. She packed her trunks and left for Darien and had she been able to catch a connecting boat there while still in the grip of her first emotional revolt she might indeed have returned north. But on arrival at the port she found that she would have to wait for another three or four days and that gave her time for reflection. As she wrote in her next entry for Elizabeth,

I cannot give way to the bitter impatience I feel at my present position and come back to the north without leaving my babies, and though I suppose their stay will not in any case be much prolonged in these regions of swamp and slavery, I must, for their sakes, remain where they are, and learn this dreary lesson of human suffering to the end.

So in bitterness of spirit Fanny returned, though according to Pierce 'for two days she shut herself in her room, lay on the bed and refused to eat or drink the produce of slave labour'. It was a characteristic gesture.

Having returned Fanny forced herself to accept the new situation. Much as it distressed her she realized that there was nothing that she could do, or at least nothing that she could do openly. Now when she went aboard the constant prayers that greeted her of 'Oh, missis, you speak to massa for us!' represented not an opportunity to help but a torture of frustration, so that whereas once she had welcomed such appeals now she only wanted to shun them. The only help she could give was to suggest that though she might not speak on their behalf at least such petitions as they might make to 'massa' should be made in her presence. Sadly she was even forced to admit that since she could not change the system Pierce might be right when he argued that to listen to their complaints and to pour out sympathy could only have the effect of making them discontented and more unhappy once she had gone and was no longer at hand to listen to their tales, tales which he believed to be exaggerations of the truth, highly coloured for her credulous ears. How far Fanny was in fact imposed upon is a question that nobody not thoroughly familiar with slavery in its historical setting can hope to answer. The Butler slaves would have been less than human if they had not played upon her sympathies. Moreover in the modern world, where slavery is rarely to be found, though it still exists, and is now condemned, as Fanny would have condemned it, as a violation of human rights, it is difficult to make an objective historical judgement on American slavery as she knew it. Her own judgement was both subjective and emotional. Whether in the cold light of truth her reactions to the conditions which she saw around her on Butler Island and Hampton Point were exaggerated is a matter of importance to the historian but not to her biographers. On Fanny herself the effect was traumatic and unforgettable.

Pierce's refusal to allow his slaves to approach him through the mediation of his wife did not, and was not intended to, put an end to all her work for their slaves. She could still give them the little favours that they asked, a trifle of sugar, flannel for rheumatic or swollen joints. She could still try to make their material conditions more decent by exhorting them to cleanliness of person and tidiness in their wretched cabins. She could still supply the comfort of sympathy; if there was nothing she could do, at least she could listen. She could still minister to the sick and the old. She did not find these things easy; if her heart was torn by pity her senses were revolted by the fleas, the dirty clothes, the horrible sores. As she told Elizabeth, 'I do not suppose that these hateful consequences of dirt and disorder are worse here than among the poor and neglected creatures who swarm in the lower parts of European cities; but my call to visit them has never been such as that which constrains me to go daily among these poor people, and though on one or two occasions I have penetrated into fearfully foul and filthy abodes of misery in London, I have never rendered the same personal services to their inhabitants that I do to Mr Butler's slaves'. When not directly forbidden by her husband, Fanny was still prepared to undermine the hated system when she could. Her willingness to teach young Aleck to read in defiance of the law was one example. The fact that she was prepared to pay wages to young lads for clearing rides through the thickets, once their daily tasks had been done, was another way of 'disseminating ideas among Mr Butler's dependants, the like of which have certainly never before visited their wool-thatched brains'. The idea that she was so busily implanting was the connection between work and wages. When finally the Butlers left Georgia in mid April Fanny's verdict was

I think I have done what I could for them – I think I have done as well as I could by them; but when the time comes for ending any human relation, who can be without their misgivings? Who can be bold to say 'I could have done no more, I could have done no better?'

She was never to return.

Yet in spite of Fanny's heartbreak it would be misleading to suggest that the four months which she spent in Georgia were all gloom and without their interludes of pleasure, even happiness. Fanny, with her passionate love of beauty, found much in which to delight. The profusion of flowers was a constant joy; in particular she loved the wild jasmine whose 'fragrant golden cups' she described as 'fit for Oberon's banqueting service'. She was entranced by the beauty of the great magnolia with its 'lustrous green foliage' and its 'queenly blossoms'. The birds too were another source of interest and pleasure. The song of the mocking-birds, the sudden flight of the waterfowl, the great turkey buzzards who spread their wings and soared over the river like 'so many mock eagles', the ungainly flight of the heron as it rose from the reed beds, all enchanted her. Once Pierce called her to look at 'a magnificent bald-headed eagle, sweeping like a black cloud over the river, his bald white head bent forward and shining in the sun, and his fierce eyes and beak directed towards one of the beautiful wild ducks on the water'. Even more enchanting than the trees, the flowers and the birds was 'the unspeakable glories of these Southern heavens, the saffron brightness of the morning, the blue intensity of noon, the golden splendour and rosy softness of sunset. Italy and Claude Lorraine may go hang themselves together'. Interspersed with her indignant and pitiful stories of oppression and suffering such word pictures constantly appear, as when, weary with having poured out her distress on paper, she went out to refresh her spirit with the evening air. She wrote,

the scene just beyond the house was beautiful, the moonlight slept on the broad river which here is almost the sea, and on the mass of foliage of the great Southern oaks; the golden stars of German poetry shone in the purple curtains of the night, and the measured rush of the Atlantic unfurling its huge skirts upon the white sands of the beach (the sweetest and most awful lullaby in nature) resounded though the silent air.

Again and again in the unhappy weeks that followed her husband's refusal to hear any more petitions through her, Fanny found her main relief in her attempts to throw off the weight of horror that depressed her by walking or by riding her new horse, Montreal, and the beauty around her never failed to soothe. As she told her friend,

I am helped to bear all that is so very painful to me here by my constant enjoyment of the strange wild scenery in the midst of which I live . . . I suppose, dear Elizabeth, one secret of my being able to suffer as acutely as I do without being made either ill or absolutely miserable, is the childish excitability of my temperament, and the sort of ecstasy which any beautiful thing gives me. No day, almost no hour passes without some enjoyment of the sort.

Plunged in misery one minute, as she rode her horse along a causeway alive with land crabs she could laugh aloud as she watched their frantic antics to escape from Montreal's hooves. It was a great and saving gift to be so possessed by beauty and so relaxed by the absurd.

Fanny's preoccupation with slavery made her somewhat unsympathetic to the local white society with whom, as Pierce Butler's wife, she came in contact. While they remained at Butler Island this was largely confined to the people of Darien with whom she exchanged visits without much enthusiasm. She thought the white women poor, ineffectual creatures, who made no effort to combat the enervating climate, languid both in their deportment and in their speech. Darien itself, in modern terms, she would have described as a 'dump'. When the Butlers moved to Hampton Point the circle of her acquaintances widened, as in addition to the Butler estates there were several other large plantations on St Simon's Island. The only person from whose conversation she derived much pleasure or information had emigrated from Glasgow in his youth, and it was from him that she received confirmation that the terrible tales that her black clients had told to her of the King regime were not, as Pierce would have had her believe, 'rubbish' and 'd—d lies', but perfectly true. Not all the plantations were run down; the Hamilton estate was prosperous and the family well housed, but what struck Fanny most were the unkempt grounds and dilapidated appearance of many of the planters' houses while some of the Negro cabins that she passed as they rode through the islands she described as 'dirty, dilapidated dog kennels' compared to which the worst of those on her husband's estates were like palaces. The southern way of life, the southern code, with its contempt for work and its exaggerated emphasis on honour, were to Fanny completely alien and if she required any further confirmation of the rottenness of that society she was to be furnished with it before the Butlers left for the north. A dispute between two neighbouring planters, accompanied by insults and affronts, led to one's shooting and killing the other after an accidental meeting in a hotel at Brunswick. What shattered Fanny was the way in which nobody looked or spoke as if anything unusual had occurred. Fanny rejoined that she was 'going away from such a dreadful state of society'. In it she could find no redeeming features; slavery corrupted both slave and master, both black and white, and an unspoken prayer possessed her as she stood on the crumbling banks of the Altamaha river:

Beat, beat the crumbling banks and sliding shores, wild waves of the Atlantic and Altamaha! Sweep down and carry hence this evil earth and these homes of tyranny, and roll above the soil of slavery, and wash my soul and the souls of those I love clean from the blood of our kind.

Well might she write 'How new and sad a chapter of my life this winter has been'.

SIX

A Clash of Personalities

It is difficult to determine just how important a part the Georgian interlude played in the break-up of Fanny's marriage. When Pierce had first rejoined his family in England the relations between them had seemed easier. Apparently this improvement was short-lived. Fanny's second pregnancy may have made her particularly nervy because early in 1838 she was again demanding to be sent home, declaring,

Since my marriage with you my life has been one long incessant privation, which was all very well when you were kind to me; as, however I will never be subjected to rudeness and ill manners from anyone, without doing that which is within my power to avoid it, I must beg you now that you will take proper means for my leaving you, as you were the only thing that kept me in this country.

She even threatened that if he would not do as she wished she would sell her gold watch and chain and go home on the proceeds, and announced that he could make arrangements for the return of the second child, when born, to the States. This letter sounds as if it had been penned by a furious Fanny after some matrimonial flare-up. Pierce's defence was that, though he was not aware of having been rude, he was so depressed by his wife's behaviour that he may well have been irritable. This may well be the truth. Fanny was not easy to live with. Even Henry James, who admired her greatly when he knew her in her latter years, admitted that at times she could be extremely annoying. Whether on this occasion Fanny did or did not carry out her threat to sell her watch is not known, but in 1839 Pierce told Elizabeth Sedgwick that 'Five or six times she has packed up all her clothes to leave me. Twice she has taken her jewels to Philadelphia and sold them in order to obtain money to travel.' This particular storm, like so many others, seems to have blown over. Her second daughter, christened Frances Anne after her mother, and known in the family as Fan, was born on 28 May, precisely three years after her elder sister Sarah, which, as Fanny pointed out, illustrated her own devotion to routine.

After their return from Georgia things seem to have got worse between her and Pierce. By the end of May that year he was so worn out and depressed that he took the unusual step, for him, of pouring out his perplexity and unhappiness to Fanny's great friend Elizabeth Sedgwick. The visit that Pierce and Fanny had paid to the Sedgwicks in Lenox in the summer of 1835 seems to have developed into a regular occurrence. Over the years Lenox had grown into something of an intellectual and cultural centre where well-known figures in the literary world could escape the heat of summer when cities like Boston became intolerable. To Fanny, Lenox was a haven for both body and spirit. It gave her everything that she most missed in the rest of America: hills which she adored – it was in the Berkshires that she first claimed kinship with them – beautiful countryside where she and Pierce could ride together, and in the evenings pleasant parties and good conversation. Fanny Appleton has left a vivid description of Fanny, her maternal duties done, attired in her riding costume, white breeches and a black velvet habit and cap, mounted on a fiery steed which she managed with consummate skill and grace. In the evening, dressed in her favourite white muslin with bare arms and neck however cold the weather, she sometimes sang old ballads, sometimes read from Shakespeare's plays, and always held her companions enthralled by the range and depth of her conversation. Only in the intellectual atmosphere of Boston was Fanny ever so happy in her adopted country. In a letter to Harriet she described the Sedgwicks as 'very dear to me and almost the only people among whom I have found mental companionship since I have been in this country'. In addition to the Butlers' spending some part of each summer or autumn in Lenox various members of the Sedgwick clan in turn stayed with them at Butler Place. On 7 May 1838 Fanny had told Harriet 'I have just been enjoying the pleasure of a visit from one of the Sedgwick family. They are all my friends, and I do think all and each in their peculiar way good and admirable'. It was natural, therefore, that Pierce should turn to Elizabeth for help in his matrimonial difficulties though, unlike Fanny, he cannot have had much in common with their more intellectual interests. Indeed from the first Catherine Maria had never thought him Fanny's equal and had questioned her wisdom in marrying him.

A matrimonial crisis had come in the last week of May when once again Fanny was threatening to leave her husband, to return to England by the next packet boat and to earn her living on the stage. On their daughters' joint birthday she had seemed happier and the day had passed off pleasantly, but that night when Pierce had gone upstairs he found a note on the table by the bed in which Fanny demanded

I now request once and for all to be allowed to return to my own country, and such friends as remain to me there. God knows how bitter a life mine has been to me for some time past. I cannot endure it any longer and will not. You can never repair the injury which you have done in marrying me, though you seem to think that your having done so is sufficient compensation for all the privations which I feel, though they are imperceptible to you. I will not remain here to be your housekeeper, your children's nurse, or what yet you make of me that is still more degrading and revolting.

What Fanny meant by this last sentence or what lay behind this out-burst is difficult to surmise. Probably Pierce told Elizabeth as much or as little of the causes of tension between them as he thought would win him her sympathy. There is for instance no mention of their differences over slavery, where he knew that Elizabeth's sympathy would be with Fanny. Yet it is difficult to believe that Fanny always managed to keep silence on a subject so near to her heart. Pierce's explanation of the present crisis was that though in the past Fanny had given him to understand that the basic cause of her unhappiness was the fact that she was separated from her family and friends, 'lately she has taken up the idea that she has become indifferent to me'. What grounds she had for believing that Pierce no longer loved her he did not say. Pierce declared that 'I have never doubted the continuance and strength of her love for me and she should never have doubted mine. I know that our feelings are as strong as when we first loved but cemented and made holy by the birth of our two daughters.' Yet he continued sadly, 'her life is passed in bitter misery, in constant tears and heartbreaking sobs'. When their marriage was in the last stage of breaking up in 1844, Fanny accused him of adultery, on the evidence of some letters which she found in his desk, though this charge was never proven. It is possible therefore that some earlier rumours might have reached her. Little is known of Pierce's private life. In 1842 a couple of Philadelphia misses credited him with having a mistress but as at this time the Butlers were again in London the supposition must either have drifted over the Atlantic or be based on a reputation earned at some earlier date. Moreover if Fanny had heard and believed such gossip she would certainly have confided her suspicions to the Sedgwicks; she was never good at keeping things to herself. A more likely explanation may have been found in Pierce's frequent absences from home. This, as Elizabeth pointed out to her friend, was not surprising when his return 'always made you unhappy, and your greeting consisted in tears, and sobs and sleepless misery'. Sometimes Fanny swung to the other extreme, shocking Elizabeth by her offhand manner towards him, and on one particular occasion when Pierce had been far from well, Elizabeth felt constrained to add 'my husband would die, if I should give him such a reception'. Coming from a friend as devoted to Fanny as Elizabeth Sedgwick undoubtedly was, this remark is at least some evidence that Pierce was not merely fabricating a case against his wife.

Indeed the letter in which he appealed to Elizabeth for her help gives the impression of a man at the end of his tether, faced with a situation that he can neither understand nor control, writing 'Alas! poor Fanny, the bitterness and misery are of her own creating, and mar my happiness as effectually as her own'. Though he admitted that though 'she must feel very much the seclusion in which we live, and constantly regret the separation from her family and early friends, nevertheless it was no 'remedy to be eternally weeping and bemoaning this as the greatest and only calamity'. When he told Elizabeth, 'She is undermining her health by this constant gloom and weeping, her nerves are very materially affected already and the tone of her mind, as regards herself, is sickly and unnatural', adding that 'the difficulty is within herself, it is inherent', he seems to be describing a woman very near to a nervous breakdown. Probably half unconsciously he even acknowledged that the tension between them was a major element responsible for his wife's mental condition, telling Elizabeth, 'It seems as if her spirit became troubled by my presence and would never settle down, but like a boiling spirit which rises out of the earth it is ever most troubled and agitated and most uneasy when we are most together and alone.' By his own admission in her dealings with other people Fanny appeared completely rational and he had nothing but praise for her management of their children. Unfortunately his own remedy for this distressing situation was to declare that 'unless she can be made sensible of this, and summon resolution to overcome this morbid state of feeling, she will be miserable for life'; something of which Fanny at this time was completely incapable.

Indeed it looks as if Fanny, at least when in the grip of such emotions, were trying to break free from the marriage while Pierce was still struggling to save it. Certainly he assured Elizabeth of his conviction that 'If we are not happy together, less happy should we be apart.' Fanny did not share his belief. Early in 1838 she had told him 'If you will take my advice in casting aside your own regard for appearances and consult only your own comfort and happiness, you will make some arrangements by which in future to be freed from it altogether.' To her husband this seemed to imply that to break up a marriage was, as he said, no more than to end 'a partnership to carry on some small retail business'. It was an ironic twist of fate that in 1844 it was Fanny who was desperately struggling to retain her foothold in the family home in order not to be separated from her children while Pierce, inspired by then by a bitter dislike of the woman he had once loved, was determined to drive her out. This tragic reversal of roles was still some troubled five years away. Elizabeth's response to his *cri de coeur* was both prompt and shocked. Clearly she thought Fanny mentally unbalanced. Her immediate advice to the harassed Pierce was, 'Try to recall that she is diseased, and treat her soothingly and compassionately, as if she were sick with an ordinary malady. She is markedly susceptible to reproof or disapproval, and for the present at least you must bear and forebear.' To Fanny she wrote a letter which, though warm and loving, was very much to the point, writing 'Your mind is positively and greatly diseased and you yourself have been the cause of all that appearance of indifference in your husband which you now believe to be the original source of all your unhappiness.' She then pointed out a fact which Fanny never seemed to have realized, that Pierce also 'has suffered deeply, intensely, though too reserved to show it', adding, 'you know the power he has of concealing his feelings, and his inclination to do so'. Later Elizabeth Sedgwick was to turn against Pierce, but this comment provides an interesting sidelight on the kind of man she believed him to be in 1839. Finally she told Fanny that, even had she been the wronged woman that she thought herself, she had no right to break up a marriage into which she had entered willingly and so deprive her children of the care of both parents. At the end of this long letter Elizabeth turned again to Fanny's mental condition, writing, 'My poor dear Fanny, my precious, almost idolized friend, do let me persuade you that your mind is diseased', suggesting that her morbid tendencies were an inheritance from her mother, who had died in 1838, and who apparently had also suffered from time to time from periods of terrible depression. Fanny's published autobiographical writings, apart from her *Records of a Girlhood*, have little to say about her mother beyond praising her capabilities as a theatrical critic, but there are hints that she was not easy to live with at times. Also perhaps it is worth mentioning that Fanny's younger brother, Henry, was so mentally disturbed during the latter years of his life that he had to be kept in a private asylum, where he died.

There is no reason to suppose that when Pierce enlisted Elizabeth's sympathy he was not genuinely unhappy, nor that he did not still love Fanny in his own way, nor that he was not struggling to preserve his marriage, believing that if only Fanny would be sensible, as he understood the term, they might still be happy together. It might have been happier for both of them if he had realized, as Fanny had, that this was no longer possible. Her husband might still love her but the whole way in which he handled this painful situation showed how little he understood her. It was not that Fanny was unwilling to try to control her feelings. This she promised to do, but for the unimaginative Pierce this was not enough; he wanted cast-iron assurances, writing,

you should not say you will endeavour to overcome your morbid state of mind, but you should say 'I will do it', and like a drunkard who dashes for ever from his lips the bitter cup that has brought wretchedness on himself and family, you should summon strong resolution, and never again allow yourself to fall into that state in which reason leaves his seat . . . It is singular that the fate of your unfortunate mother does not act as a warning and that the sad example that she gave you has not been shunned.

This bracing masculine advice, which Fanny was clearly incapable of taking, was all the more maladroit because, having given it, Pierce then poured out his heart to her, declaring,

Never doubt the strength and continuance of my affection for you – that can never cease. It is true you have it in your power to make me unhappy, to cause my home to be distasteful to me and to force me away from you and my children – but you cannot make me cease to love you. You cannot drive me to seek pleasure or enjoyment away from you; if I cannot have happiness in my home, it is nowhere for me. I may not be happy with you; I cannot be happy without you.

Pierce was probably assessing the situation accurately in thinking that he and Fanny could be happy neither together nor apart. Though most of the evidence on which any judgement must be based comes from Pierce, because in later life Fanny took drastic precautions to see that her letters, when they dealt with her matrimonial troubles, were destroyed, some indications remain that in between her bouts of frustrated misery, Fanny still felt the pull of her old love for her husband. It was incompatibility, not indifference, that destroyed them. In 1839, if his wife were suffering from some mental disturbance, Pierce himself was physically far from well. Fanny, in her brief allusions to the matter, gives the impression that his complaint was some sort of rheumatism. He had been ill while they were in Georgia and the trouble had persisted after his return. In June he decided to try the hot sulphur springs in Virginia and Fanny told Harriet that as there was no suitable accommodation for herself and the children they might not be able to go with him; the general tone of her letter indicates that this was something she regretted. Finally she and the children went to Lenox. One wonders if in spite of the friction between them she would still have preferred to be with him. The friction certainly continued when they were together again. In the autumn of 1839 John and Pierce were to return to Georgia and Fanny expected, and hoped, to go with them. Preparatory to doing so the Pierce Butlers shut up Butler Place and moved into John's house in Philadelphia. Their departure was delayed by Pierce's continued ill health and Fanny, who resented not being in her own house, blew up once more. She threatened to walk out unless he found them a place of their own. It was the old, sad story; neither could see the other's point of view. Eventually John and Pierce went to Georgia alone and Fanny returned to Butler Place with disappointed hopes. John at least had apparently not welcomed the idea of his sister-in-law's disturbing presence on the plantation.

Cut off from Philadelphia by bad weather and bad roads, Fanny spent a boring, monotonous winter. During the day she had the solace of her children's company and the interest of teaching young Sarah, now an engaging imp of five, to read. But when she and baby Fan had gone to bed Fanny found the house depressingly quiet. In the evenings she occupied herself with reading Gibbon's *Decline and Fall*, and with worsted work, to which she was much given, but when ten o'clock struck she was glad to have an excuse to go to bed herself. She confessed to Harriet, 'I am longing for the spring as I never did before.' Then at least she could find pleasure in her garden which, apart from her children, was now her main interest. She had even managed to create some semblance of an English lawn. Nevertheless the spring, when it did come, brought with it new domestic problems. She discovered that Margery, the children's nurse, was trying to turn little Sarah into a Roman Catholic, and Protestant Fanny felt that her daughter could no longer be left under so dangerous an influence. This was a grief to Fanny. The two women had been through much together: terrifying Atlantic crossings, the appalling journey to Georgia and the strangeness of plantation life with its limited accommodation. In other ways too Margery had been an excellent nurse. Writing to her cousin Cecilia, now married to George Combe, in 1835, some six months after Sarah's birth, she had told her how much she attributed her baby daughter's progress to Margery's continual talking and playing with her. If she could Fanny would have liked to keep Margery with her as her personal maid while finding another nurse for the children, but financially this was not possible. Before Pierce had gone south there had been indications of financial difficulties. Fanny had already spent her annual allowance of pin-money and had been turning over in her mind some means of getting hold of what she described as 'a few dollars'. She had controlled her income for too long; she was used to spending it as she wished and she found it irksome to be dependent on Pierce, particularly when their views so often clashed. Often she regretted having been quite so lavish in handing over all her American earnings to her father when she married. Then it had not seemed to matter. Fanny was in love and had not tasted the bitter fruit of financial dependence. Now as the strain between her and her husband grew she found it more and more distasteful. Because Fanny's aspirations had always been literary it was to be expected that she should look to her pen to meet financial emergencies. Pierce, on the other hand, remembering the reverberations of her American journal and her desire to give publicity to her views on slavery, was basically opposed to any such activities on his wife's part. During Fanny's last stay in England society had been shaken by a scandal which had involved a well-known man of title, Lord de Ros, in a charge of cheating at cards. By the convention of the times men might not pay their bills, they might seduce other men's wives; but they did not cheat at cards. This suggested to Fanny a possible plot for a play, which she started to write and which she entitled *The English Tragedy*. In the summer of 1838, when she was at Lenox with the children but without the inhibiting presence of Pierce, who had stayed in New York to have medical treatment, she finished her final draft. When however she consulted Theodore Sedgwick on the possibility of finding a publisher for it, Pierce opposed the whole idea, thinking the substance of Fanny's new play quite unsuitable for publication in the country where she was living under his name. He apparently had less objection if it were published, or even performed, in England. Fanny accordingly sent it to Macready, who had once appeared under her father's management and who was a leading figure on the English stage. His verdict was to pronounce it 'one of the most powerful modern plays I have seen – most painful, almost shocking, but full of power, feeling and pathos'. But as he and the men he consulted thought it too strong meat, even for the London stage, one can understand Pierce's reluctance to see it appear in Philadelphia under the name of Butler. By 1839 hints were appearing to the effect that it was not only Fanny who was short of money. When Sidney Fisher had ridden out from Philadelphia to visit Butler Place he got the impression that the Butlers were rich and lived in great style, but Pierce, judging by his subsequent financial record, was a bad manager and man of business. He had a weakness for speculation and it is likely that his investments had been affected by the financial collapse and national crisis in 1837. In 1840 a further proof of the need for economy came when, as Fanny told Harriet, she had to give up her personal maid, as they were forced to cut down their establishment. Servants were always a problem because Americans despised domestic service, so that more and more Fanny found herself dependent on the raw Irish variety. In consequence on the day on which the new nurse was off duty Fanny found herself forced to forgo 'the usual decency of changing my dress for dinner, from the utter incapacity of my housemaid to fasten up my back'. Perhaps the modern generation should be more grateful than is sometimes the case for zip fasteners.

March 1840 brought more serious distress. Fanny received a miserable letter from her husband who was ill in Georgia. This news coincided with a letter from Elizabeth in which her friend had felt compelled to repeat to her some of the contents of Pierce's letter written in the previous May. Fanny was shattered by this revelation of his misery and his love. Even her devoted Elizabeth seems to have thought it strange, as she told Pierce that 'the idea of her ever having made you unhappy seems to be an entirely new revelation to her', but here she may have been mistaken. On 3 March Fanny had written 'I grieve to hear of your low spirits, though 'tis some relief to me to think that I am not now near you to wear and harass you, and produce the depression you complain of.' The letter ended 'God Bless you. Ever your own wife.' It is fascinating to contrast the tone of the letters that passed between this ill-yoked pair when distance divided them and those outpourings by the irritated and frustrated Fanny when they were under the same roof. The existence of the latter, though a boon to a biographer, is nevertheless puzzling. Why did she have to pour forth her irritation and demands for repatriation on paper when she was seeing her husband every day? It is not as if Fanny were ever at a loss for words; her reputation as a brilliant conversationalist is too well attested by strangers and friends alike. Compulsive letter-writing is a recognized form of neurosis and it may have been merely a symptom of her disturbed state of mind. A possible, or perhaps it would be more correct to call it a subsidiary reason, is suggested in one of the letters that Fanny fired at Pierce while waiting for the birth of her first child. In it she wrote 'My feelings towards you, and with regard to my own situation, are such as to render it utterly impossible for me to speak calmly upon the subject.' She may have felt that she could only state her case in writing. This domestic correspondence raises another question. Why did Pierce keep the letters which she wrote to him so that he was able to quote them so fully in his own correspondence and later to publish them in his own self-justifying Statement? Was it his lawyer's training? Did he think as early as 1836 that he might one day need evidence of Fanny's irrational behaviour? May there not also be something a little ingenuous in his Statement that though he was not in the habit of making copies of the letters that he wrote he happened to have rough drafts of the ones that he quoted? Against this must be weighed the fact that men with legal training did very often keep copies of the letters that they wrote, as witness the many volumes of George Combe's correspondence now in the National Library of Scotland.

The news of Pierce's ill health, combined with the effect that

Elizabeth's letter had produced, had the predictable result of sweeping Fanny away on a tide of remorseful grief. On 19 March she wrote distractedly, 'I am almost in despair; I thought that once freed from the gloom and disquietude which my thrice unhappy temperament seems to throw over you, and alone with John in that favourable climate, you would have had at least a temporary relief from pain and depression. Oh, Oh! My dearest what can be done for you?' After suggesting that perhaps with John as his companion (she did not propose going with him herself), he might try the curative effect of a German spa, she ended her letter 'God bless you, my darling, dearest Pierce.' After reading Elizabeth's letter she told him that she felt as if the 'iron indeed was entering my soul; forgive me my dearest, dearest Pierce, if I have so bitterly cursed your existence. I cannot write any more; I am blinded with crying. Ever, ever your own wife, Fanny.' Pierce returned in May and once again the storm-tossed couple seem to have found happiness together. They enjoyed such distractions as Philadelphia had to offer. When the famous European dancer Fanny Ellsler visited that city they went to see her performance every night. This Fanny told Harriet was 'an extraordinary effort of dissipation for me, who hardly ever stir abroad in the evenings'. If the present were pleasant, the future was still uncertain. Even Fanny herself was not sure what she wanted to do. Part of her longed to be back in England and to be with her father and Adelaide, who was enjoying her first success as an opera singer, having made her debut at the Fenice Theatre in Venice as Norma, later to be one of her favourite roles. Yet much as Fanny wished to be with them she told Harriet, 'My roots are beginning to spread in my present soil.' The worst period of her homesickness was now behind her. She no longer felt, as she had felt in 1838, that every letter that she received from 'the other side is to me what the drop of water would have been to the rich man in Hades'. On one thing at least Fanny seemed to be determined; if she came to England it must be with her husband from whom at the moment she seems to have been genuinely anxious not to be separated. Pierce's own plans were uncertain but they do not seem to have included a visit to England in the autumn. He did not want to leave the country when a presidential election was pending. He was a strong supporter of Van Buren, and Fanny, much as she wanted him to agree to come with her to England, was prepared to admit that in this case he had sound reasons for not doing so. She was at last beginning to show some interest in American politics, largely motivated by what she described as 'that best woman's reason, sympathy with the politics of the man I belong to'. Such a comment might even be construed as holding out some hopes for future matrimonial harmony. It was not only politics which seemed likely to detain Pierce; there was also a decision to be made about whether he would return once more to the Georgian plantation. If so Fanny was anxious to go with him. She wanted to continue with the work among the women slaves that had absorbed so much of her energies on her first visit and she wanted to continue her first-hand writing up of the journal which she had kept while there. Being Fanny, she was honest enough to realize that this could never be published without the consent of both her husband and his brother. She was also honest enough to feel that she must make her intention to continue with her journal plain to Pierce before she went south with him. If he should go south without her then on one thing she was determined. She would not spend another winter alone at Butler Place. Rather than face that prospect she would go to England, even if it meant going alone.

The situation was finally resolved by the news that Charles Kemble was seriously ill. This decided Pierce to go with his wife and children to England, in spite of his interest in the forthcoming election, when the problem of the annexation of Texas to the Union loomed large, and in which as a slave owner he was interested. Accordingly the whole family, including the children's new nurse, Anne Martin, a capable American girl, sailed from New York. The report on Charles Kemble when they reached London was bad, so bad indeed that at first the doctor forbade Fanny to see her father lest the excitement should prove fatal. However after a slight change for the better she was allowed to do so and from that day he improved steadily. On their arrival Pierce had put up at the Clarendon, a well-known hotel, until he could make more permanent arrangements. Finally he rented a house in Clarges Street, where in April Charles Kemble joined them. Fanny's happiness was complete when in May Adelaide returned to London after a successful continental tour and Harriet came over from Ireland. The Butlers were soon caught up in a whirl of engagements; when they dined with Fanny's old friends the Egertons there was nobody there, except themselves, below the rank of a viscount. For Fanny the great event was a concert given by the Duchess of Sutherland at Stafford House in aid of Polish refugees. This was to be the occasion of her sister's first semi-public appearance in England; she was to sing, the great Rachel to recite, and Liszt to play. It was a gay and brilliant scene. Pierce also was enjoying the delights of sophisticated London society, of which he was now a part, and showed no inclination to go home. The lease of the house he had taken in Clarges Street having expired, another was rented in Harley Street and the Butlers settled in for the winter of 1841. Not all their time was spent in London; like the rest of Society during the summer months they were engaged in a round of visits in the more salubrious countryside. Fanny took Pierce to stay at Worsley, her old haunt, with the Francis Egertons, and reported their visit as 'prosperous and pleasant'. It was certainly a distinguished house-party, including as it did the corpse-like Rogers, the Irish poet Moore, and that brilliant talker and historian Macaulay. In a letter to Lady Dacre, Fanny described him as 'like nothing in the world but Bayle's Dictionary, continued down to the present time and purified of all objectionable matter. Such a Niagara of information did surely never pour from the lips of mortal man.' Among their visits there was one to the Lansdownes at Bowood. Once again it was a distinguished party, which included Dundas, Lord John Russell and the diarist Charles Greville, Lady Francis Egerton's brother. Fanny herself was much in demand and entertained the party with readings from *Much Ado About Nothing* and *The Hunchback*.

This halcyon period was coming to an end. In December things once more began to go wrong between Pierce and Fanny. From the beginning of 1842 their marriage seems to have moved steadily towards disaster. On the surface it was Fanny's views on slavery that occasioned the reopening of the rift between them but underneath its cause was their diametrically opposed conceptions of the roles of husband and wife in the institution of marriage. This was the rock on which their marriage was finally wrecked. During the happy interlude that had followed Pierce's return from Georgia Fanny seems to have struggled to restrain her passionate attempts to convert him to her own views on slavery, realizing rather belatedly that early habits and prejudices were too strong for her to break down and that her reasoned arguments were apt 'to degenerate into passionate appeals, the violence of which is not calculated to do much good in the way of producing convictions in the minds of others'. It was therefore a cruel stroke of fate that she and Pierce should once again be involved in a clash of wills that turned on the issue of slavery. Fanny's views were no secret, and towards the end of 1841 she had been approached by Maria Childe, the

Abolitionist, who herself had made great sacrifices for the cause in which she passionately believed. She must have known that Fanny had kept a journal while in Georgia and now wrote suggesting that she might be allowed to publish some part of it. On this occasion Fanny had acted correctly. Deep though her detestation of slavery was, she had always regarded her Georgian experiences as confidential. Her journal had been intended only for Elizabeth and as a means of recording her own day-to-day impressions. It was not ammunition to be placed at the disposal of the Abolitionists without her husband's consent, which she must have known would never be given. She wrote accordingly to Mrs Childe suggesting that, though she could not allow any part of her journal to be published, she could furnish her with an account of their journey to Georgia in the course of which 'some observations on the effects of slavery, as they were apparent wherever I went, necessarily occur'. To Fanny this was a compromise that satisfied her conscience; she could serve the cause in which she believed without betraying her husband's confidence or appearing to criticize his way of life. This was a process of moral hair-splitting that a man like Pierce could never have appreciated. Having written her letter Fanny gave it to her husband to be posted, together with one addressed to Elizabeth Sedgwick. Some time later Fanny found both letters, still unposted, in her husband's desk. Thinking this to be just one more instance of Pierce's carelessness she picked them up and posted them, as any wife might do. When she mentioned the fact and found that his action had been deliberate she was furious, immediately declaring her intention of writing to Mrs Childe to explain why she had received no earlier reply to her letter. The result was a bitter quarrel; Pierce declared that if she sent it against his express wishes it would be tantamount to ending their marriage. Fanny remained obdurate and Pierce was forced to appeal for help to one of Fanny's American friends now living in England. This was Fanny Appleton's elder sister Mary, now Mrs MacIntosh. She was able to persuade the enraged Fanny that such a letter, used by Mrs Childe for publicity as it might be, should not be sent. Reluctantly Fanny gave way. This patched up but did not heal the wound that the quarrel had caused. Pierce brooded on the fact that his wife had given way to the persuasion of a friend when she would not yield to the express orders of her husband; Fanny felt sore and ill used. She was prepared to accept the fact that in marriage the final decision-making must rest with the husband; in the main she was prepared to allow her pattern of life to be dictated by his wishes and judgement. It was the limit which she placed on the absolute duty of obedience that was at the root of the clash between them. 'A woman', she told Harriet, 'should love her husband better than anything on earth except her soul, which I think a man should respect above everything on earth but his own soul.' It was at this level that her hatred of slavery on grounds of conscience and her rejection of Pierce's conventional conception of the role of husband and wife were linked. It was against God's laws for any man to own another individual. Every person must be allowed to possess his or her own soul, and therefore even a wife could not give unquestioning obedience to her husband. She once told Kate Sedgwick that she could not 'under any *circumstances* of *misery whatever* give my conscience into the keeping of another human being or submit the actions dictated by my conscience to their will'!

By April 1842 the situation had become so tense that Fanny decided on flight, following standard practice in leaving a note behind her. She must have been turning over plans of this kind for some time, for in March she had announced to Kate that as she could not allow herself to be maintained by a man who had cast her off she intended to return to the stage. Apparently she also intended to return to America, because she asked her friend about the possibility of buying a plot of land in the Berkshires, and inquired how large an annual income she would need to run a modest establishment consisting of herself and two servants. By April this must have seemed a more unpleasant course than being maintained by Pierce, for in the note she left him she wrote, 'I have full confidence that rather than see me return to the stage to earn my subsistence you will allow me sufficient for my maintenance (I care not how little) till my father dies, when I hope you will be freed from the charge of me.' People unsympathetic to Fanny might feel that such a threat amounted almost to a form of blackmail, though in her strung-up condition it is unlikely that she looked at it in this way. The mention of her father's death referred to the arrangement by which the capital sum that she had made over to him, with the purpose of giving him an income for life, would revert to her on his death. Having fired this broadside Fanny departed from Liverpool intending on her arrival to ask the proprietor of the Adelphi Hotel to get her a ticket on the steam-packet leaving for Boston the next day. Pierce does not yet seem to have lost all affection for his wayward wife; later the same year he could still assure her that he believed 'the strong bond of love which first attached us to each other . . . as strong now as ever it was'. Whether driven by love or the desire to avoid publicity, or a combination of the two, Pierce set out in pursuit and caught up with Fanny at Birmingham. They then travelled to Liverpool together and by the morning he had persuaded his wife to give up her plan of immediate flight, promising that if she were still determined to leave him he would at least accompany her back to the States and so avoid a scandal. In other words he gave Fanny time to cool down. The Butlers then returned to London and for a few more months maintained an uneasy truce.

Outwardly their lives followed their normal pattern; the visits, the parties, the social round went on. They stayed with the Duke and Duchess of Rutland at Belvoir as members of a cheerful house-party where grandeur combined with gaiety. From there they went on to Lord and Lady Willoughby at Grimsthorpe. Their next visit was to Comford House, to see old Lady Berkeley, one of the few personal contacts that Pierce had in England. When her fifth son had been travelling in America he had met Pierce in Philadelphia. They had struck up a friendship, and it had been he who had given his young friend an introduction to the Kembles. Fanny thought he had had a bad influence on Pierce and that his way of life was profligate, but she liked his mother. Lady Berkeley's own life had been unconventional; she had been a butcher's daughter, had won the love of the then young Lord Berkeley, had become his mistress, borne his children and finally married her noble lover. Her life reads like the plot for a romantic novel and bears out the old adage that truth is stranger than fiction. But for the most part the circles in which Pierce moved were those to which he had the entree through his wife.

To Fanny fell the distinction of royal notice; Queen Victoria indicated her wish that Fanny should be presented at court. This gracious notice gave her no particular pleasure; she was worried at the expense that it would involve. However, Pierce decided that she must go. A dress was bought and jewels were hired for the occasion, the safety of which caused their wearer considerable anxiety. Fanny herself was surprisingly agitated and self-conscious; later she declared that all she saw of the ceremony were Prince Albert's legs. Pierce also had his moment of social glory. He was presented by the American ambassador at a levee on 6 May. Democratic Anne Martin was horrified that he, an American, should kneel and kiss the Queen's hand. Hardly were these excitements over before Fanny was caught up in private theatricals organized by the Egertons, who proposed giving a performance of *The Hunchback* with Fanny in her famous role of Julia. May was spent in rehearsals and the play was given at Bridgewater House. It was a trying experience for Fanny to return to her past, even among friends. She told Harriet that she had been desperately nervous in case she had by now forgotten how to act. Her fears were unjustified. Charles Greville declared, 'Mrs Butler acted as well as Fanny Kemble did ten or twelve years ago.'

But behind the social façade Fanny was growing more and more irked by her financial dependence on Pierce. In May she had confided in Harriet that she was 'rather in want of money', and that 'I cannot help sometimes regretting that I did not reserve out of my former earnings at least such a sum as would have covered my personal expenses.' Financial independence, particularly at the moment when relations were so strained between her and Pierce, raised a moral issue. Though she admitted that her present 'pecuniary position would now seem to most people very far preferable to my former one, but having *earned* money, and therefore most legitimately owned it, I cannot ever conceive that I have the right to the money of another person'. Her immediate difficulty was that she owed a Mademoiselle Devy the not inconsiderable sum of £97, which would have represented a trifle over three weeks' salary when she first played Juliet at Covent Garden. Her dress allowance being already spent, in their present circumstances she was clearly unwilling to ask her husband to foot the bill. Instead she told Harriet that she intended to earn the money herself. With this intention Fanny set about translating and adapting Dumas' *Mademoiselle de Belle-Isle* for the stage, and providing her father, who much to her dismay had again accepted the unlucky management of Covent Garden, with a ballet based on the story of the Indian Princess Pochontas. She also considered once again using the non-controversial part of her Georgian journal, which dealt with their appalling journey to the south. Then one night, while she was brushing her hair, she had a sudden impulse to sketch out a sequel to Kotzobue's *The Stranger*, the equivocal ending of which had long intrigued her. Having no paper at hand she snatched up Sarah's copy-book and started writing it scene by scene and act by act until the spell was broken by the sudden appearance of Pierce, so that she told Harriet 'The short-lived triumph of the spirit of inspiration died away under the effect of a conversation by which it was interrupted and I collapsed like a fallen omelette soufflée.' From the rest of the letter it would seem that what deflated Fanny was Pierce's pointing out that whatever she earned was not her own property but that of her husband, a harsh legal fact that in her moment of enthusiasm she had forgotten. Legal it might be; just, she felt, it was not. As she exploded to Harriet she could not accept that 'what I invent – create in fact – can really belong to any one but myself; therefore if anything that I wrote could earn me £97, I am afraid that I shall consider that I, and no one else, had paid my bill'. Fanny's situation was one that faced many talented and independently minded Victorian women who had been unfortunate enough not to have marriage settlements that secured to them some money under their own control and who therefore were totally dependent on their husbands' generosity. As Fanny ruefully declared, 'a deal of love must be thrown into one or other or both scales to make the balance hang tolerably even'. Between her and Pierce this 'deal of love' was no longer sufficient to prevent her from feeling, as she told Harriet, 'something very like wrathful indignation, impotent wrath and vain indignation to be sure – but not the less intense for that'. To her, injustice was injustice, whether sanctioned by convention or not, and irrespective of whether Pierce did or did not enforce his legal rights to their limit. To remind her coldly of the position was enough for her to feel all the fury aroused by an unloving restraint.

Moreover as a wife and a mother she had other worries. They were living extravagantly and Pierce seemed incapable of managing his affairs with prudence. For some time Theodore Sedgwick, who appears to have been looking after the Butlers' financial interests while they were in England, had been urging Fanny to use her influence with her husband to get him to return, and she declared herself that she was quite wretched at their prolonged absence. This put an added strain on their already strained relations. Whatever persuasion or pressure that she used failed. Pierce did not want to leave England and when the lease of their Harley Street house was up he moved his family back into the Clarendon Hotel until they could take possession of another rented house, 25 Upper Grosvenor Street. While they were at the Clarendon another bitter quarrel broke out. Though it was nearly two o'clock in the morning, Fanny ordered the hotel porter to call her a cab and told Pierce that she was leaving him. Again we have only his account of the incident, according to which he first remonstrated with her, pointing out that in any case they were leaving the hotel next morning and asking her to delay her departure at least until then. Fanny refused; Pierce's temper snapped and he told her that if she did so he would take both children with him to Liverpool and catch the first steamer back to America, and that she would never see her children again. Under this threat Fanny gave way to the extent that she sent the cab away, but next morning she went to her sister's house. Pierce took the children and their new English governess, Miss Hall, with him to the house in Grosvenor Street. It was the most serious breach that had yet occurred, and this time there was no last-minute reconciliation. Fanny did not return to her husband and children, but continued to stay with her sister. Though the bond between them was very close, the two sisters were quite different in temperament. Adelaide had a sweetness and a steadiness which endeared her to all who knew her. Earlier in life Fanny had been surprised, and even a little shocked, that the literature which had moved her to tears had left her sister unaffected and even a little critical. Young Anne Thackeray said of Adelaide, 'Her beautiful head was like that of some classical statue nobly set upon her shoulders. But no classical statue ever looked at you as she did; her eyes and mouth spoke before she uttered.' Later, when for a time she was living in Paris in the Rue Royale, where she had an apartment, Anne thought it seemed like a Paradise on earth because Adelaide 'liked glorious things full of colour, Italian, sumptuous, and she liked them used for daily life and pleasure'. When Fanny fled to her she was able to give her unhappy sister a home because in the previous September she had married Edward Sartoris, giving up her career to do so. Fanny, in view of her own experience, had been full of apprehension, writing to Lady Dacre,

'It seems amazing to abdicate a secure fortune, and such power, power to do anything so excellently (putting its recognition by the public entirely out of account) for that fearful risk [continuing] to see my sister, that woman most dear to me, deliberately leave a path, where the sure harvest of her labours is independent fortune, and a not unhonourable distinction . . . for a life where if she does not find happiness, what will atone to her for all that she has left?'

Fanny's fears that history might repeat itself were groundless. Adelaide's marriage was a happy one and in Fanny's troubled future she and Edward were to do what they could to ameliorate her distress. But for the moment there was nothing to be done.

By now the conflict had been narrowed to one thing – the question of Fanny's total submission to her husband's will. The letters that passed between them at this time are those submitted by Pierce and Fanny as evidence in their later divorce proceedings and doubtless each selected those most likely to further their own case. Even so they illustrate very vividly the differing moral stands adopted by them in the impasse that their matrimonial difficulties had reached in 1843. Fanny, while not prepared to give way on a matter of conscience, made an emotional appeal to her husband 'to save yourself, Pierce, and me, and our darling children from a ruin worse than worldly beggary, from self-condemnation and condemnation of each other, from a daily and hourly departure further and further from all noble and holy influences'. To Pierce this was so much hot air; he had come to the end of the road. In reply he wrote, 'Much as I wish to be reconciled to you and much as I am impelled to give way to the impulse of love and affection which attracts us mutually towards each other, we had better not do so unless our union is to be permanent and unless our future mode of life is to be different from the past.' He then went on to say that this could only be achieved if it were based on a clear understanding 'on which we are to live together for the future'. It was no good merely patching up another reconciliation based only on 'the strong bond of love'. They had done this before but such reunions had only resulted in

temporary happiness; after a short lull the same old grievances had given rise to the same unhappy and miserable differences between us; indeed so that with few intervals our whole married life has been a troubled existence, disturbed by contentions and disputes. This must not be so for the future; either we must live apart, wretched as such a life is for ourselves and unfortunate and injurious as it will be for our children or we must live on better terms.

These Pierce then proceeded to particularize:

If you will govern your irritable temper, and if you can consent to submit your will to mine, we may be reconciled and may be happy. I firmly believe that husband and wife cannot live happily on any other terms and it would be vain for us to be reunited unless upon a clear understanding of the conditions I propose and a full determination to abide by them. I have put these in plain language, and in a way perhaps calculated to wound your pride; but as I wish you to be under no delusions as to what I expect from you; it is better to do so.

Fanny's reply was equally forthright and unequivocal. With regard to his first point she wrote, 'I have already promised to *endeavour* to control my temper – to promise more, with my nervous, excitable temperament, and the temptations to irritation which naturally spring out of our differences of disposition, would be unwise and unwarrantable.' She then went on to his second condition that she should submit herself to his will. This she declared to be completely unacceptable, something she could not entertain for a moment as, 'I consider that it is my duty *not* to submit my conduct to the government of any human being,' adding with her usual devastating honesty, 'though I love you better than any other living creature my affection does not so far blind my judgement as to suggest you as fit for such a charge.' The breach could not be hidden from their more immediate circle, and Charles Greville, that acute and industrious diarist, provides a searching analysis of the situation in which Fanny was entangled. When his diary was first published she was still alive and good taste dictated that its editors should omit the following passage, which has been incorporated in more modern editions. After outlining her story Greville wrote

She has discovered that she has married a weak, dawdling, ignorant, violent tempered man, who is utterly unsuited to her, and she to him, and she is aware that she outlived his liking as he has outlived her respect and esteem. With all her prodigious talents, her fine feelings, her noble sentiments and lively imagination, she has no tact, no judgement, no discretion.

Greville's final summing up was:

She has acted like a fool, and now he has become a brute, the consequence is that she is supremely and hopelessly wretched. She sees her husband brutal and unkind to her, ruining himself and the children by his lazy, stupid management of his affairs, and she lives in perpetual terror lest their alienation should at last mount to such a height that she shall be separated from them for which alone she desires to exist.

This was written in December, when Fanny and her husband were still living apart. A new twist was given to the situation when the Sartorises' plans necessitated their giving up their house as they were going away. This meant that Fanny would be without a home. Fanny wrote to Pierce offering terms, her own terms. She suggested that he should give her independent quarters in his present house so that she could return and be with her children without having any contact with him. The reason she gave for this rather cool request was that though he was now indifferent to her she had loved him too much to meet him on neutral ground. To do so would be daily torture. For

Fanny it was always all or nothing. If he refused to allow her to return to the matrimonial home and live separately there, then she would take lodgings near her father. Apparently she must have been too tense even to wait for a reply, or perhaps she preferred shock tactics; late next night after the servants had gone to bed Pierce heard knocking at the front door. It was Fanny. Whether from affection or fear of a scandal, Pierce let her in. For the time being Fanny had won her point; she and Pierce lived under the same roof but separately. It was an uncomfortable situation and once again their friends tried to mediate between the warring couple. Mary MacIntosh explained to Fanny that all that Pierce expected was a general compliance with his wishes, a compliance that any wife, including Adelaide, would show towards her husband. He was prepared to concede that no husband had the right to ask his wife to do anything morally wrong, and this he had never done. He was prepared to go further. Through bitter experience he knew that this was an issue on which Fanny and he might clash, Fanny perceiving a point of conscience which to him did not exist. All he would ask of her therefore was that, if disagreement should arise on some such point, Fanny should consult her own friends and if her obedience could not be construed as a betrayal of her conscience she would conform to her husband's wishes. On this basis the negotiations, if they can be so described, continued. Finally, though Fanny reserved the right to refuse obedience in the last resort on grounds of conscience, she was prepared to promise that 'I would endeavour heartily to do my duty better henceforth than I have done hitherto. More than that I dare not say for I know myself most fallible,' making the admission 'I am aware that I have so often been at fault towards you that though I may not have much hope for the future I have much regret for the past.' Pierce accepted his wife's declarations of good intentions and by February she and Pierce were once more living together as man and wife. Fanny then wrote happily to Kate, telling her, 'The terrible and long enduring difference between myself and my husband has been adjusted and for the first time for many a day I am possessing my soul in peace and breathing an atmosphere of affection and happiness.' It was the last reconciliation before the final breach. The Butlers sailed for America in May.

The period of renewed harmony between them was brief; Pierce's financial embarrassments soon put a new strain on their fragile relationship. The Butlers had left London in one of Pierce's characteristic blazes of extravagance; he gave a farewell party to some two hundred of their friends. The fashionable caterers Gunters supplied the refreshments, and six policemen were needed to control the traffic. While in England, Pierce seems to have had little regard for the amount of money needed to keep his family in the style of living that they had adopted. Return to the States meant retrenchment; Butler Place was to be let and the Butlers were to live in a Philadelphian boarding-house. Fanny loathed American boarding-houses, where her privacy was at constant risk, even though the family had its own quarters. Before she returned she had told Catherine's brother Theodore that she felt 'a tightening of my heart, to think that the only place which I have known as a *home* in America is not what I am to return to', while she reported that poor little Sarah had cried bitterly at the news. Though in later life Fanny referred to Butler Place as her purgatory the news that they were not to return there was a severe blow; now there would be no garden for her to tend and for the children to enjoy. She was only too well aware of her own propensity to irritation and dreaded the strains that she knew must arise out of such uncongenial conditions as now faced her. A bad crossing, during which for the most part she lay prostrate in her bunk, left her exhausted. Briefly she sought fresh strength by seeking out Dall's grave while she was in Boston, telling Harriet, 'her lovely virtues seemed to call to me to get up and be of good cheer, and strive to forget myself even as she had done'. Such comfort as she got was short-lived; it was a joy to be with the Sedgwicks again but otherwise the future looked bleak.

The breaking point did not come until the autumn but even before that there were signs of strain. The heat of summer in Philadelphia was almost unbearable and in July Pierce sent Fanny, the children and Miss Hall to Yellow Springs to avoid the city at its worst. This was a somewhat shabby spa, where Fanny found the accommodation unsatisfactory, but at least it was cooler than Philadelphia. Also there were facilities for bathing and swimming which she enjoyed. They were there for a month. Then in a letter to Theodore Sedgwick Fanny described how Pierce had descended on them on 15 August with orders to pack up immediately and return to Philadelphia, adding her comment 'I do not know in the least whether we are to remain here now, or go elsewhere, or what is to become of us.' There was another side to this apparently dictatorial action on her husband's part. Fanny had always been a law unto herself and the arrangements at the baths at

Yellow Springs had offended her sense of privacy. She disliked the American practice of providing one communal dressing-room for women bathers; on her first visit to Rockaway years earlier she had commented on it adversely in one of her letters home. Accordingly at Yellow Springs Fanny adopted the routine of waiting until the time allotted to female bathers had almost expired, so that the changing-room was deserted, before entering the water herself. This caused acute embarrassment among the male bathers, who could not use the baths until she had left them. Their annoyance at this inconsiderate behaviour was increased by the fact that this left them insufficient time for their own enjoyment of the baths before the hour fixed by custom for dining. When Pierce was told what was happening he rushed to the spa and moved his family forthwith. The reason he later gave for his precipitate action was the fear that if Fanny persisted in this practice she might be faced with a very unpleasant situation at the hands of the irate gentlemen. Later, when marshalling his grievances against Fanny, this was one of the instances of her unreasonable behaviour that he quoted and, as he went so far as to get an affidavit from the proprietor of the baths, the story cannot have been the mere product of his malice. After a week of the heat in Philadelphia Sarah and Fan grew pale and Pierce sent his family to West Chester. It was a wearing, hot, unsatisfactory summer and it was with relief that Fanny was able to go to her friends in Lenox for a short break. The uneasy matrimonial peace was maintained a little longer. On her way back from Lenox Pierce met her in New York with the news that the actor Macready was due to arrive in New York and that, as they had now no place of their own in Philadelphia where they could entertain him, they would do so at Astor House in New York. Fanny Appleton, in her diary, recorded that Henry Longfellow met the English actor when he dined with the Butlers in that city on 14 October. But rumours were already flying round and later Macready prided himself on having repressed his ungentlemanly inclination to probe into their truth. This brief interlude in New York must have been one of the last social occasions on which the Butlers appeared together.

Tempers and nerves on both sides had clearly become frayed when during one of Pierce's absences in New York that autumn Fanny came across some letters in his desk which made her highly suspicious. According to Pierce's own statement their seals were still intact until his wife broke them and read the letters. They had been written several years before and were unsigned but 'apparently in the writing of a female'. When he returned Fanny charged him with having been unfaithful to her even in the early days of their marriage. A bitter quarrel followed. Pierce was furious with his wife for having read his private letters, and it must be admitted that had the roles been reversed Fanny would have been equally furious. The result of this mutual explosion, as stated by Fanny in her rebuttal of the charges made against her by Pierce in their divorce proceedings, was that 'the last hope of reunion was extinguished, our intercourse as husband and wife totally ceased, the relation itself practically terminated and thereupon an arrangement of separation was entered into under which we continued to live'. With such scanty evidence on which to base conclusions, Fanny herself admitted that she had no legal proof of her assertion and could not quote it as a fact, and it is impossible to know how much justification she had for her accusation. That Pierce had been involved with some woman seems very probable but this may have fallen short of actual adultery and the unopened letters would suggest that Pierce had tired of the entanglement, if entanglement it was, before the woman who wrote them. In a letter to the Unitarian minister, Mr Furness, who subsequently became caught up in trying to sort out the Butlers' matrimonial problems, Pierce wrote 'I solemnly declare that my treatment of her has been just and kind, and my conscience fully acquits me of any one act towards her, of which a reasonable woman could justly complain', and even the most reasonable woman might 'justly complain' of adultery. Fanny, on the other hand, told a friend that in a moment of exasperation her husband had admitted to one of her own friends that he had been unfaithful to Fanny but that without the letters and the knowledge of by whom they had been written his wife had no proof. Fanny herself therefore seems to have had no doubts that Pierce was guilty, and turned for help and support to the Sedgwicks. Theodore came to Philadelphia to see how far he could sort out the facts and Pierce, who still regarded him as an impartial friend, gave him the letters to read in order 'to let him see that their contents would not sustain the inference she had drawn from them', continuing, 'he too must have thought so, for they were certainly never called for by her counsel, as they certainly might have been if judged to import criminality.' This in itself is not conclusive proof that Theodore thought them innocent. As a lawyer he may merely have realized that as evidence they were inadequate. As yet, therefore, the question of divorce did not arise, but as the marriage had clearly broken down Theodore's task was to arrange mutually acceptable terms between the estranged husband and wife. These were that Pierce would give Fanny one third of his income, but never less than $2,500 a year, paid either quarterly or monthly as she chose, that he would not object to her taking her own apartments in the boarding-house in which he and the children were living, and that Fanny should have free access to them. In return for her financial settlement and these concessions she was to promise not to return to the stage, not to advocate Abolitionist causes in print and not to publish anything of which her husband disapproved. The terms were not ungenerous but the sympathies of Elizabeth Sedgwick, to whom Pierce had turned for help and comfort in 1839, were now with Fanny, Clearly, whatever her brother-in-law thought, she considered Pierce the guilty party, writing to him 'I regard you as having deliberately and deeply injured the dearest friend that I have on earth out of my own family.' According to his Statement, Pierce discovered that it was not only Elizabeth who had turned against him. Theodore seems to have been involved in an attempt to find more substantial evidence of Pierce's adultery, even instituting inquiries in London in the hope that something to discredit him might emerge. This Pierce considered double dealing. He had regarded Theodore Sedgwick as a mutual friend of himself and Fanny. Now he discovered that Theodore considered himself as Fanny's legal adviser and, after a strained correspondence, Pierce wrote telling the lawyer that he declined to hold any further communication with him. Henceforth he evinced the bitterest hostility to every member of the Sedgwick family.

As to whether Pierce had actually been physically unfaithful to Fanny at some time in their married life, the only safe verdict would seem to be the Scottish one of 'non-proven', but Fanny's attempts, aided by the Sedgwicks, to make the charge of adultery stick in order to gain the legal custody of her children destroyed any last vestiges of affection for her which her husband might still have cherished. On this he is quite explicit. In his eyes Fanny had forfeited all claims to be considered as a wife and even as a mother. In his own words she 'had already done me and my children all the harm that can be done.' Once he had thought that only death could have ended his love for her but now he wrote:

she fairly wore out, crushed and extinguished my affection . . . all was at an end between us; there was no desire on the part of either to be reunited; that indeed had become impossible, for no trace of attachment lingered in the heart of either, we were no longer one; not even formal friends, she had become my calumniator, and exulted over the victim of her envenomed slander.

These were bitter words and, though they were written later to justify both his determination to divorce Fanny and the harsh tactics that he employed to drive her from his house, tactics which alone made divorce possible, from the time that she accused him of adultery his attitude hardened into an implacable determination either to make her completely subservient to his will or to break the marriage. The wheel had come round full circle. Now it was Fanny who was fighting for the right to live in the same house as her children. Her failure to secure evidence to press home the charge of adultery, which she hoped would have given her custody of the children, faced her with the stark alternative of either complete submission or exile.

While the Butlers continued to live in the same boarding-house though with separate apartments, an uneasy truce prevailed. Mr Gerhard, Fanny's lawyer, continued to pay her the agreed allowance of $280 a month; no restriction was placed on the amount of time the children spent with her. This solution could only be temporary. Pierce was planning to move into his own house in Walnut Street, and Fanny, desperately anxious to continue to be with Sarah and Fan, inquired via her legal adviser as to Pierce's future plans, expressing at the same time her wish to be under the same roof as her family. Pierce's reply was coldly correct; he intended to move into the new house in May and on 1 July to take the children for two months to Newport to avoid the summer heat. If Fanny wished to be with her children he would not prevent her provided – and here came the sting – she was prepared to accept certain conditions. He stipulated that if Fanny wished to remain a member of his household 'all acquaintance and intercourse, of whatever kind, whether by word or letter, shall, at once cease' between any member of the Sedgwick family and his wife. Henceforth Fanny must agree to treat the people who had been her dearest friends in America 'in every respect, as entire strangers, and as if she had never known them'. His second condition was that his wife should not keep up any acquaintance with persons of whom he disapproved, the third that neither in conversation in America nor in her letters to England should his wife 'mention any circumstances which may occur in my house or family and that she will in like manner cease to speak of me in terms of reprobation and reproach'. In essence these terms meant that if Fanny returned to the family home she returned in utter dependence on her husband, cut off from every influence that might stiffen her own resolution to resist. To this ultimatum Pierce demanded a reply within two days. He was putting his wife in an impossible situation and of this he must have been well aware. She had not yet got to the stage of desperation when she could agree to renounce her friends, sign away her independence and muzzle her conscience. Also she was too honest to agree to terms which she knew she could not bring herself to keep. On 5 May Pierce was informed that she found herself unable to comply.

Philadelphia must already have been full of gossip about the Butlers' matrimonial differences. Fanny certainly seems to have made no secret of them. But once Pierce and the children moved into Walnut Street, the breach between them could no longer be glossed over. Early in June therefore the Unitarian minister, Mr Furness, remembering the many kindnesses that he had received from Pierce's mother in the past, wrote to offer his services as a mediator. These Pierce, while expressing his gratitude, turned down on the ground that he did not think they would be in any way helpful. Fanny also made a last effort at compromise by offering terms which she could fulfil. On 13 June Mr Meredith, who was now acting as her legal representative, wrote asking Pierce if he would waive his three conditions if Fanny on her part would promise to make no reference to the past, obviously meaning what she still thought of as Pierce's adultery. Pierce's reply was a cold one. He declared that there were no circumstances in his past which he wished to bury and that he now considered Mrs Butler's rejection of his terms to be final. On his part there was no more to be said. Even then he did not prevent Fanny from seeing her children while they were in Philadelphia, though her opportunities of doing so were restricted. Fanny had by then moved into a new boarding-house near to Pierce's residence and Sarah and Fan were allowed to spend two hours each day with her. In a letter to Harriet dated 14 July 1844, Fanny told her,

I walk before breakfast with the children from seven to eight. Three times a week I take them to the market to buy fruit and flowers; an errand I like as well as they do. The other three mornings we walk in the square opposite the house. After breakfast they leave me for the morning, which they pass with their governess or nurse.

In the evening their mother was allowed to take them out again for another hour, after which Fanny returned to her boarding-house and a lonely dinner. When they went to Newport Fanny was deprived even of this fragment of their company. When she suggested going to Newport herself in order to be near them Pierce told her that if she did he would bring the children back to Philadelphia in spite of the heat. This was a risk Fanny could not take and in this way she was deprived of their company, notwithstanding the previous arrangement that she should have free access to them. Pierce's own attitude was that when she refused to accept his terms by which she could once again have become a member of his household she had forfeited her rights as a mother as well as of a wife.

When the children returned to Philadelphia Fanny complained bitterly that innumerable petty excuses were used to curtail the time that under the old agreement they had been allowed to spend with her. If she met them in the street with their governess, Miss Hall hurried them past their mother, to whom they were not even allowed to speak. Once when Fanny managed to snatch a word with Sarah, asking her how she could behave so cruelly to her mother, the child replied that her father had ordered her to obey her governess. For making the attempt Fanny declared that her children were then not allowed to see her even within the agreed period for a week. These instances of the policy of pinprick persecution which Fanny now had to endure at her husband's hands are taken from the evidence which she submitted to substantiate her claim that far from having deserted her husband voluntarily she had been driven away by his cruel behaviour. It is probable that they lost nothing in the telling. Even so it would appear that Pierce was now making Fanny's position untenable and was doing so deliberately. In these miserable months, living in a boarding-house and with the time she could spend with her children precarious, Fanny suffered another loss, less devastating than that of their company, but hard to bear in a life as empty as hers had become. Riding continued to be her greatest means of relaxation and she was devoted to her horse, Forrester. Once she had described him to Harriet in glowing terms,

He grins with delight, like a dog, when I talk to him and pat him. He is a bright bay, with black legs and mane, tall and large and built like a hunter with high courage and good temper. I have had him for four years and do not like to think what would become of me if anything were to happen to him. It would be neccessary that I should commit suicide, for his fellow is not to be found in 'these United States'.

After the Butlers had returned to the States in 1843 Pierce, exercising his legal rights, sold Forrester to a livery stables. The details are obscure. His motive may have been economy or a desire to curb Fanny's independent habit of riding where and when she would in defiance of her husband's wishes; Pierce did not think she should ride alone, Fanny persisted in doing so. To sell Forrester was at once a punishment and a restraint on her freedom. Fanny refused to be browbeaten. She managed to sell a volume of her poems, poems which gentle Fanny Longfellow thought too bitter to be written by a woman, and with the proceeds bought her beloved horse back. Pierce apparently did nothing to prevent her. Her pleasure was short-lived; Forrester slipped on a treacherous surface, injured his leg and eventually had to be put down.

The matrimonial situation was becoming too much even for Fanny; she confessed to being nervous and spiritless though for a time she still felt that she must struggle on. Then in December somehow she heard that Pierce had told friends of his in Philadelphia that he regretted her separation from her children. Adelaide also, with whom he seems to have kept in touch, and other English friends, urged Fanny to make another overture to her husband. His reply was that if she wished she could still return to her home and her children if she were prepared to accept the conditions which he had previously proposed. He did however add a warning that, 'in consequence of her desertion of the children, I have been for a year past to assume the entire direction of them, and that the arrangements that I have made for their studies and education must in no ways be interfered with.' Once again Pierce demanded an immediate answer. Fanny was shattered; clearly her husband was not prepared to make the slightest concession. She must return on his terms or not at all. Moreover the terms he now demanded seemed to her to be even more unacceptable than those she had rejected a year ago if, as his warning implied, she was to be debarred from interfering with the upbringing of her own daughters. Again she hesitated and asked for time to consider what she claimed were new terms, a request which Pierce took as a proof of her insincerity in making fresh overtures. This he argued had merely been a device to put him in the wrong, and he denied that his terms were different from those he had originally offered. In one sense this was true; a year had created a different set of circumstances; to some extent Pierce was justified in insisting that Fanny must not now upset the established routine of the children's education. To Fanny this was to reduce her to a mere cipher in her own household. Nevertheless on 18 December

1844 she gave in; she could no longer bear to be cut off from her children.

If she expected to be allowed to move in immediately she was disappointed, and became convinced that Pierce was deliberately delaying her return. At her request Mr Furness, who had been active in trying to bring about a happy reconciliation between husband and wife, took the matter up with Pierce. His reply was that he was quite as anxious as Fanny to get the whole matter settled but that it would take a little time for Fanny's rooms at Walnut Street to be made ready for her. Moreover the original financial arrangements that had applied when Fanny was responsible for her own board and lodging had to be modified. Pierce now suggested an allowance of $200 for her personal expenses; the rest would be borne by him, including the provision of a personal maid. He even showed some consideration for her comfort in asking her whether she would prefer to bring her present one with her, but there his consideration stopped. This time there were to be no loopholes for misunderstanding of the terms on which she once again became a member of his household. He insisted that she sign a formal agreement, setting out the conditions on which she was to return to his house and containing a declaration that if she failed to abide by them she would leave. Again Fanny demurred and protested, but again she gave way. On 3 March she returned to her husband's house. Before doing so she wrote her last letters of farewell to her dear Sedgwick friends. They make sad reading; Pierce could have imposed no harsher or more wounding conditions. It is interesting nevertheless to notice that Edward Sartoris, Adelaide's husband, found nothing objectionable in them. Writing to Pierce on 4 February, having expressed his pleasure that Fanny was once again to be united with her children, he went on,

Against your conditions I confess I have nothing to urge. Total separation from the Sedgwicks was, I agree with you, indispensable. I have never ceased to lament Fanny's connection with people who, in my opinion, have always given her the very worst possible advice; and I think the other conditions require nothing but what every woman is bound to do to preserve peace and quiet in her interior.

Clearly, taking a masculine viewpoint, he considered that his sister-in-law had been largely the authoress of her own troubles through what he described as 'the rashness of her proceedings'. At the same time he gave Pierce some advice which, had he been able to take it, might have given the new compromise some faint hope of success. Knowing Fanny as he did, he pointed out that Pierce must 'allow her a fair share in the general care and education of her family'. To deny her this would be both to outrage her sense of justice and to 'remove the natural vent for a mind already so restlessly active'.

Unfortunately for their domestic peace Pierce's resentment against Fanny was now so deep that he was no longer capable of making the slightest concession towards her. Perhaps he did not even wish the experiment to succeed and his sole motive in taking her back was an exercise in public relations. If he were deliberately trying to make life impossible for her Fanny's own conduct did nothing to make the situation easier. She had had few illusions when she had decided to accept her husband's conditions as to what awaited her and confessed in a letter to Kate Minot, Elizabeth Sedgwick's daughter and now Mrs Edward Minot, that she viewed what she described as her martyrdom with dismay. The situation in which she had placed herself was intolerable to anyone of her proud, independent and active temperament. Fanny in any circumstances could never have submitted to being a cipher, least of all in her own home, and that was the role she was now forced to accept. The breach between her and Pierce was in no way bridged. Fanny had her own apartments and her own maid; her personal contact with Pierce was confined to verbal trivialities when the family met for dinner. Otherwise he had insisted that all communication between them must be in writing. The children's education and conduct remained in the hands of Miss Hall. Cut off from her friends and her natural responsibilities there was nothing for her to do except dwell on her grievances and kick against the pricks.

This did not make for domestic calm and by April there was a major confrontation between them. Whether this was due to a deliberate trick on Pierce's part to trap his wife into a breach of his conditions or was merely intended to be a test of her intention to keep them is not clear; he gave Fanny an envelope containing an unopened letter from Miss Sedgwick. Surprised, but thinking that for some reason her husband wished her to read it, she opened it and did so. She was soon disillusioned. Pierce wrote furiously, 'You have lived in this house little over a month, and you have already violated the principal condition by which you bound yourself to observe while living under my roof.' This he declared made her in his eyes 'a person utterly wanting in truth and good faith'. In reply Fanny attempted to explain that, far from intending to break her word, she had assumed that the letter in question had been passed to her by Pierce because he wished her to read it. Though he counter-argued by asserting that she ought to have made the situation so clear to the Sedgwicks that they would not have tried to communicate with her in the first place, even Pierce was forced to admit that there had been a genuine misunderstanding and that his wife had been guiltless of any deliberate attempt to break the restrictions he had placed upon her. Meanwhile the wisdom of Edward Sartoris's advice to give Fanny some scope for her restless nature became more and more justified when, according to Pierce, she bombarded him with 'rapid epistles to remodel almost every department of the domestic administration'. This had the effect of making him increasingly irritable and he seems to have retaliated by subjecting her to a series of petty slights and humiliations, all dredged up and recorded in the 'Narrative' which she submitted as a rebuttal of the charge of desertion which Pierce brought against her during the divorce proceedings. When, for instance, she spoke to him in front of the children, he would ignore her and continue to read the newspaper. With the idea of destroying her authority with her own children on one occasion, when Fanny sent back some shoes that had been bought for little Fan on the ground that they were too small, Pierce immediately had them brought back and insisted that his daughter wear them. On the children's joint birthday, when their father planned to take them to spend a day at the farm in the country, Fanny was informed that Pierce, Miss Hall and the two children would go in the carriage but that there would be no room for her. If she wished to come she would have to follow on horseback or in a hired cab. When Fan saw how upset her mother was she impulsively threw her arms round her, declaring, 'Don't cry, mother, I'll go with you,' a sacrifice of the child's enjoyment which Fanny refused to accept. Inevitably, in the struggle between the parents, the children suffered. After a long absence in which Sarah and Fan had been used only to the authority of their governess and their father, it was natural that Fanny should have some difficulty in reasserting her own authority, particularly with her high-spirited elder daughter. Sometimes this resulted in scenes. On one occasion Fanny in a blazing temper dragged Sarah, who had plainly been defying her mother, to Pierce with the demand that he insist on her obedience. For the sake of discipline he complied, but in a letter dated 29 June, he forbade all future interference on Fanny's part with

Sarah, writing in wounding phrases that 'the total loss of affection, duty and obedience which she shows for you is the result of your own violation of all the duties of a wife and mother'. This on Pierce's part appears to have been wishful thinking. He attached too much importance to the childish disobedience of an eleven-year-old who was conscious that she could play one parent off against the other. There was no loss of affection for their mother on the part of either Sarah or Fan. In spite of the stormy home atmosphere and the long separation that followed Fanny's final departure, both children managed to retain their love for both their parents in spite of the contention between them.

This domestic situation involved a third party, the shadowy Miss Hall, who had been engaged as the children's governess while the Butlers were in England. Like many Victorian governesses she was gently born and later, when she finally returned to England, in a letter to her brother expressing regret at her departure, Pierce spoke of her 'gentleness, amiability and kindness'. There is no indication that Fanny disliked her personally. Indeed before the break-up of the marriage in 1843 she had gone out of her way to show her kindness. While the Butlers were still at the Clarendon Hotel and Anne Martin, the nurse, had returned to America, Miss Hall dined with the family – a somewhat unaccustomed honour for an English governess, who was more usually treated as a kind of upper servant and relegated to the schoolroom. Moreover Fanny went out of her way to prevent the governess being slighted by the hotel servants. But once Fanny had rejoined her husband's household in 1845 there was bound to be trouble when Fanny saw Miss Hall's authority being preferred to her own. Both Fanny and Pierce were ahead of their time in that neither of them believed in corporal punishment and on one occasion when an exasperated Miss Hall administered a sharp slap to Fan, who was being naughty and disobedient, Fanny hurled an outraged note at her husband in which, according to him, the slap was magnified into 'a whipping', and bad-tempered cries into 'screams of terror'. This situation, in which Fanny was constantly made to appear of no importance beside the governess, was bound to create comment of an unfavourable kind on Miss Hall's character and on the relationship between her and her employer. Whether local gossip was rife or not it is difficult to know but in England Fanny's friends and family were up in arms. In June Adelaide wrote to Pierce entreating him to modify that most unjust and intolerable arrangement by which Miss Hall (a hired instructress) supersedes my sister in her right and control over her children. No woman would bear such an intolerable insult as this! There is but one opinion about it here, and that is, that from the moment my sister returned to take her proper place, Miss Hall ought to have been dismissed at once. All your and our friends are in the extremest despair that this should not have been arranged by you previously to Fanny's return to your house.

This was an opinion which Mary MacIntosh, who had played such a benevolent part in their matrimonial troubles while the Butlers had been in England, shared. There is nothing to suggest that Miss Hall and Pierce were sexually involved or that Fanny thought they were, but when Pierce, in one of his usual long self-justifying communications to Fanny, declared that he was at a loss to understand why Miss Hall's presence in his house should be construed as an insult to his wife, he must have been singularly naive. Justified or not, her presence was bound to cause gossip. He was soon to be enlightened. Friends of Miss Hall in England informed her of the current gossip that she and Mr Butler were lovers or, in Victorian terms, that there was a criminal connection between them, and that that was why Mrs Butler had left her husband. Pierce was furious, believing, or affecting to believe, that Fanny was herself the originator of these scandalous reports.

When charged with it Fanny, probably out of a mixture of hurt pride and fury, refused to give Pierce the categorical denial that he demanded. Instead with cold logic she pointed out that as he considered her to be a liar in any case, there was very little point in her so doing, and that she could not be held responsible for what either his or Miss Hall's correspondents in England might have written. One of the conditions which Fanny had accepted was that she should make no mention of any of her husband's concerns, but it is perhaps legitimate to suppose that in her letters to Adelaide and Harriet the ban on the discussion of what was taking place in the household in Walnut Street was little observed. It is more than likely that in so far as she must have poured out her heart to them her correspondence was to some extent the source of the rumours that had now reached Miss Hall. Certainly Adelaide knew the position or she would not have written to Pierce as she had. Miss Hall's own position remains ambiguous. Why did she stay? Why did she allow herself to become Pierce's tool in the humiliation of his wife? It looks as if her sympathies must have been with him. Was this the result of his charm or of Fanny's tactless behaviour? Was she merely a typical Victorian woman who believed that the man must be head of his own household and master of his family? One would like to know more of Miss Hall.

In July the sweltering heat of Philadelphia produced a fresh crisis. Pierce decided to send his daughters to a small farm that he owned about six miles from the city as he was unable to take them, as he had done in the previous year, to Newport. Naturally Fanny wished to go with them but instead Pierce sent them in the charge of their old nurse, Anne Martin, who he declared was one of the few people who had ever been able to manage them. When Fanny remonstrated with him his reply was that the farm was too small to accommodate Fanny as well as the nurse and the two children and that there was nothing to prevent her from seeing them as often as he did himself. Fanny counter-attacked, arguing that if the farm were not large enough for both her and Anne Martin then she was 'at least as competent as a hired attend-ant' to look after her own children. The bitter epistolary warfare went on, Pierce affirming that as Fanny had deliberately absented herself from the family home for so long she had now no right to complain, and Fanny asserting that what Pierce was doing amounted to a deliber-ate attempt to separate her from the children. This, in spite of his reasonable sounding explanations, is probably true. In the Narrative which Fanny later compiled in the effort to prove that far from volun-tarily having deserted her husband and children Pierce had made it impossible for her to remain, she declared that the children having gone into the country, Pierce handed the house in Walnut Street over to workmen, leaving her to face all the resulting discomfort while he went to live with his brother. Again Pierce had a reasonable explana-tion which was that when Fanny had rejoined the household he had given her the best rooms at the front, that his own at the back were insufferably hot, and that this was why he slept at his brother's. More-over he accused her of exaggerating the discomfort of having work-men about the place, declaring that they were only repainting the lobby and entrance hall.

Determined to secure what she felt were her rights, Fanny prepared to put whatever pressure on her husband that she could. When there-fore he asked her to sign a legal document for which, in view of her dower rights on his estate, her signature was necessary, realizing that this was important to him, she refused until he showed more considera-tion for her position as a mother. She also determined to move to the

farm where, she declared, the farmer made no difficulty about providing her with lodging. In a furious temper Pierce arrived at the farm
late in the evening, collected the children, without even giving them
time to say goodbye to their mother, and took them back to the
sweltering heat of Philadelphia. Fanny followed early next morning
and finding that Pierce had departed for an unknown destination
(later he said it had been to find other country accommodation for the
children), she herself took them back to the farm, where, she declared,
they were delighted to be once more. There she left them, determined
not to jeopardize their health by provoking Pierce to remove them
once again. Meanwhile, as a punishment for her refusal to sign the
legal document that he needed, her husband both cut off her allowance
and forbade her to go to the farm. Fanny could go on no longer. She
was too intelligent and good a mother not to realize how bad it was
for the children to be treated as shuttlecocks, tossed to and fro between
battling parents. For their sake she would have to go. Her father and
Adelaide were now advising her to return to England, but without
funds this also presented difficulties. Tortuous negotiations followed
between Pierce and Fanny's legal advisers on the question of the
allowance he was prepared to make her once she was no longer a
member of his household. Pierce's suggestion was that she should
renounce her dower rights and in return he would make her an allowance of $1,000 a year secured on Butler Place and the Walnut Street
house. This Fanny was reluctant to do. She feared that Pierce's extravagance might jeopardize her children's future financial prospects.
In a letter to the eccentric and wealthy Boston lawyer Sam Ward,
who was a valued member of the circle of her Lenox friends and on
whom she relied for advice in such matters, she told him that she
thought that Pierce intended to keep her without funds, drive her back
to the stage and then somehow secure a divorce. In August she was
still struggling to wring some formal agreement out of her husband.
Then on 11 September Fanny once again left her husband's house and
moved to Sanderson's Hotel where she waited for a reply to her last
application to Pierce. Eventually an informal agreement on her allowance was reached. Fanny signed the document that Pierce required to
extinguish the ground rents and Pierce promised to allow her $1,000 a
year, but from Fanny's point of view this was not a satisfactory
arrangement as it was not safeguarded by a legal agreement, and she
therefore remained dependent on Pierce's goodwill for its payment.

Then, free at last from the hated conditions on which she had returned to him, Fanny went back to Lenox to be once again with the Sedgwicks and her other friends before sailing for England. According to her Narrative she was forced to borrow her passage money from a friend; according to Pierce's Statement she left debts behind which he was forced to settle. Fanny sailed for England on 16 September 1845.

The last few months, full of humiliation and misery for Fanny, and disfigured by Pierce's cold hostility, are a sad comment on the early days of their happy courtship. It is an ill business for outsiders to attempt to apportion the blame when a marriage breaks down as utterly and with as much bitterness as did that of Pierce and Fanny Butler. As her father wrote, 'What can I, what can anybody, what ought anybody to say between man and wife? All may see their altered conduct towards each other; but who shall presume to divine the causes of that conduct and to judge between them?' However vindictive and petty Pierce's behaviour in the last years of their marriage, he, no less than Fanny, felt himself to be the victim of his partner's malice. To a husband with all the backing of Victorian convention behind him Fanny's refusal to submit her will and views to his must have seemed monstrous. Her stormy temperament, strong will, driving energy and uncongenial views, above all her putting principles before affection and wifely duty, made Fanny in his eyes a bad wife and a bad mother. He had no desire that his daughters should grow up to be like her, or remain under her influence. Fanny was at once too honest, too independent and too intense, always sure that justice and right were on her side, to have been a helpmate to a man of Pierce's temperament and traditions. The tragedy was not so much in the breakdown of their marriage as in the fact that it ever took place. So, at the age of thirty-six, Fanny had to leave the land of her adoption, her dreams, her home, and above all her children, and to build afresh on her English foundations.

SEVEN

Frustration and Divorce

In the autumn of 1845 Fanny Kemble, in her own laconic words, 'returned to [her] father's house in London'. Emotionally bruised and battered, she ceased, for a time at least, to struggle against the impossible situation in which her husband had placed her. Charles Kemble no longer lived in a house of his own and at the time of his daughter's return was in comfortable lodgings in Mortimer Street. Here Fanny found her refuge. Her position was sufficiently distressing. Apart from her allowance from Pierce she was dependent on her father. Nor had she even the comfort of his continual companionship as often he was away fulfilling some professional engagement. Occasionally he would pay her a flying visit. Once, Fanny told Harriet, 'he marched in, looking extremely well, kissed me, opened his letters, wrote me a cheque for £10' and then rushed off to Brighton. Fanny's London friends however left her little time to brood and she was soon caught up in a whirl of social life; a whirl to which once again she had to accustom herself. In a letter to Harriet she wrote,

London with its distracting quality of *things* to do, is already laying hold of me; and the species of vertigo, which I experience after my lonely American existence, at finding myself once more overwhelmed with visits, messages, engagements, and endless notes to read and answer, is pitiable. I feel as if I had been growing idiotic out there, my life here is such an amazing contrast.

At least she did not suffer the mortification of finding that her friends had forgotten her and that her absence had cooled their affection for her. Initially Fanny had not expected to be in England for long; there had been talk of her and her father's repeating the American tour.

What Fanny's reaction to this scheme was there is no way of knowing. She certainly intended to return to America as soon as circumstances would permit her to do so; this is clear from scattered references in her letters to Harriet. Moreover she was now to some extent dependent on her father, and would be totally so if Pierce should discontinue her allowance. Even had she not been, when she returned to his protection her sense of filial duty would have made her as ready now as she had been in the past to fall in with his wishes and plans.

Early in November she was trying distractedly to see as many of her friends as possible before sailing once more to the States. While Charles Kemble was still in Brighton she went to see her old friend Lady Dacre, who pressed her to stay with her at Hoo. Harriet, who was staying with her great friend Dorothy Wilson in Hastings, was equally anxious that Fanny should spend time with them. Somehow too she must contrive to see her brother John and his German wife. Emotionally drained, Fanny for once could neither think nor plan, nor even make up her mind. As she told Harriet,

I am full of care and trouble and anxiety, and feel so weary with all the processes of thinking and feeling, deliberating and deciding that I am going through that I must beg you to decide for me . . . I have a sense of mental incapacity, amounting almost to imbecility; and I feel every now and then, as if my brain machinery were running down and would presently stop altogether. Seriously what with the greater and the lesser, the unrest of body and disquiet of mind, I feel occasionally all but distracted.

It must have been a relief when five days later Fanny heard from her father, who was still in Brighton, that he had given up the idea of crossing the Atlantic. At least there would now be some respite during which Fanny could begin once again to get her nerves under control, and she went down to stay with her friends the Grotes at Burnham. Harriet hoped that there her nerves would become 'tranquillized' and soon Fanny was able to tell her friend how much she was revelling in 'the delight of being in the country and the ecstasy of a fifteen miles' ride through beautiful parks and lanes'. To be on a horse again was for her the best relaxation, even though the horse was not her beloved Forrester. Moreover, Mrs Grote had assembled a house-party of interesting people, including the economist Nassau Senior. Fanny described him as 'a very clever man, a great talker, good upon all subjects, but best upon all those on which I am even below my average depth of ignorance, public affairs, questions of government, the science of political economy and all its kindred knowledge'. It was one of Nassau Senior's views that a factory's entire profit came from the last hour of labour, which had provided the textile manufacturers with a cogent argument against the reduction of the existing twelve-hour day worked in the mills, a reminder of the grim life led by the working people of Britain at a time when Fanny was enjoying all the luxury of the English country house. Fanny herself was not unaware of the social problems of the period; Manchester and Liverpool, two cities where insanitary conditions and deplorable housing helped to produce so high a death rate among children under five that it dragged down the average expectation of life for manual workers to sixteen and seventeen years, were cities in which she had frequently played. When in the troubled year of 1848 Europe was aflame, and in England the Chartists were much in evidence, her evangelical conscience made her describe 'the monstrous inequalities in the means of existence' as 'the crying sin of modern Christian Civilization', declaring that in England 'it is more flagrant than anywhere else on earth ... We are the richest and the poorest people in the world, as the extremes of rampant luxury and crawling poverty are wider asunder here than anywhere else on earth.' The statement is questionable; the generous sympathy that prompted it is not.

Burnham itself, set in the lovely countryside, was far from any scenes that might give rise to such thoughts, and Fanny found

the intellectual life with which I am surrounded in England is such a contrast to my American existence that it acts like a species of perpetual intoxication. The subjects of literary, critical and social interest that I so constantly hear so ably and brilliantly discussed, excite my mind to a degree of activity that seems almost feverish after the stagnant inertia to which it has lately been condemned; and this long withheld mental enjoyment produces very high nervous excitement in me too.

Yet much as she craved such mental stimulus her evangelical conscience could not be completely smothered when she reflected on what she called 'the low moral level' which provided the platform for so much intellectual brilliance. Everything that was within her that was luxury loving, intelligent, lively and intellectually aware responded to the life lived in houses such as Bannisters or Oatlands or Hoo, where good manners and good conversation against the elegant background of England's great country houses provided a pattern of living as pleasant as it was cultured. In spite of her agony of grief at having left her children it made Fanny's spirits rise to be once again part of this congenial circle. Never temperate in her emotions, one of her great assets was her elasticity of spirit which again and again carried her out of the deep trough of her depression. This was a fact of which she was well aware, writing to Harriet,

I know no one who has such a capacity (that looks as if I had written rapacity – either will do) for enjoyment, or who has so much of it in mere life – when I am not being tortured as I have. I ought to be infinitely thankful for my elastic temperament; there was never anything like it, but the heroine of Andersen's story, 'The Ball' who had 'a cork in her body'.

However exhilarating as Fanny found staying with her wealthy aristo-cratic friends she was still troubled by 'the stupid shallowness of society' which she attributed to the fact that they devoted 'all their energies and all their faculties to mere amusement, as they have no right to do'. In consequence of this lack of direction, of which her evangelical con-science could not but disapprove, they were 'neither well amused, nor well occupied, nor well anything else', a judgement which Lord Chesterfield, who has never been credited with an evangelical way of thought, would have been in hearty agreement when warning his son against the dangers of idleness.

In spite of moods of relaxation and even enjoyment, in the months after her return to England Fanny remained a deeply unhappy woman. Her nerves were still so raw that once, when her father came into the room unexpectedly while she was playing the piano and spoke to her she burst into tears and was seized with such a fit of trembling that for some minutes she could not manage to stand. Often when she went out so gallantly to parties in the evening she had spent the morning sitting on the floor weeping. During December she wrote 'No, dearest Hal, it would be impossible for me to tell you how sad I am; and instead of attempting to do so, my far better course is to try to write of something else.' Her financial position added its own nagging anxiety. The most obvious way of mending her fortune would have been to return to the stage, and she was uncomfortably conscious that this is what her father wished her to do. Pierce in his own Statement certainly gives the impression that he was still paying her the somewhat meagre allowance that had been agreed but in Fanny's letters there is no mention of this. She writes as if she were mainly dependent on her father, telling Harriet that it was a 'wretchedly uncomfortable position, but compared with all that had gone before, it is *only* uncomfortable'. Instead of returning to a life she had always disliked she still hoped that she might achieve at least a modest independence with her pen. She still had some verses in manuscript, which she thought some magazine might take, and if this did not materialize there was always the chance that her *English Tragedy* might find a publisher. Much to her relief therefore on 12 December she heard from Blackwood's that they would publish her poems and would pay well for what in her opinion was merely 'trumpery'. She knew well enough however that such expedients were merely putting off a final decision; if she were not to return to the American stage some alternative form of earning a living must be found. Here fate, in the form of her sister Adelaide, intervened. Having given up her own operatic career in favour of matrimony she and her husband spent much of their time in Italy. Now she wrote to Fanny suggesting that she might join them. To visit Italy had always been one of Fanny's dreams, and it was ironic that it should come as the result of the break-up of her marriage and the loss of her children. Nevertheless, with her usual buoyancy Fanny declared herself 'enchanted at the bare suggestion'. Everything however depended on her father's reaction to the scheme as it was he who would have to find the money for the journey. Apparently he did approve, and even toyed with the idea of accompanying her, a suggestion which again Fanny found enchanting. Soon she reported that he was deep in maps and guide-books, and busy planning a route. Even then a cloud of uncertainty hung over the project. Charles Kemble in the end decided not to travel to Rome with his daughter and Fanny reported to the patient Harriet with some dismay, 'he has neither determined my line of march, nor said a single word to me about my means of subsistence while I am abroad'. Finally the route was agreed and the date of departure fixed for 20 December and in the depth of winter Fanny and her maid – it would have been inconceivable for her to travel alone – set out for Rome. In these days of the international express, the aeroplane and the package tour, Rome is only a few hours away. In 1845, railways were still a novelty. Fanny sailed from Southampton to Le Havre. There she took a diligence to Rouen where, foreshadowing the motor-rail, the conveyence was placed on a train as far as Paris. The French diligence, which corresponded to the English stage coach, was divided into compartments which might almost be described as first, second and third. The best portion was the coupé, which held three people and which Fanny and her maid Hayes hoped to secure for themselves by paying for all three places. This gave them almost the convenience of a private chaise. It was a lengthy journey and, once they had left Paris, was full of difficulties, delays and discomfort. At Château Chinon they were actually snowed up for some days before reaching Marseilles. There they caught a steamer to Civite Vecchia, completing the last stage of their journey by carriage. Finally they arrived at Adelaide's house at Trinita dei Monte in April. Fanny spent nearly the whole of the next year with them, a year in which she was gradually able to unwind, in so far as Fanny, with all her problems facing her, could unwind. When later she wrote an account of her travels she called it *Year of Consolation*. Unlike her *Journal of a Residence in America* it throws very little light on her private life. It was written for publication, not, as the earlier journal had been, for her own pleasure. As she told Harriet, 'I should certainly preserve no record whatsoever of my impressions but for the very disagreeable conviction that it is my duty to do so, if there is, and I believe there is, the slightest probability of my being able by this means to earn a little money and to avoid drawing on my father's resources.'

By now Fanny had achieved a certain reputation as a writer. She had to her credit two plays, *Francis I* and *The Star of Seville*, which had been performed in America in 1838, and a volume of verse; moreover the name Fanny Kemble still had a certain publicity value. It was a period when travel books were fashionable. Catherine Maria Sedgwick had kept a similar journal of her travels in England, and Fredrica Brenner was to publish her impressions of America in the fifties, to mention only two people within Fanny's own orbit. Travel was not yet easy but it was very much part of upper-class life and there was already a market for a mixture of travel and memoirs; people who had visited foreign places themselves were eager to compare their impressions with those of lately returned and observant travellers; people compelled to stay at home enjoyed the vicarious experience of seeing foreign lands through other people's eyes. To Fanny this kind of writing, undertaken solely for financial reasons, was distasteful and certainly not a labour of love; she was writing for a public in which she was not interested. As, with her usual honesty, she told Harriet in the same letter, 'I have a great contempt for the process, for the barren balderdash that I write; but exchange is no robbery, a thing is worth what it will fetch, and if a book seller will buy my trash, I will sell it to him, for beggars must, in no case, be choosers.' The basic trouble for her was that because her motives for writing were not creative she felt unable 'to give fresh interest to a mere superficial description of things and places seen and known by everybody, and written about by all the world and his wife for the last hundred years'. Nevertheless, because she had a vivid pen and an eye for detail she produced a competent and readable piece of work which, duly published, received for the most part favourable reviews, though once again, as in the case of the American journal, she was criticized in some quarters for using unladylike words, such as 'stinking', when describing the filth that disfigured many of the sites in ancient Rome. For the biographer it has less to offer than any of Fanny's writings. It is an external account in which the reader will receive much information on the sights that Fanny saw but little insight into her personal life.

For this one must turn again to such letters to Harriet as survive. Harriet had, it will be remembered, visited Italy in company with her friend Dorothy Wilson while Fanny had been in America, and what she wanted was not descriptions of Rome's antiquities but Fanny's reaction to the Italian scene. One thing to strike Fanny was the similarity in matters of climate between that country and America, a similarity that it is easy to overlook because the civilizations were so different. To English people visiting Italy for the first time the brilliance of the sky came as a revelation but her years in America had made Fanny familiar with that blazing blue. As she pointed out, Boston is on the same latitude as Rome, and both experience the same unbearable summer heat; and what to English visitors was strange, luxurious vegetation merely reminded Fanny of Georgia in winter. Just as she found Philadelphia unbearable in the summer so she found the climate of Rome most trying. She declared that the sirocco wind 'destroys me body and soul while it lasts, and there is a sultry heaviness that gave me at first a perpetual headache'. Yet once she started the serious sight-seeing necessary for her journal Rome stirred her imagination in spite of its filth. Nevertheless it was with pleasure and relief that she escaped with Adelaide and Edward to Frascati in May. The surrounding country reminded her of her beloved Lenox hills, though she was forced to concede that those round Frascati were grander and that the likeness was purely physical. On the credit side there were no ugly American clapboard houses and utilitarian villages to spoil the natural beauty with which she was surrounded; on the debit side there was what she described as 'the over-population of the countryside'. In the Lenox hills she could walk for hours without meeting a soul; in Italy it seemed impossible ever to get away from the human presence. Nevertheless Fanny loved to wander alone, slightly to the disquiet of her family, dipping her hands and face in every wayside fountain she came to and 'sitting down by it, only to get up again and wander on to the next spring of living water', which, as always, fascinated her. Such solitary expeditions gradually helped to relax the tensions of the past years. Fanny was slowly coming alive again. As she wrote to Harriet in the July of 1846, 'in spite of abiding sorrow, I often have hours of vivid enjoyment, enjoyment which has nothing to do with happiness, or peace, or hope; momentary flashes, bright gleams of exquisite pleasure, of which the capacity seems indestructible in my nature; and whatever bitterness may lie at my heart's core, it still leaves about it a mobile surface of sensibility, which reflects with a sort of ecstasy every ray of light and every form of beauty'. This exercise in self-analysis brings out Fanny's receptiveness to the beauty round her which is reflected in much of her early versifying, and in her descriptions of the American country-side which in the happy days of his wooing she had explored with Pierce.

The bond between Fanny and Adelaide was close, in spite of the gap in their ages and in spite of their different temperaments. Anne Thackeray recalled how Adelaide had once told her,

I do not know if you will think it very conceited of me; but it always seems to me that no one I ever talk to seems able to say anything clearly and to the point except myself and my sister Fanny. When she speaks I know exactly what she means and wants to say; when other people speak, I have to find out what they mean, and even then I am not certain they know it themselves.

Adelaide was still a teenager when Fanny went to America in 1832; when she returned for her first visit to England in 1837 the gap between the sisters had narrowed. Adelaide was already beginning to make a name for herself as a singer and Fanny Appleton, who was also in London at that time, has left a charming description of the two sisters singing together to entertain their guests when Charles Kemble gave an evening party. Fanny had been intensely interested in her sister's operatic career and very proud of her, though privately she had thought that her potential as an actress even greater than her perform-ance as a singer, and it was with apprehension that she had seen her give up that career for matrimony. During Fanny's second troubled visit to England Adelaide had provided a refuge for her when she had been living apart from Pierce and had done her best to bring her sister and Pierce into a better relationship. Nevertheless, grateful as Fanny was to Adelaide and her husband for giving her time to lick her wounds and to have a year's respite in which to gain some tranquillity of spirit, she realized that Italy could only be an interlude. She had always intended to return to England by the end of 1846 and eventually to go back to America in the spring, as soon as the weather would allow her to make the crossing without too much wretchedness. There is nothing in her letters to indicate that she felt she had permanently cut herself off either from her adopted country or from all hope of being reunited with her children. As far as one can gather from her heavily self-censored correspondence, there had been no talk of a divorce, apart from her remark to Sam Ward that she thought Pierce intended by keeping her short of money to drive her back to the stage and then to divorce her. Meanwhile money remained a major consideration both for the immediate and for the more distant future. She did not feel that she could exist on her father's bounty while she was in England and she wished to accumulate a small capital which would give her some independence when she returned to the States. In one letter, it is true, there is a trace of anxiety as to the best way of preventing Pierce from exercising his legal rights as a husband to her property, but he certainly had not done this when she had earned enough money to buy back her horse Forrester. Perhaps he felt that this would be bad publicity.

Slowly Fanny had come to recognize that if she wanted money there was only one way in which it could be earned in adequate quantities. Though she emphasized how much she disliked having to depend on her father, this in itself might not have been enough to force her to return to the stage. She told Sam Ward before she returned to England in 1845 that part of Charles Kemble's income was 'the fruit of my former labour' and that in accepting money from him she would be in some sense living on what she had earned. But to return to America with some capital behind her would require more than her father could be expected to provide. To return to the stage was a painful decision. It was also to some extent a hazardous one. It was nine years since she had acted in public, and audiences have notoriously short memories. Moreover Fanny was no longer the 'pin-up girl' of her debut when, as much later Thackeray laughingly told her, he and his fellow students had been at her feet. Instead she was, in her own words, 'a stout, middle-aged, not particularly good looking woman', who had lost what had been one of her main attractions, youth, without having gained the acting experience that would have enabled her to play the more mature parts of Lady Macbeth and Queen Catherine in *Henry VIII*, which previously she had found so difficult. She would undoubtedly have preferred a London engagement, where she had friends and where she now had a headquarters, having rented a house belonging to her old friends the Fitzhughs. But, since money was the supreme consideration, she was determined not to turn down any opportunity of earning it. Accordingly, having had a good offer from Manchester, where in her early career she had often acted, she accepted it, writing to Harriet, 'The step I am about to take is so painful to me that all petty annoyances and minor vexations lose their poignancy in the contemplation of it.' She also confessed that her nerves were so 'terribly shattered' that she did not think she could bear to see 'reflected in eyes that I love that pity for me which I shall feel only too keenly for myself, on the first night of my return to the stage'. One friend at least was there. Henry Greville, brother of Lady Francis Egerton and the diarist Charles Greville, had long been an admirer of hers. The family seat of the Egertons was at Worsley, where Fanny had often stayed, and he had been a member of the happy group connected with those private theatricals where long ago Fanny had met her first love at Oatlands, another Egerton family seat. Like his more famous brother, Henry Greville also kept a diary, and in it he describes how, having called on Fanny when she returned from Italy, he had stayed three hours and 'as usual, was excited, amused and interested by her conversation, as I always am, more than by that of any other woman. She is so eloquent, so droll, so sad and so gay, and so unlike the rest of the world.' When she went north Henry and his friend Count Potocki travelled for part of the way with her and then rejoined her in Manchester in time for her opening night. Fanny was to appear in *The Hunchback*, playing her famous role of Julia, and when the day arrived she derived some comfort from the fact that Henry was to be in the audience. Even when she had been playing regularly the welcoming roar from a too enthusiastic audience had always produced in her a feeling of terror, and it was this which she most dreaded having to face once more. The Manchester audience did give her a great reception, delighted to welcome their old favourite back to the stage. From Henry Greville's account of the evening it 'overcame her so much that she acted the first scene of the play with less effect than usual, but recovering herself by degrees, she came out with all her former spirit and energy in the last two acts. I have no doubt,' he added, 'that she will act the elder parts much better now than formerly.' Fanny was less concerned herself with the merit of her performance than with the more practical aspects of her new venture. She was relieved to find that she could still stand up to the mere physical strain in spite of the fact that after the first night she developed 'a dreadful cough and sore throat' and that her feet and ankles swelled as a result of so much standing. As a compensation she thought that her voice was stronger than when she had first gone on the stage; all in all she felt that she would be able to carry on for another couple of years. In spite of her friendly welcome Fanny could hardly hope to attract the large audiences that had once flocked to see and hear her; accordingly she planned to move from one town to another to make sure that by playing to fresh audiences she might retain sufficient popularity, or rather not to wear out that which she still had, 'to secure the small capital upon which I can live independently'. For the next eighteen months this was her main preoccupation.

In addition to Julia in *The Hunchback*, while at Manchester Fanny played Mrs Siddons' old part of Lady Macbeth and in lighter vein what she described as a 'rather pretty foolish part' in *The Honeymoon*. Her return to the stage had been made less unpleasant than she had anticipated in that the manager was kind and considerate, the supporting company she considered 'very fair', the plays carefully produced and the theatre itself 'beautiful'. What probably gave her the most confidence and pleasure was the fact that the Manchester audiences liked her. This always meant much to Fanny, who described them as 'most exceedingly kind and cordial'. In addition to the money that she earned her return to professional life kept her so busy that she had little time to brood over the past. In the old days Aunt Dall had taken charge of Fanny's stage wardrobe but apparently her maid Hayes was incapable of managing in the same way, so that Fanny had to be responsible for her theatrical costumes, as well as for rehearsing new plays. Then there were letters to write, social engagements to be fitted in and somehow time to be found to correct the proofs of *The Year of Consolation*. It was an exhausting life, made more so by having to be constantly on the move in what Harriet called her 'zigzag progress' between her various engagements. For instance on 4 March Fanny was playing in Liverpool, on the 14th in Dublin. Fanny had been doubtful as to the propriety of giving theatrical performances in Ireland when the majority of the people there were in the grip of the terrible potato famine, but needs must when the money devil drives, and Fanny did not feel in a position to turn down the offer of employment. Also her brother Henry was stationed in Ireland and to play there would give them an opportunity to meet. They had dinner together every night when Fanny was not at the theatre; all her spare time was devoted to him – she even refused Lady Bessborough's invitation to the St Patrick's ball. Dublin therefore brought her some measure of happiness but her rapturous welcome there was a thing of the past; there were no longer hordes of young men laughing, cheering and dropping on one knee to look under her bonnet as she hurried from her coach. Later she found herself in a position to do something towards raising funds for Irish famine relief. Henry Greville and his friends were then busy organizing a couple of charity performances at the St James Theatre in London. The company were to be amateurs but, as in the Oatlands days, Fanny was asked to take the lead. The plays were to be *Hernani* and *The Hunchback*. Fanny had just managed to secure a month's engagement at the new Princes Theatre and this put her in a somewhat difficult position because Maddox, the manager, did not wish her to appear on the London stage before then. As this was to be her first London appearance the occasion was too important for her future plans for Fanny to dare to break her contract. However eventually, realizing that it might be penny wise and pound foolish to affront all the society notables who were sponsoring these amateur performances, Maddox reluctantly consented and the organizers were able to go ahead. Fate again played an odd trick on Fanny. When she had consented to play the lead in *Hernani* she did not know who the rest of the cast were to be. Later she discovered that her first love, Augustus Craven, was also to play his old part in what she described as 'very different circumstances'. Of her own feelings she makes no mention. They had of course met since then; Fanny had dined with the Cravens on her first visit back to England in 1837. Playing with Fanny once more seems to have fanned into life her old attraction for him; certainly when she was playing in Bath in the following June she described to Harriet how he had called at her lodgings, accompanied by a young niece, and made a long visit. Two days later he called again, this time alone, for another long visit. Fanny's only comment was 'certainly novelists invent nothing more improbable than life'. It would be interesting to know what passed between them on this second visit.

Fanny's movements, once her appearance at the Princes had finished, are difficult to follow. She was in Bristol in May, noting on her journey there how the traditions of a non-mechanized past persisted into the new railway age where the stokers had dressed their engines with huge bunches of hawthorn and laburnum 'as formerly stage coach horses used to be dressed with bunches of flowers at their ears on May day'. During June she played in Bath, Exeter and Plymouth. Later she seems to have been in Yorkshire and then in Scotland where she acted in Glasgow, Perth, where she played a couple of nights, Dundee and Edinburgh. There she had the pleasure of staying with her old friend George Combe, now married to her cousin Cecilia, Mrs Siddons' daughter. They had married in 1833, to Fanny's great delight, and later had themselves visited the States where George had given a series of lectures on phrenology. But there was sadness as well as joy in their reunion. Andrew, the 'dear doctor' was dead. No longer could Fanny drive round Edinburgh in his dog-cart or hold him to his promise to dance with her on his sixtieth birthday.

It was a joy to be back in her beloved Edinburgh, though she found it changed not for the better, and deplored the railway line now running through the Castle Gardens, which she thought 'cruelly spoilt' them, even though from Princes Street this new sign of the times was invisible. Then in November she moved southwards again, staying with Lady Dacre's granddaughter Barbarina, now Lady Grey. In all her wanderings and throughout her troubles Fanny could always rely on her friends in whom, in spite of her quirks, eccentricities and uncomfortable candour, she inspired deep and genuine affection. She needed such consolation and support. The future was uncertain. Fanny hoped for a longer engagement in London for the new winter season but negotiations with Maddox hung fire and Fanny was forced once again to go on tour. Her letters to Harriet are depressed. The venue was East Anglia, the weather chill and bleak and audiences often small. In Norwich she reported dolefully that she had been 'obliged to stand bare necked and bare armed and almost bare footed (for the thin silk stockings and satin shoes are a poor protection) on the stage to houses, I am sorry to say, as thin as my stockings'. Things were no better at Yarmouth where she complained that she was 'very cold and very comfortless in these horrible theatres' which she described as 'damp barns'. They are now, for the most part, only a memory but the delight-fully restored eighteenth-century theatre at Richmond in Yorkshire, with its underground dressing-rooms, gives some idea of the inade-quate conditions backstage. By the end of January both her fortunes and her spirits were at their lowest ebb. At the beginning of February she was seriously thinking of braving 'the winter passage across the Atlantic', in the hope of finding work in America. The one thing that held her back was the fact that Adelaide and Edward Sartoris were expected to return to England in May, and Fanny could hardly bear to go without seeing them. In the meantime she had been trying to make alternative plans. She would much have preferred to read plays than to act in them, but filial affection had prevented her from doing so since Charles Kemble had made this field his own. However it now seemed possible that he might be giving up these 'readings' and Fanny had been sounding out the possibilities of starting them herself when her father apparently reversed his tentative decision. For Fanny, enduring the rigours of East Anglia, this was the last straw. She broke down and 'cried like a baby the whole of the day', afterwards excusing herself by explaining 'of course my nerves were out of order, or I should have chosen some less rubbishy cause among the various excellent reasons for tears I have to select from'. Fanny was in the Slough of Despond. Then suddenly, in January 1848, the tide turned. She was offered a month's engagement, with the possibility of a further month, to play at the Princes as Macready's leading lady, and was able to write to Harriet 'I am most thankful that the depression and discouragement under which I succumbed for a while has been thus speedily resolved.'

Nevertheless the prospect of acting with Macready was daunting. Born in 1793, he was the youngest of the four leading actors who had dominated the London stage in the eighteen twenties, the others being Charles Kemble, Charles Young and Edmund Kean. By 1848 he stood alone; Charles Young had retired, Charles Kemble was a spent force, Edmund Kean was dead. Though Macready had owed his first London engagement to Charles Kemble, when he appeared at Covent Garden in 1816, his relations with the Kembles had not been without strain, a strain accentuated by their very different styles of acting. Both Charles and Fanny had been trained in the tradition of John Philip and Sarah Siddons which demanded a dignified, sonorous delivery of Shakespearean verse. With Macready, dramatic action was more important than the way in which Shakespeare's lines were spoken.

When he had seen Fanny play in the amateur performance of *Hernani* at St James he had castigated her performance as 'affected, monotonous, without one real impulse, never in the feeling of her character, never true in look, attitude or tone'. Quite apart from the professional jealousy that made him resent Fanny's being billed with him as a co-star, she was not the leading lady he would have chosen. After their first rehearsal of *Macbeth* on 19 February his comment was 'I have never seen anyone so bad, so unnatural, so affected, so conceited.' Fanny for her part was more charitable and perhaps more understanding. She thought him a good tragic actor, though quite without comic power of any kind and that

his want of a musical ear made his delivery of Shakespeare's blank verse defective and painful to persons better endowed in that respect. It may have been his consciousness of his improper declamation of blank verse that induced him to adopt what his admirers called the natural style of speaking it, which was simply chopping it up into prose – a method easily followed by speakers who have never learnt the difference between the two, and that blank verse demands the same care and method that music does, and when not uttered with due regard to its artificial construction, and rules of rhythm and measure, is precisely as faulty as music sung out of tune.

But though Fanny condemned his delivery of Shakespeare's verse she was ready to praise his skill in the production of visual effects on the stage, saying that he 'had a painter's feeling for colour and grouping and scenic effects'.

It was not the differences in their styles that worried Fanny so much as Macready's reputation for personal violence on the stage. He would be so carried away when acting that he was capable of inflicting genuine physical pain on whomever was unfortunate enough to be playing opposite him. The Kemble–Macready partnership did not get off to a good start. When Fanny arrived at the theatre she discovered that he had appropriated the star dressing-room, which had been hers on her previous engagement, and that she had been relegated to another smaller room which had no fireplace and which could only be reached by a steep flight of stairs. Maddox, when approached, hedged and made excuses, explaining that Macready used so much musk and scent that the dressing-room was impregnated with it to such an extent that he did not like to put Fanny into it. As a result of her protests he did manage to find her a better room with a fireplace but she still had to use the flight of stairs, which was a source of annoyance to her as it made it difficult for her to hear the call-boy. It would have been more convenient to use the Green Room while waiting but this, in her position as the leading lady, she would not do. Macready did not even give himself the trouble, or pay Fanny the courtesy, of attending the first rehearsal of *Macbeth*, and though he did come on the second day Fanny reported, 'He is not courteous, or pleasant or even well bred; remains seated when one is standing and talking to him.' She soon found she had more to put up with than mere bad manners. Innovation was not a feature of contemporary presentations of Shakespeare and Fanny expected the familiar stage set. To her dismay she discovered that Macready had rearranged the position of the great table in the banqueting scene. This completely ruined her own movements, robbing them of their dramatic intensity. It was in vain that she remonstrated with him against 'this unwarrantable selfishness'. He remained adamant. All she could do was to say bitterly that 'Since it is evident that Mr Macready's Macbeth depended on where a table stood I must contrive that my Lady Macbeth shall not do so.' These were brave words, but she confided to Harriet that though she had played the first scene fairly well the rest of her performance had suffered because she had found his style of acting disturbing and distracting throughout most of the play. Fanny found him difficult to act with after the conventional productions to which she had been accustomed, complaining,

he keeps no specific time for his exits or entrances, comes on when one is in the middle of a soliloquy, or goes off when one is in the middle of a speech to him. He growls and prowls and roams and foams about the stage in every direction, like a tiger in a cage, so that I never know what side of me he means to be, and keeps up a perpetual snarling and grumbling like the aforesaid tiger, so that I never feel quite sure that he *has done*.

It was not, Fanny thought, that in all this he was being deliberately unfair to his fellow actors, he was merely 'absolutely regardless of them'.

Macready was not only unpredictable; he was terrifying. Fanny was horrified at the mere thought of having to act Desdemona to his Othello.

I do not know how Desdemona might have affected me in other circumstances but my only feeling about acting it with Mr Macready is dread of his personal violence. I quail at the thought of his laying hold of me in those terrible passionate scenes, for in *Macbeth* he pinched me black and blue, and almost tore the point lace from my head . . . as for that smothering in bed, 'Heaven have mercy upon me', as poor Desdemona says. If that foolish creature would not persist in *talking* long after she has been smothered and stabbed to death, one might escape by the off side of the bed, and leave the bolster to be questioned by Emilia and apostrophised by Othello; but she will uplift her testimony after death to her husband's amiable treatment of her and even the bolster would not have been stupid enough for that.

Fanny then made an intriguing comment on the death scene, arguing that Othello's bungling attempts to kill Desdemona were a witness to his own agony of mind; otherwise as a soldier and a powerful man he would have had no difficulty in dispatching her completely and quickly. The rehearsal went better than she had feared. Fanny's dread of Macready, combined with the horror of the play itself, she said, 'took such hold of me that at the end I could hardly stand for shaking or speak for crying', with the result that Macready seemed quite mollified by her condition. On the night of the performance she was in less danger than she had feared, 'the actual smothering being arranged to take place behind the drawn curtains of Desdemona's bed', and Macready showed her more consideration than Fanny had expected. This may have been due to the fact that when Fanny, overcome with horror in her scenes with Othello, fell down in a state of genuine hysterics, he took this as a tribute to his acting and no longer found her affected and conceited. Nevertheless playing with him was a constant hazard, as the poor actress who was playing the Queen in *Hamlet* discovered in the closet scene when, having grasped Hamlet's hand at what to Macready was the wrong moment, he knocked her down with such violence that the poor woman had bruises all across her breast. Though nothing so brutal happened to Fanny, who charitably decided that she 'really believed that Macready cannot help being as odious as he is on the stage', even she did not get off unscathed. Once, when having lately broken her little finger in a carriage door, Fanny was playing with him in *Macbeth*, he nearly made her faint with the violence that he crushed it and by way of apology merely remarked coolly 'that really he could not answer for himself in such a scene and that I ought to wear a splint'. No wonder she declared that if she had to act with him much more she would require 'several splints for several broken limbs', adding that she would not have accepted a further engagement with him for £50 a night.

By March, Macready's violence on the stage was being matched by violence in the streets. In 1848 Europe exploded in a series of revolutionary outbreaks when Louis Philippe was driven from the throne of France and when the authoritarian regimes in Italy, Austria and the German states were threatened. The Chartists in England were revivified by these happenings abroad and Fanny, remembering the tumults and excitements over the passing of the Reform Act, was keenly interested. One of her more endearing qualities was her keen and genuine concern for the cases of individual suffering and hardship which she came across in the course of her travels. Her sympathy was always for the underdog, the helpless and the exploited. Once when she saw a small five-year-old standing in front of a 'poor mean kind of pastry-cook window looking with eyes of poignant longing' at its contents, Fanny stopped and discovering that the mite wanted baked apples for 'his poor little brother who was sick' she not only gave him the money to buy enough of the coveted goodies to send him home laden, a generous spontaneous gesture that many people would make, but she followed it up by going immediately to see his parents and discover what help she could give. On another occasion in the cold of a December in Hull, she saw what looked more like a bundle of rags than a small child. Kneeling beside him, Fanny learnt that he was sleeping rough because he had been deserted by his mother and his stepfather, and that when he had gone to the workhouse he had been refused admission because he had no written order signed by the right authority. Fanny went into action. She took charge of the boy and bullied the workhouse official so effectively that she left her protégé seated by the fire and provided with food. Nor did her activities on his behalf stop there. Fanny's reason for being in Hull was that she had been giving a series of readings to the Literary and Scientific Institution there, and she now pledged the proceeds of one of these to provide the boy with sufficient funds to place him as an apprentice in a trade of his own choice. Here Fanny was spending not only time but the money she was working so hard to accumulate to help a miserable victim of the red tape of the new Poor Law. Nor was this an isolated incident. In London she had similar tussles with both the police and the Poor Law officials for the way in which unfortunate girls found sleeping in the parks were treated by them.

Fanny was not alone in her awareness of the hardship and suffering that the growing pains of a new industrialized society brought with it. Many people feared that discontent with the established order would lead in England, as it had done on the Continent, to violence. In the early days of March London seemed on the brink of serious disturbances. On the 8th Fanny wrote

We are quite lively now in London with riots of our own – a more exciting process than merely reading of our neighbours across the Channel. Last night the mob in its playful procession throughout this street, broke the peaceful windows of this house. There have been great meetings in Trafalgar Square these last two evenings, in which the people threw stones about and made a noise but that is all they did by all accounts. They have smashed sundry windows and the annoyance and apprehension occasioned by their passage wherever they go is very great.

But unless the soldiers were called out she did not think that the riots would be very serious. Fanny's letters contain much shrewd comment on the contemporary scene. It is, for instance, interesting to note that although the metropolitan police, the 'Peelers', were by now a well established force, it was still the military who were felt to be the last protectors of law and order. At the same time Fanny was well aware that to call on them to deal with the rioters would only acerbate the trouble. The mass of English people had never been prepared to tolerate military action and the dislike of a standing army was a deeply ingrained tradition among them. Though Fanny believed that change was both inevitable and desirable she did not expect, despite the riotous crowds in the streets, that they would be accompanied by any 'violent convulsions', arguing that 'in spite of the selfish passions of both rich and poor, our own people do fear God more, I think, than any other European nation, and recognize the law of duty, and there is good principle enough in all its classes, I believe, to meet every rational change with firmness and temperance.' In so thinking Fanny was right for the wrong reasons. The great Chartist movement fizzled out like a damp squib, and the forties and fifties saw a gradual improvement both in the comforts available to the working classes and in new remedial legislation dealing with urban sanitation and the employment of women and children in factories, which indirectly also lightened the labour for able-bodied men; but it was the Evangelical faith of a section of the middle classes and of men like Lord Shaftesbury, combined with the administrative drive of men of the calibre of Edwin Chadwick, rather than the piety of the masses, that led to these improvements. She was more in accordance with the facts in writing 'the wisdom and wealth of the middle classes is a feature in our social existence without parallel; it is the salvation of the country'. Here it is possible that Fanny was being over-generous to her own kind; some credit at least should go to a ruling class that knew when to retreat in the face of changing circumstances. But, however momentous the changes that were to bring into being a fairer and juster society, Fanny was convinced that come they must, writing, 'I believe in them nevertheless for I believe in God's law, and in Christ's teaching of it and in the obviously ordained progress of the human race.' This was her fundamental belief, underlying all her thinking about society, and even about mankind, asking, almost with desperation,

will the days ever come when men will see that Christ believed in humanity as none of His followers have done since, that He, knowing its infirmity better than any other, trusted in its capacity for good more than any other? We are constantly told that people can't be taught this, and can't do t'other; and He thought them nothing short of absolute perfection. 'Be ye perfect as your Father in heaven is perfect.' Are we to suppose He did not mean what He said?

It is impossible to understand what made Fanny 'tick', or what her attitude was to all the problems that confronted her unless we remember that whatever her application of it to a particular issue might be, all her thinking was based on this sure faith in God.

Before the end of 1848 Fanny was going to need all her faith and all her courage but by the end of her engagement with Maddox her future prospects seemed encouraging. At last it looked as if she might be on the threshold of a more congenial way of earning a living. Shakespeare she loved, and she had many of the qualities of a fine actress – a beautiful voice, an ability to speak blank verse and an insight into character. It was the artificiality of the stage, the false glamour, often the poor or indifferent plays which she had to act, that she disliked. By the forties an alternative was becoming popular. People who were hesitant about going to a theatre because of religious or moral scruples could enjoy, without feeling guilty, hearing Shakespeare's plays read aloud. Reading aloud was popular even in the high social circles in which Fanny so often moved. At a time when people relied on their own talent and that of their friends for much of their entertainment, it was the normal practice for the guests at a house-party to entertain the company in the evening with music or, when one of the company happened to be a famous actress, like Fanny, to ask her to read to the assembled guests the plays with which she was generally associated. Fanny often did so.

Her friends at Lenox were used to ask for the same favour and the pupils at Elizabeth Sedgwick's school there thought it a high privilege when she read aloud to them. It was therefore a skill of which she was very much the mistress, but the fact that Charles Kemble, when he came to find the strain of theatrical performances too great as he grew older, or when suitable engagements were not forthcoming, employed his talents in a series of highly successful readings, precluded his daughter from entering into rivalry with him. It was not until he abandoned these that Fanny could consider giving such readings herself as an alternative to remaining on the stage, where it may be that her drawing power was in any case no longer bringing in her previous earnings. She had already been asked by the Provost of Eton, via her friend Mary Anne Thackeray, to read to the school, which she did with great success though she refused a fee for what she declared 'will be such a great pleasure to me'. She was also giving a reading in Hull in the December of 1847 when she came across her 'bundle of rags' in the street on that cold night. Here certainly she was accepting a fee because part of it she donated to secure an apprenticeship for her little protégé, but she does not seem to have embarked on a full-scale professional programme of readings until March 1848, when she gave the first of her well-known readings at the Highgate Institute. The project had been thoroughly discussed before then. Driven by the cold and discomfort of acting to poor houses in Norwich in January of 1848, Fanny had decided that as soon as she returned to London she would 'take measures about my readings which I think I had better begin in earnest'.

Beginning in earnest meant finding a manager who would assume the financial risk of promoting the new venture, someone who would pay Fanny a fixed fee and keep the profits, or shoulder the losses, himself. There were difficulties. Fanny was determined to prostitute neither Shakespeare nor her own talent. She refused to confine her readings to the more popular plays, for which she could always have got full houses, and she refused to give more than three, or at the most four, readings a week. To do so would have been to risk losing her own enjoyment and to grow stale. So it is not surprising that Mr Mitchell, with whom she was in negotiation, was hesitant to take on so formidable and determined a character as Fanny. At one point in early February he actually refused to consider the proposition further. Her friends Dr Harness and the two Greville brothers rallied round with suggestions and Henry urged her 'to undertake the speculation of giving readings at my own cost, hiring a room and sending out advertisements etc; but this,' Fanny declared, 'I will not do. I am willing to work hard for very little gain, but not to jeopardize any portion of the small gains, for which I have already worked so hard.' Instead she tried to follow up feelers that had been made elsewhere, writing to the Secretary of the Collegiate Institution at Liverpool, which had shown interest, before she had concluded her engagement with Maddox who had been prepared to offer her twenty guineas a night for six nights. Apparently it was also then that the Highgate Institute had been in touch with her. Clearly there was a potential market for such readings and finally Fanny and Mr Mitchell came to terms. Anxious though Fanny was to find a manager-promoter, she continued to make difficulties. He naturally wished the price of the seats to be whatever the traffic would bear. Fanny had scruples and wanted a lower figure, but Mitchell seems to have stood out for ten shillings, asking how he could possibly insult someone like Lord Lansdowne by only charging him five shillings for the pleasure of hearing Fanny Kemble read. Finally the last difficulties were sorted out and Fanny embarked on her new career. She was an immediate success and her devoted friend Henry Greville wrote enthusiastically that he had been to hear her read the *Merchant of Venice* and later *Much Ado About Nothing*, declaring, 'It is wonderful the effect she produces, it is like seeing the *whole* play admirably acted, and delightful to hear the beautiful poetry, which is usually so murdered on the stage, spoken by her melodious voice, and with her subtle expression.'

Fanny at last had found her medium and the future looked bright in so far as the modest independence which she sought now seemed a reasonable possibility. It would mean some postponement of her return to America but even this had its compensation. She would now be in England when Adelaide and Edward returned from Italy. Fanny had already arranged engagements worth some £500, she told Arthur Malkin, when the blow fell. Pierce commenced divorce proceedings against her. Whether this had always been his intention is speculation but in April 1847 he had told his lawyer, John Cadwaller, that his wife had no intention of returning and asked him if legally he would be entitled to ask for an absolute divorce. This the laws of Pennsylvania, unlike those of Britain, permitted him to do; divorce could be granted after two years of wilful desertion. Accordingly in March 1848 he filed his application in the Court of Common Pleas at Philadelphia.

Rather less than a month later Fanny received a summons to attend on 5 June. This was a possibility that she seems to have considered when Pierce was dragging his feet over the question of her maintenance once she had left the family home in Walnut Street, but her fears appear to have been allayed once her husband had agreed to make her an annual allowance. There is no further indication that she had expected so decisive an action on his part and she seems to have been taken utterly by shocked surprise. In some ways Fanny always had a one-track mind; she was apt to plan ahead without taking contingencies into consideration. Her intention had always been to return to America as soon as she could carry out her plan of saving enough to enable her to buy a small property in Lenox and live there quietly. Because so many of her intimate letters were destroyed or suppressed her intentions have at times to be surmised from incomplete evidence, but it would appear that she thought that, with her own house in Lenox and her 'modest independence', she would be able to resume her link with her children. This had been temporarily interrupted. When she had first left America Sarah and Fan had been allowed to receive letters from their mother but when Fanny, feeling that she should explain to them why she was returning to the stage, had attributed this to lack of funds, an implication that Pierce found damaging, he refused to allow his daughters to receive any more letters from their mother. Possibly the outlines of the future had always been a little hazy in her mind. She concentrated on seeing her children again without facing the possibility that Pierce might have other ideas. What she could not accept was a charge that she had wilfully abandoned both her children and her wifely duty. This offended both her sense of justice and her pride. To her it was clear that Pierce had driven her out by making the continuance of their life together impossible and it was unjust that she should be publicly branded by the divorce as a bad mother and a bad wife. In a letter to Elizabeth she told her that much as she dreaded the inevitable wretchedness that lay ahead she had no alternative but to return and fight the case. Fanny then booked a passage on the Hibernia and after landing in America went straight to Lenox, where she deposited her answer to Pierce's allegations with Charles Sedgwick, the clerk to the Lenox court.

So indignant was she, and so determined to prove that Pierce had driven her out, and that she had ample reason in his treatment of her for leaving him, that to the formal denial of the charge she appended her Narrative, from which quotations have already been made. This complicated rather than helped the subsequent legal proceedings. Had Fanny confined her case to the denial of the charges the issue would have been straightforward, and could have been tried either with or without a jury. To supply this kind of evidence before it had been asked for was to prejudice the issue. The Narrative was inadmissible evidence which had to be struck out; the trial was then fixed for 16 April 1849. Fanny demanded a trial by jury; this was something that Pierce, always averse to washing dirty linen in public, was anxious to avoid. He wanted to be rid of Fanny; he did not want the attendant publicity. Accordingly the rest of the year, until Fanny was finally persuaded to withdraw her defence, was taken up with a flurry of negotiations, as Pierce tried to settle out of court. The trial was postponed until September and by then an agreement had been reached. Rumours had been circulating to the effect that Pierce was financially seriously embarrassed, if not already insolvent. Fanny, knowing his unbusinesslike habits and his proclivity towards extravagance, found no difficulty in believing this and was seriously worried about her children's future. If she could succeed in tying up his property, so that it eventually would be secured for them, then she was prepared to withdraw her defence. Pierce began these negotiations by suggesting that Fanny surrendered her dower rights on his property which he would then will to his daughters. This proposition Fanny rejected. She was not prepared to drop the substance of her dower rights for th shadow of his promises. The wheeling and dealing went on, during which she confided her hopes, fears and difficulties to her Lenox friend, Sam Ward, the Boston lawyer, on whose loyalty she felt she could depend. Meanwhile she had to remain in Philadelphia, where local opinion seems to have been on Pierce's side. In one letter to Ward she commented bitterly on 'the glamour with which everything connected with Mr Butler seems enveloped here – a hallucination so strong that I think if I remain here much longer I shall come to perceive that he is a paragon of every earthly virtue and myself a monster of iniquity'. She was further deeply hurt by the action of the University Committee. Money was something of a problem. Fanny had had to leave England while still short of her financial target; in America there were lawyers to be paid and other expenses. She had no alternative but to give a series of Shakespeare readings in order to raise funds. When a formal application was made for the use of a lecture-room at Pennsylvania

University she was, as she told Ward, 'a good deal surprised and shocked' to find it 'respectfully declined'. Though she took the snub in dignified silence as far as the public was concerned, it did not make her love Philadelphia any the better.

Nevertheless Fanny had to stay in Philadelphia until she could discuss the terms of her settlement with Mr Joshua Fisher, her contact with Pierce. There was however one supreme consolation. She was able to see Sarah and Fan every day, which was an 'inexpressible happiness' to her. Pierce had gone south to the Georgian plantation and had left his daughters in a boarding-house. At one time Fanny had been terrified that he might drag them to Georgia with him. Once she had seen Fisher she had been forced to leave them there herself in order to spend a couple of months in New York giving the first series of her readings in America. Catherine Sedgwick, who was in New York, writing to her niece Kate, reported an enthusiastic reception. 'There is a real hearty, enlightened enthusiastic admiration for her here. One old lady, sans eyes, sans teeth, sans everything but ears, rose after a morning and said she wished she would read oftener in the morning, for she could not come over from Jersey City at night.' Another witness to Fanny's success was her old friend Mr Hone. Writing in his diary on 13 March 1849 he described how

The fashionable world is agog again upon a new impulse. Mrs Butler, the veritable Fanny Kemble, has taken the city by storm. She reads Shakespeare's plays three evenings in the week, and at noon on Mondays in the Stuyvesant Institute in Broadway, a room which will hold six or seven hundred persons, and which is filled when she reads by the elite of the world of fashion; delicate women, grave gentlemen, belles, beaux and critics flock to the doors of the entrance, and rush into such places as they can find, two or three hours before the lady's appearance. They are compensated for the tedious sitting on hard seats, squeezed by the crowd, by a hour's reading, and very fine certainly, for Fanny knows how to do it – of the favourite plays of the Immortal Bard, she makes $2,000 or $3,000 a week and never was money so easily earned.

With the money Fanny was able to fulfil a long-cherished plan; she bought a house in Lenox, the Perch, and so at last was able to live among her friends in her beloved Berkshire hills. It was a slightly comical-looking house, made up of a three-storied tower with a high pitched roof, attached to a more conventional two-storied building adorned with a portico. It stood some half-mile outside the village and, because it was flanked by some oak trees, it was sometimes supposed that Fanny had bought it because of its resemblance to a house in the English countryside. This, like so many ingenuous explanations, was false. Fanny's reason was more prosaic; she had bought it because it happened to be on the market.

Meanwhile the negotiations about her settlement dragged on. After Fanny had finally seen Mr Fisher she wrote more cheerfully to Sam Ward, reporting 'something like two thousand dollars a year saved for my chicks – a brand snatched from the burning verily, for if all the tales I hear be true Mr Butler is insolvent, which indeed I have supposed to be the case ever since I heard of his embarrassments.' Here rumour and Fanny were anticipating events; it was not until 1856 that Pierce was forced to hand over the running of his estates to a friendly syndicate. Moreover what Fanny finally secured was something rather less than the $2,000 a year she had anticipated. The money was placed in the hand of trustees, one of whom was to be Joshua Fisher, a prominent Philadelphian. It is revealing of Fanny's feelings about that city that when the final arrangements were under discussion she wrote to Sam Ward saying that though she had perfect confidence in Mr Fisher's moral qualities,

I have not the same reliance on his judgement and discretion. Moreover Philadelphian people appear to me so very different from any other I have ever met with in any other part of the world that I am determined to leave my children's property in the hands of two trustees and as Mr Butler seems himself to indicate Mr Fisher as one, the other with my consent shall not be a Philadelphian.

Before the case was due to be heard in September agreement had been reached and Pierce obtained his divorce without further opposition from Fanny. This was the price she paid for the sake of her children's financial future, though it appears to have been made somewhat more acceptable by a provision that the children should be allowed to spend one month a year with their mother. Certainly they spent September with her at Lenox but Fanny returned to England in 1850 and apparently did not return to the States until 1856. Why she allowed so long a time to elapse is not clear, but there are indications that perhaps Pierce, as he had done in the past, contrived so many obstacles that Fanny found it impossible in practice to spend any time with them while their father remained in sole control. Another chapter of her life was over; Mrs Butler was replaced by Mrs Fanny Kemble. Pierce never married again. Whatever his motive in divorcing Fanny it does not appear to have been a desire to ask another woman to be his wife.

EIGHT

Building a New Life

Having allowed Pierce to divorce her, as the only means of securing her daughters' financial future, Fanny was faced with the necessity of rebuilding her own shattered life. This was no easy task for a woman in her fortieth year. Nevertheless she was fortunate in that the success of her readings, to which Mr Hone had borne such convincing testimony, had already provided her with a foundation on which to build. For some twenty years they were to provide her with an income, gain for her a reputation on both sides of the Atlantic, and dictate the pattern of her life. At last Fanny had found her true medium. At last she was able to give expression to her deep devotion to Shakespeare without the tawdry trappings of the stage. As her main source of income the readings were important to her but she held to her resolution never to prostitute her veneration for him for the sake of money. With truth she claimed, 'I have never consciously sacrificed my sense of what was due to my work, for the sake of what I could make by it.' Had she been prepared to pander to popular demand she could have made still more by concentrating on his best-known plays. This, to the despair of her agents, she steadily refused to do; she insisted on reading the less well-known ones also. Moreover her pride and sense of her own dignity were such that she refused to make any concessions in the shape of cheap effects. The routine which she followed was almost ostentatiously simple. With a slight acknowledgement to her audience she would take her place behind a simple table furnished only with a reading desk and a glass of water. The only concession that she made to dramatic effect was to wear a sombre dress for tragedy, a lighter colour for comedy and for historical plays a facsimile of the Garter in solid gold on its blue ribbon across her chest. This was an ornament which she valued greatly, not merely for its intrinsic value but for its associations. Anxious though Fanny always was to earn enough to secure for herself that decent independence which meant so much to her, she was generous in giving both her time and her energy to what seemed to her deserving causes. Amongst these was the George Society, the aim of which was to assist Fanny's countrymen who had fallen on hard times in America. As an acknowledgement of the funds which she had raised for the Society she had been presented with what from a distance appeared to be an exact replica of the Garter, though a nearer inspection would have shown on one side the motto of the Society, 'Let mercy be our boast and shame our only fear', and on the other a grateful inscription. Occasionally her wearing of this decoration led to speculation. Henry Greville, at the end of one of her readings, heard two gentlemen debating the point, one voicing the view that it must be some foreign order while the other replied testily, 'I tell you it isn't, she was never *ordered* abroad or at home by anybody', a remark which made Henry Greville observe that 'the gentleman knew you'. With no other aids than her wonderful voice and expressive face Fanny could hold her audience spellbound.

As a means of earning her living her readings had an additional advantage; they were likely to be equally profitable on both sides of the Atlantic. After Sarah and Fan had gone back to their father there was little beyond her New England friends to keep Fanny in America and increasingly her thoughts seem to have been turning to her own country. Her father's health was once more giving cause for concern, though he did not in fact die until 1854, and she was longing to see Adelaide, whose return to England she had missed by two days when she had been forced to make her precipitous rush to America in 1848 Nor had she any reason to suppose that her readings would be less successful in England than they had been in the States. Accordingly, writing on 4 February 1850 to her brother John's old friend Arthur Malkin, she told him that though she had not 'quite finished making my fortune in spite of the magnificent accounts of the wealth with which the newspapers abound' she thought she 'would put the finishing strokes to it among my own people'. When she wrote she seems to have been contemplating returning in the autumn, but she apparently changed her plans as on 25 July, when Henry Greville and Adelaide were dining together, she surprised them by unexpectedly walking into the room. Until she could once more be sure of free access to her children there was little to tempt her back to America and she remained based in Britain. Here her trans-Atlantic successes were repeated. The theatre critic Crabbe Robinson, whose memories of her went back to the days of her Covent Garden triumphs, went to hear her read *Hamlet*. The impression that she made was on the whole favourable, indeed he rated her above Mrs Siddons, writing, 'She has a fine, clear voice and reads with admirable distinctness, so that at the bottom of a long room I scarcely lost a word.' Of her interpretation he made some minor criticism, writing,' I thought her occasionally too violent and exaggerated but generally the expression was such as I could (have) sympathy with. She gave great effect to the light and comic tone of Polonius but on the contrary was somewhat bombastic as Laertes.' Henry Longfellow, a great admirer of hers and married to her young friend Fanny Appleton, thought that she was better in tragedy than comedy; her *Lear* and *Anthony and Cleopatra* he described as 'stupendous'. Not everyone was quite so enthusiastic and even Longfellow felt forced to endorse Charles Dickens's criticism of the way in which she pronounced 'Henery' in the historical plays. Young Henry Irving, who when still a clerk had gone with great expectations to hear Fanny read *Hamlet*, had not been impressed either. In a light-hearted account of his reactions he once described to Ellen Terry how Fanny had swept on to the platform with flashing eyes, pounding the volume from which she was about to read with terrific energy while pronouncing in thrilling tones, '*Ham-a-lette* by Will-i-am Shake-es-peare.' He liked her interpretation as little as he approved of her diction, thinking it far too melodramatic for the melancholy Dane. Fanny was very much her father's daughter and Mrs Siddons' niece; she belonged to the grand manner of acting, a manner which demanded 'every emphatic word underlined and accentuated'. According to an article which Fanny contributed to the *Cornhill Magazine* in December 1863, 'On the Stage', Charles Kemble had always insisted that this was necessary 'lest he should omit the right inflection in delivering the lines'. It was not a style that commended itself to the newer school of acting which Irving was to represent.

Nevertheless in the fifties Fanny could still command her audiences and she devoted herself to the task of making money. This imposed on her a restless, exhausting life. Her headquarters continued to be in London but her many engagements forced her to go 'up and down the whole length and breadth of Great Britain'. Where possible, she combined pleasure with business by staying with friends. On one occasion her host was an old Cambridge friend of her brother, the poet Edward FitzGerald, best known today for his very free translation of *Omar Khayyam*. He lived in seclusion at Woodbridge, and Fanny called him an 'amiable hermit'; they were firm friends and active correspondents. Out of his regard for her, on the occasion of this particular reading, when Fanny came on to the platform and, in accordance with theatrical practice curtseyed to her audience, the poet rose to his feet and bowed in return. Promptly the rest of the audience rose likewise, a gesture which caused her to be 'not a little surprised, amused and confused by this general courtesy' on the part of her audience. Such visits were a pleasant interlude in a dreary round of hotels. Once she threatened to write a guide to those of Britain based on her own experience. It would have made interesting reading, a kind of nineteenth-century Michelin guide. Her accolade was bestowed on the Bedford at Brighton, with the Royal at Lowestoft in second place. Certainly Fanny had ample opportunity to be well informed on such matters. Except when she was lucky enough to have a series of readings booked in one of the major towns, she was perpetually on the move; often literally here today and gone tomorrow. To give one random sample, based on letters written at the end of September, Fanny was at Canterbury from the Sunday to the Wednesday, followed by two nights at Dover. Then, in transit to keep an engagement at Bury St Edmunds, she spent a night at her London lodgings before going on to Suffolk. In her younger days she had become inured to the constant movement demanded from her and her father on provincial tours, but these to some extent had been regulated by the lack of quick communications. By the fifties England had an efficient railway system which, though it made her whirlwind tours less physically exhausting than they had been in the old coaching days, also made it possible to crowd more separate engagements into a week. In spite of the occasional break, or a visit to friends (Fanny seems to have spent some time with Harriet in the autumn), she grew increasingly stale and weary. In her memories of these years there is no zest; they are singularly flavourless, scrappy and irritatingly vague.

It was not just the reaction of picking up her life again; Fanny had personal reasons for being out of spirits in 1852. The details are obscure but some time in January that year she learned that Henry had fathered an illegitimate son while he had been stationed in Ireland. Apart from the moral issue she was particularly distressed by her brother's apparent lack of responsibility towards him. This was something to which she returned again and again in her letters to George Combe, with whom at the moment she was also in correspondence over some difficult and annoying legal and financial business. Apart from a wish to be able to see his son occasionally and to have him brought up as a Protestant, Henry appeared perfectly willing to have him adopted, thus relinquishing all claim to him. This apparent detachment may have been due to the fact that Henry was now becoming increasingly unstable emotionally. By the next year he had become sufficiently mentally deranged to have to be placed in a private asylum, where Henry Thackeray visited him. Writing to his friend Mrs Proctor in March 1853, Thackeray somewhat ruefully compared his own lowness of spirits with the general air of euphoria which Henry Kemble had displayed. Far from realizing his position he imagined himself to be staying at a gentleman's country seat and boasted of his prowess both in the hunting field and with the ladies.

It was on Fanny that the burden fell. When she wrote to George Combe on 30 January 1852 she told him that in view of Harry's lack of concern she was approaching her father to see if he would either take the child or make some contribution to its keep. 'Harry's boy', as Fanny called him, was not her only worry. Another factor in the situation was a certain Mrs Glyn, with whom she told George Combe her father was infatuated. Then in April Fanny discovered that in addition to Henry's illegitimate son there was a daughter in Ireland. When Adelaide and Edward Sartoris returned to Italy, where they spent much of their time, Fanny felt even more forlorn, and in 1853 decided to join them. It would be a relief to turn her back on her problems that for the past year had beset her and to be able to enjoy the comforting companionship of her sister.

Though Italy was not one of Fanny's favourite countries – she found the volcanic atmosphere of the region 'utterly repugnant' to her constitution – it provided her with a very necessary breathing space. Moreover she found Sorrento 'enchantingly beautiful'. The Sartorises had been fortunate enough to secure a house with a terrace from which they had a view over what Fanny described to Harriet as 'earth, sea and sky'. Nevertheless, as modern tourists still discover, there were drawbacks even to this scene of loveliness. Fanny complained 'There is no beach and the cliffs being very high, and all crowded with gardens or orchards of private dwelling houses, one is debarred from that familiar intercourse with the sea'. Moreover, though she acknowledged its beauty, she explained her lack of response to it by the fact that

The species of loveliness in this part of the world is the least attractive possible to me. That which is sublime, severe, stern, dark, solemn, wild and even savage, is far more to my taste than this profusion of shining, glittering, smiling, sparkling, beaming, brilliant prospects and aspects.

Like all tourists, Fanny and the Sartorises 'did the sights'. They explored the famous Blue Grotto at Capri and, more adventurously, were carried up in chairs in the moonlight to the very rim of Vesuvius. There, wrapped in blankets, they passed the night. This expedition at least satisfied Fanny's sense of the dramatic; she pronounced 'Vesuvius is undoubtedly a great deal more like hell than any imagination that can be formed of hell can be'. In the cooler October weather Fanny and the Sartorises returned to Rome. There she was caught up in the brilliant, distinguished coterie of English residents and visitors among whom Adelaide was a leading figure. One of these was the young Anne Thackeray, who promptly fell under Fanny's spell. Her *Recollections*, written in later life, contain some vivid sketches of Fanny when she first knew her. Anne often heard her say that 'It was a hard and difficult time of her life when she needed all her courage to endure her daily portion of suffering.' Her heart was with her children and she grasped hungrily at any scraps of news that friends, such as the Ellesmeres, then visiting America, could send to her. As ever Fanny's moods swung from one extreme to another. Often she would sit, a silent figure, dressed in black, doing her inevitable worsted work, withdrawn from the vivacious company that flocked to Adelaide's salon. On other days her energy would bubble over. Then she would take Anne with her, telling the coachman, when he asked for directions *'Andate al Diavolo'* and they would drive over the Campagna, with Fanny singing at the top of her voice, to the acute embarrassment of her young companion. As always, when she could Fanny rode until one day her horse stumbled over the uneven ground of the Campagna and threw its rider, so that Fanny dislocated her right shoulder. In the early summer of 1854 she returned to England, partly because of her pressing need to earn money, partly through anxiety about her father's health.

She thought her father was 'looking younger and better, and is, I verily believe, stronger than any of us'. Henry, she reported, was 'suffering horribly from what I suppose to be inflammatory rheumatism'. By now Charles was an old man and very deaf. Crabbe Robinson, who had met him at Talfourd's in the July of 1853, said that with the aid of a tube he could still maintain a *tête à tête* conversation, and that except for this he still found him a very agreeable person with whom to converse. By the November of 1854, five months after Fanny's return, her father was dead. In 1857 Henry died and as John also died in the same year, the two sisters made themselves responsible for Henry's children, Adelaide apparently providing for the daughter and Fanny for the son. At one time Fanny seems to have contemplated taking him with her to America. As understandably there is no mention of any of these family problems in Fanny's published memoirs, and as the story has to be pieced together from her letters and stray allusions, the details are tantalizingly vague.

For two more years life stretched drearily before her, then in 1856 her long heartache came to an end. Sarah was now twenty-one and a free agent. There was nothing now to prevent Fanny from seeing her elder daughter. She returned to America and to her New England friends in Lenox and there at last Sarah joined her. In spite of the emotional strain that the breakdown of their parents' marriage must have imposed on them, Sarah and Fan seem to have remained attached to them both. The two sisters were very different in temperament. Sarah was a northerner, sharing her mother's views on slavery, and her roots remained in Philadelphia. Fan, in contrast, accepted her father's outlook and traditions; her heart and sympathies were with the south. On the other hand she shared her mother's love of mountains while Sarah, when her mother tried to persuade her to embark on an expedition to the Adirondacks, was most uncooperative. As Fanny explained she was not at all savagely disposed, and sleeping on hemlock pine branches, getting her hair matted with resin, had few charms for her. Once again the pattern of Fanny's life altered; once again America would have to be the base of her operations. Though, as she once confessed 'God knows America is far from being as pleasant as England at any time, but my children, being Americans, and America their undisputed home' the greater happiness was once again to be with her daughter. Each summer she could enjoy her company, and when Fan also became free of her father's control in 1859 she described this time as 'the one blossom of my year'. Each autumn, Fanny resumed her reading-tours.

Though these were successful, travelling and living in hotels was exhausting and very expensive. Fanny, returning to the United States, was horrified by the cost of living. After one year she wrote with a kind of irritated anguish to Arthur Malkin, declaring,

It is not very likely, my dear Arthur, let me live as long as I will, that I shall ever be a rich woman, if I am to live in America; the cost of one's existence here is something fabulous, and the amount of discomfort one obtains for money that purchases a liberal amount of luxury as well as comfort in Europe, is by no means a small item of annoyance in one's daily life.

Once, after what the indignant Fanny considered to be a blatant case of overcharging, she sent the following letter to the editor of the local paper, the *Milwaukee Sentinel*. 'Sir, I think the person who made the accompanying charges for one week's board and lodging for myself and maid is probably insensible to shame, and therefore the publication of this extortion will not affect him, while it may at least cause the amusement of astonishment to your citizens.' She then particularized the various items, which included 25 cents for the bar and $10 for the use of a piano, commenting 'The 25 cents put down for the bar is for three lemons, which I asked for on occasion of having a duck for dinner. In Chicago I had a new piano sent in from a music store for a fortnight and the charge for it was $3.' Even in the minor matter of a hotel bill Fanny refused to accept exploitation without protest; as always she was ready to carry the war into the enemy's camp. Her quarrel was not only with high prices. Though appreciative of much that she found in America her English sense of values made her equally critical of the way in which Americans spent their money. To her far too much went on outward show and not enough on the more solid comforts of life. As an instance of this she contrasted her hotel sitting-room in New York, which had 'three large looking-glasses set in superb frames, green and gold satin curtains and furniture and carpet and rugs of all the splendid colours of the rainbow' with her bedroom, which did not even boast the luxury of a fireplace in a climate where the winter temperatures varied from zero to twenty-one degrees below freezing-point. 'Does not the juxtaposition of such a drawing-room and such a bedroom,' she asked indignantly, 'speak volumes for the love of finery and the ignorance of all decent comfort, which are alike semi-barbarous?' Though Fanny still found her most faithful and favourite audiences in New England, her engagements were no longer confined to the east coast. The America which she had first known in 1832 was being transformed with a rapidity that almost stuns the imagination. By the eighteen forties the great movement to the prairies and hunting-grounds of the west was well under way. The slogan for success was 'Go West, young man'. When she had first come to the United States an increasing trickle had been doing just that. In 1836 Arkansas, and in 1837 Michigan, had achieved statehood; after the depression of that year Congress had encouraged the western flow by passing new land laws to make land more easily and securely available to people prepared to settle there. The discovery of copper and coal tempted miners to follow; then came the discovery of gold in California and the great Gold Rush that inspired hundreds of families to cross the prairies and the deserts in their covered wagons. In spite of all the drama of the Western movies only those who have done the journey in person, whether by car or coach or on one of the great trans-continental railroads, can even begin to appreciate their courage. Not all the people who made the great trek were of American stock. Even before the famine the Irish were coming in some numbers; after it they poured across the Atlantic in a steady flood. So did the Germans, particularly after the abortive risings against the autocratic European regimes in 1848. Demand created transport and transport accelerated the movement towards the west. By 1846 Iowa became a state; Wisconsin followed in 1848. The middle west had already become a social entity by the time that Fanny resumed her readings and, like everybody in search of profit, she too went west. In the winter of 1856 she penetrated as far as St Louis and beyond the Mississippi to the farther shore of Lake Michigan. Before the days of the railroad and the Erie Canal this would have been an unbelievable journey, which, even if possible, would have been pointless. In the early days of pioneering there would have been no demand for Shakespearean readings; whatever funds the settlers might possess would have to be devoted to sterner purposes. That Fanny should have gone west at all was a proof of the extent to which the civilizing influence of wealth and success had extended. Fanny was deeply impressed by all that she found there and not least by the pace of life, writing 'the rapidity, energy, and enterprise with which civilization is being carried forward baffles all description, and, I think, can hardly be believed but by those who have seen it'. Everywhere she found new cities, adorned with what she described as magnificent streets and houses, in addition to warehouses, wharves and quays built to cope with the new and growing traffic once the Great

Lakes had been linked to the east by the Erie Canal. Even more important was the coming of the railways. The horrific early journeys that
Fanny had made down to Georgia were now things of what seemed a
very distant past, though barely twenty years had elapsed. These at
first had been concentrated in the east, tying together the economies of
the Eastern seaboard where population and industry alike were thickest.
By 1857 the scene had been transformed; as many as nine lines all now
converged on the lake port of Chicago. So it is not surprising that the
shops in the new cities were full of luxuries from Paris; as Fanny had
observed when she first came to the States, American women were
avid for the fashions from France. It was a strange experience not only
for Fanny but for the pioneers themselves to be in the midst of a new
urban civilization where, fifty years before, the bison, the Indians and
the trappers had roamed. Nevertheless she was glad to get back to New
England which she always declared 'is more like Old England than
any part of this huge and wonderful country'.

In the May of 1859 Fan became twenty-one. At last Fanny could
have both her daughters with her without her ex-husband's agreement.
Whether she had seen her younger daughter between her return to
America in 1856 and Fan's birthday is not clear. There is no mention
of her having done so in her *Further Records*, but these are so disjointed
and inaccurately dated that the absence of any such mention is by
itself no proof. When she and Pierce had finally worked out the terms
in return for which Fanny had agreed not to fight the case, there seems
to have been some mention of Fanny's being allowed access to her
daughters for a portion of each year, but the only time when it is
certain that she did so was when they were both with her at Lenox,
before Fanny returned to England and they were sent to school. Of
Pierce's feelings towards Fanny after this date there is no record. Things
had not gone well for him. His financial difficulties had increased so
that in the summer of 1859 he was driven to the humiliating expedient
of having to sell a portion of his slaves, 436 in all, in order to meet his
debts. Fanny, on the other hand, was making a good income in spite
of the expenses of which she complained and in 1859 she arranged that
when she returned to Europe for the summer Fan should come with
her. As the link between Pierce and his younger daughter was clearly a
close one it seems a fair inference that had her father been opposed to
the plan Fan would not have gone. Sarah did not go with them. She
had fallen in love with a Philadelphian doctor, Owen Wister, whom she

married. For Fan it was an exciting and almost new experience. She had been only five when her parents had returned to America from England in 1843, and her memories of her mother's country must have been dim. It was almost in the nature of a miniature Grand Tour. Fanny took her daughter to Paris and to her beloved Switzerland before returning to spend the autumn in England among her English friends where, among other activities, Fan sampled the thrill of cub-hunting. When finally mother and daughter returned to New York in October they were met by Sarah and her new husband. The Wisters were an old Philadelphian family with a long medical tradition, and Sarah's marriage meant that not only through her father, but also through her husband, she would unquestionably be accepted by that exclusive society which had never quite approved of young Mr Butler's marrying an actress, however celebrated. Fan returned to Philadelphia with her sister and Fanny once more turned her energies to an autumn and winter tour. She had, however, as well as the memories of her trip with Fan, a new experience to look forward with happy expectations. Sarah was expecting her first child, and in 1860 Fanny became a grandmother.

It was well that her personal life was, for once, running smoothly because the political situation was growing ever more threatening. Soon after Fanny's return to the States in 1856 she had written a letter to Henry Greville that was full of fears for the future, telling him that 'The terrible and inevitable slavery question is beginning to weigh like an incubus upon the whole country, pressing every day nearer and nearer to some solution which threatens to be a hideous catastrophe.' Just as Fanny's own involvement with this cancer had been the chief bone of contention between her and her husband, now it was threatening a breakdown on a national scale between the southern slave-holding, cotton, rice and sugar-growing states and the north and rapidly expand-ing middle west. It was not solely a question of outlook and tradition, though these were important; the economic interests of north and south seemed almost too diverse to be contained in one political union. By the end of 1859 the flash-point was very near. In her letter Fanny described how a fanatic from Kansas had tried to excite a slave rising in Virginia which 'has thrown the whole South into a frenzy of terror, which has drawn forth the contemptuous indignation of the North. The poor wretch is hanged, but from his grave a root of bitterness may be disunion and civil war between the North and South of the country.'

She wrote prophetically. The 'poor wretch' was John Brown who, with a small band of Abolitionists, had led the raid on Harper's Ferry with the intention of seizing the government arsenal there and arming the slaves, and whose soul was henceforth 'to go marching on' though 'his body lies a-mouldering in the grave'.

Fanny's attitude to the state of things in America was clearly coloured by her evangelical outlook. Earlier, even before the crisis had seemed so threatening, and shortly after her return to America in 1856, in a letter written in the September of that year, she had told Greville that

The whole state of the country, moral, social and political, makes one's hair stand on end with amazement and apprehension, and to what issue it is driving, with its magnificent freight of unparalleled material prosperity, it is hard and sad to surmise.

A month later, continuing in the same strain, she wrote,

Anything like the universal contempt for authority, which pervades the body social and political here, it is impossible to conceive. The country is really in a portentous condition of material prosperity and moral degradation. The best people speak with shame and despondency of the national condition. Thoughtful people predict inevitable consequences of the most tremendous kind to the utter demoralization which seems to pervade all classes.

It was against this background of despondency that Fanny began to feel that, just as for the erring individual suffering was a necessary ingredient for the amendment of life, so the American people seemed to require

some great national trial or trouble. The material prosperity has turned the head of the whole people. The government is despicable and despised, public and private morality at a miserable ebb and the whole country presenting the portentous aspect of the most rapid superficial progress and retrogression in all that makes the true glory and safety of a people.

For some little time yet however the lowering storm held off. Fanny had seen Sarah happily married, had taken Fan to Europe and had become a grandmother. Sarah's first child was a son, christened Owen after his father and later to achieve some fame as the author of *The Virginian*. Fanny admitted to feeling 'a most grandmotherly yearning' to see the infant when next she was able to visit Philadelphia.

An event of a more public nature that afforded Fanny much interest was the visit of the young Prince of Wales to the United States, which took place in November 1860. Thinking that Henry Greville would be interested, she sent him a long and shrewdly written account of the royal visit:

The visit of Prince Albert Edward to his grandfather's rebellious provinces is one of the most curious and interesting events in modern history and it will be well if His Royal Highness has received and can retain a pleasing impression and a cordial feeling of and towards America, for though she can scarcely need England other wise than commercially (and the need may diminish quite as readily as increase with the development of her own gigantic resources) the day *may* come when England may be glad of the support of her vigorous offspring, and together assuredly they may command the world, while any event that made them antagonistic of them would be even more disastrous to the human race in general than to the two nations themselves.

This pronouncement, which Fanny made as early as 1860, considerably less than a hundred years since the United States had become an independent power, is a testimony to the soundness of her political thinking. Nevertheless she could not help but be amused by the extent to which her democratic and republican friends allowed themselves to be caught up in a species of ecstasy by the presence of royalty. She found it difficult 'to imagine a more curious spectacle than the excitement of the whole American people at the sight of a true prince'. Fan, who had the honour of dancing with His Royal Highness at a ball, seems to have escaped the general infection. Perhaps her English blood and a few months of English society, combined with the American enthusiasm for equality, had produced some measure of immunity so that she merely described him as 'a nice little fellow' and laughed at her mother's suggestion that she should keep as a souvenir the gloves that she had worn on this royal occasion. Fanny, used to the deference that England paid to Victoria, was a little shocked and shaken by her daughter's nonchalance.

But even the Prince's visit could not for long divert either Fanny's or the nation's attention from the situation at home. In the same letter she included another piece of information significant for the future:

I am happy to tell you that the presidential election is going on favourably for the Republican party. The man at the heart of it (Lincoln) is obscure enough even for an American President, but the triumph of the party is the triumph of political reform, order, good government and humanity.

Despite the obscurity on which Fanny commented, Lincoln carried every state in the populous north and had a clear majority in the electoral college, though his share of the popular vote was only 39 per cent. Within a month of his election South Carolina had seceded from the Union and was followed by Georgia, Mississippi, Florida, Alabama, Louisiana, and Texas, and under Jefferson Davis the Confederacy had been born. For a time the remaining southern states wavered, but when Lincoln called for volunteers, and ordered a naval blockade of the southern ports, after the attack on Fort Sumter, Virginia, North Carolina, Tennessee and Arkansas threw in their lot with the Confederate States. The Civil War had begun. To Fanny this brought anxiety and grief. Partly because of her love for New England, partly because of her hatred of slavery, her sympathies were entirely with the north. This she had made abundantly clear during the crisis of 1850, which turned on the terms on which California should be admitted to the Union. Both north and south were extremely sensitive on this question of admitting new members lest the balance between the slave-holding and the free states were upset. In the end a compromise was reached, but for a time it almost looked as if the south might stage a breakaway. It was in these circumstances that Fanny, who had been giving a reading of *As You Like It* before the Mercantile Library Association in Boston, surprised her audience by coming to the edge of the platform, book in hand, and reading Longfellow's *The Building of the Ship*. In his diary Longfellow described how, 'trembling, palpitating, and weeping, and giving every word its true emphasis', Fanny read his poem. It stirred the whole audience, particularly when she read the last well-known lines,

> *Thou too sail on, O ship of State,*
> *Sail on, O Union, strong and great!*
> *Humanity with all its fears*
> *With all the hope of future years*
> *Is hanging breathless on thy fate.*

to great political enthusiasm, though to modern readers Longfellow's peroration may bring to mind Fanny's own comment that 'he was not a great poet' and that even her verdict that even so 'he was among the first of those who are not the greatest' owed something to her personal affection for him.

As the crisis grew nearer Fanny was increasingly anxious that her English friends should see the situation from the American angle, and understand the problems of the north. From the beginning of 1861 she bombarded Henry Greville with letters dealing with the current situation, explaining her views, and these, in view of the importance of the events she was describing, he copied into his diary. Like his brother he was a confirmed diarist. As a result of his industry we are provided with an interesting commentary on her political acumen and judgement. 'I think', she wrote in the January of that year, 'the secession of the Southern States, sooner or later, inevitable,' going on to express a characteristic wish that 'the cowards on all sides will not be able to poultice up the festering sore which *must* break out again and will only have gangrened the whole body of the nation still deeper.' Though Fanny felt so passionately about the issue of slavery, she saw, as many then and since have seen, that this was a symbol rather than a cause of the growing division of the nation, telling Greville,

The fact is that the Southern States see and feel very bitterly the immense pre-ponderance of wealth, activity, industry, intelligence and prosperity of the North. They neither see nor believe what is the truth, that slavery and nothing else, is the cause of their total inferiority in all these particulars, and are acting upon the insane belief that separation from the bond of the Union will turn the scale of national importance in their favour.

For her part Fanny would have let them secede, thinking it 'not only inevitable but desirable that the South shall separate from the North. Slave-holding produces a peculiar character which has nothing in common with a Christian republic founded by Englishmen of the eighteenth century.' In particular she attacked the idealized picture that the southerners tried to present of a benevolent, paternal society presided over by gentlemen, declaring that 'the Southerners are fond of calling themselves the chivalry of the South' but that in truth they were as 'ignorant, insolent, barbarous, and brutal as an ironclad robber of the middle ages. They are, in fact, a remnant of feudalism and barbarism.' Holding these views it seemed to Fanny that to fight to retain them in the Union against their will was stupid. Left to their own resources she was convinced that the Southern States would go down-hill so rapidly that soon 'the whole white population will abandon them'. The result would be a fertile wilderness, inhabited only by the Negroes, which could easily be re-occupied by the north, who would then abolish slavery throughout the entire American continent. In so prophesying Fanny was showing something less that her usual political sense. In a world greedy for cotton the south could have survived and in the fullness of time economic pressure would itself, in all probability, have led to the gradual disappearance of slavery.

Though Fanny hated slavery as much as ever she was no longer tormented by the knowledge that the Butler wealth was the product of slave owning and that no longer would it be her daughters' fate to 'inflict injustice and oppression, or tremble before impending retribution' because, owing to what she called 'their father's unprincipled extravagance', his share of the Butler slaves had by this time been sold to pay his debts. Had the Civil War not come she might have rejoiced too soon. Pierce still owned the plantation and in April he returned to Georgia, apparently with sufficient funds to buy more slaves, and with the intention of remaining in the south. To Fanny's great distress he took Fan with him. According to her mother this was in spite of the protests of all his friends and the remonstrances of Sarah and the entreaties of Fan herself. This last statement must be open to question. Fan was now twenty-three, and in view of her mother's earnings she was not financially dependent on her father. Moreover there was a tough streak in Fan; like her mother she would do what she thought right even in the face of difficulties, as her determination later to run the plantation single-handed was to show. Fan may have entreated her father not to go in face of the threat of Civil War but when these entreaties failed the decision to accompany him must have been her own. Whatever the reason for their return Pierce's plans do not seem to have materialized; by the summer father and daughter were back in the north. For Pierce Butler the expedition had an unpleasant sequel. In August he was arrested on a charge of high treason, it being alleged that he had been involved in buying arms for the south and arranging for their transport. Fanny thought the charge likely to be true. If this was so then his ostensible reason for going south had been a cover-up, which would explain why he appeared once again in a position to buy slaves. For a time Pierce was imprisoned in the fortress that guarded the approach to New York Bay, where with some difficulty Sarah and Fan got a special order to visit him. Even then the authorities must have considered him sufficiently dangerous to arrange that the visit should take place in the presence of a prison officer. Fanny, with memories of both his southern sympathies and his obstinate nature, thought he might well spend the rest of the war as a prisoner rather than take the oath of allegiance to President Lincoln. Here she was wrong. After five weeks' experience of prison Pierce Butler gave his word not to take up arms against the north and was released. As to his reasons, or whether his daughters had managed to persuade him to submit to circumstances, Fanny has nothing to say.

Apart from her worries concerning Fan, in contrast to the storm on the political horizon, 1861 had been a pleasant year for Fanny. Once again she spent the summer at her beloved Lenox where Fan stayed with her for four months. Sarah was able to join them for a month; apparently she had still not quite recovered from the effects of her confinement and she came without young Owen. When at the end of the month her husband came to fetch her home he too stayed a week. Unfortunately, as Fanny put it, two of his patients 'took the opportunity of dying shabbily and disgracefully without his assistance', so that his mother-in-law had doubts as to whether he would dare to leave his practice for future visits. As it was over a year since she had seen her grandchild, she was then looking forward to being able to pay a visit to Sarah in Philadelphia. It would be interesting to know whether on these occasions Pierce was still living in Philadelphia and with what skill her daughters managed to avoid a meeting between their parents. Certainly in her *Records* Fanny has nothing to say on what must have been an embarrassing possibility.

If her domestic life was causing her few anxieties in 1861, she was less happy about the political situation. In particular she was distressed and disturbed by the pro-southern sympathies of the English press. Most educated English opinion thought of the conflict as arising out of the right of the Confederate States to leave the Union and had not yet come to regard it as turning on the issue of slavery. For this there was some justification. In the early stages of the Civil War Lincoln himself had seemed to take his stand on this – it was not until the September of 1862 that he proclaimed that by the beginning of 1863 all slaves in the rebel states would be freed. Among many of the English upper classes their sympathy with the southern cause was based on a romantic notion, shared and disseminated by the southerners themselves, that the north represented crude materialism and was dominated by industrialists and money markets while the southern states were governed by gentlemen like themselves. This was a view that enraged Fanny. Her own views, based on personal experience, were that 'an elegant young Carolinian or Georgian gentleman, whip in hand, driving a gang of "lusty women", as they are called here, would be a pretty version of the "Chivalry of the South" '. The term 'lusty woman' was a euphemism for a pregnant one. This was the picture that she was struggling throughout the next two years to convey to her English friends. She had cause for concern. By the closing months of 1861 diplomatic relations between Britain and the Union were at their lowest ebb owing to the repercussions of the Trent affair. Jefferson Davis had sent a couple of representatives to England to plead the cause of the south to the British government, which hitherto had maintained an official policy of strict neutrality. To prevent any likelihood of diplomatic incidents British subjects were forbidden to enlist on either side or to equip ships of war. What the Confederacy hoped to achieve by their mission was, if possible, diplomatic recognition as an independent state, but at least a more benevolent neutrality. The two agents managed to book a passage on an English ship, the *Trent*, but in mid-Atlantic they were forcibly removed by the captain of an American man-of-war. Both Britain and the north reacted violently, the former with popular fury, the latter with extravagant praise for the high-handed captain whose action was regarded as a convincing demonstration of the new might of the United States. To defy the ex-mother country still brought to many Americans a glow of national pride, a defiance of fate at the time that the Union itself was threatened. At this moment it did not look as if the benefits that Fanny had seen in the visit of the Prince of Wales were likely to materialize. If neither side backed down the possibility of war was grave; Britain was preparing a stern ultimatum demanding the return of the captured envoys and an apology in terms which the Union could not possibly have accepted without considerable humiliation. The immediate crisis was averted by the tact of the almost dying Prince Consort, who persuaded Lord Palmerston, then Foreign Secretary, to rephrase the ultimatum in such a way that the Union could comply without too great a loss of face. This was done but the incident left feelings on both sides of the Atlantic high and the question of British ships running the blockade contained all the potential for future crises. Fanny felt, with some justification, that the north had received a bad press and that English politicians did not understand America. On 19 January 1862, she wrote to Henry Greville warning him that,

If they are forced to fight they will; for whatever you may think to the contrary, they are not in the least cowardly; but, wanting in common sense, as I do think they are (more than any people in the world, I begin to think) they will assuredly do everything they can to avert such a catastrophe, and I do hope most fervently that no evil feeling for their past vulgar insolence and folly, and no desire to open their cotton market for their own use again will induce England to aggravate their present troubles by taking any ungenerous advantage of them.

In defence of the Union Fanny then went on to assert that the people of Britain had no idea of the difficulties that had faced the north when confronted with all the problems of organizing effective armies in the field. As she reminded Greville, the armies of revolutionary France, which so long had dominated Europe, were in their early campaigns untrained and unsuccessful. It would not be wise, she implied, to prophesy final failure from the lack of early victories. In March she wrote more optimistically. General Grant seemed to be gaining control of the upper Mississippi valley above Vickersberg, while General McClellan was on the way to organizing an effective military force. Fanny wrote almost jubilantly, 'The theory of State Rights and the practice of slavery have both, I think, received their death blow.' Though both prophesies were eventually to prove correct in the short term, Fanny was too hopeful. When McClellan, in command of the Army of the Potomac, invaded Virginia he was driven back by General Lee. For a time, to her dismay, the Confederate troops seemed to be making headway.

Fanny did not allow the war to interfere with her periodic visits to England and when she returned to Europe in the summer of 1862 she brought Fan with her. Henry Greville, who saw her on her way through London on her way to Switzerland, said she seemed well and in good spirits though disinclined to discuss the war, which at that time was going badly for the north. Fanny loved Switzerland for whose scenery, in her own words, she had 'a sort of enthusiastic affection'. Though she described herself as 'old and fat and rheumatic', and though she accepted the fact that the years would make her 'older, and fatter and rheumaticker' she was still determined to tackle the Swiss passes, declaring that if her own legs would no longer carry her then she would ride a mule, and if that should prove impossible, why then she would be carried in a chair by eight men as, years ago, she had been carried up Vesuvius. In 1862 she was exaggerating her handicaps. She was only fifty-five and though undoubtedly she had put on weight and suffered from sundry aches and pains she was still active enough to make an expedition with Fan to Grindelwald to show her daughter a glacier. When she returned to England it was with the intention of spending the winter there. Once back she continued to fulminate against what she regarded as the misrepresentations of *The Times* in reporting on the fighting in America. When she dined alone with Henry Greville on 28 December he noted in his diary that 'I found her in great distress at the disaster of the Federal army in the late battle of Fredericton and retreat across the Rappaharmah; I think even she begins to despair of success.' It can hardly be coincidence that towards the end of that year, when the northern armies were doing so badly, Fanny decided to publish her *Journal of a Residence on a Georgian Plantation*, which hitherto she had felt that she could not do. Not only was the war going badly for the north, a new and ugly diplomatic situation was threatening to cause dangerous tension between the Federal government and Great Britain. In 1862 a couple of fast vessels had been built on Merseyside for the use of the Confederacy. What is more, they were suspected of having been commissioned by southern agents not merely to run the blockade of their ports but to act as armed raiders against the northern shipping. In spite of the efforts of northern representatives to alert Her Majesty's Government to this possibility, possibly more through muddle and delay than active ill-will to the Union, both raiders, the *Florida* and the better-known *Alabama*, were allowed to sail. Once at sea the damage that they did to Federal shipping was extensive, indeed so extensive that after the end of the war as a result of arbitration the British government handed over fifteen million dollars in compensation. Though the victory and the award were in the future; what concerned Fanny was the fact that, apart from the working class of northern England, who in spite of the hardships which they suffered as textile workers through the shortage of cotton, remained firmly anti-slavery, the majority of English people would have viewed the break-up of the Union and the independence of the southern states with equanimity. To Fanny the picture which most of them had of life in the slave-holding south was so far removed from the reality of her own experience that she must have felt driven to do what she could to lift the veil of their ignorance. The publication of the journal might therefore do something to create more sympathy for the north, particularly as in September 1862 President Lincoln had declared his intention to abolish slavery wherever it could be found in America. Unfortunately from the point of view of propaganda for the north Fanny had waited too long. Inevitably there must always be a gap between the decision to publish and the appearance of a book. By the time that Longman's had brought out the *Journal* the crisis was over, not so much in a military as in a moral sense. Once the slaves had been pronounced legally free at the beginning of January 1863 the Evangelicals rallied in support behind Lincoln. Fanny's broadside was delivered too late. How much effect it had in strengthening this growing Evangelical support must be uncertain. The name of Kemble still meant something; her Shakespearean readings had made her personally known to many people; what she had written was likely to be read with interest. Nevertheless when the *Journal* was at last published in the May of 1863 she was largely preaching to the converted. It is unlikely that it ever had as wide an emotional appeal as Harriet Beecher Stowe's *Uncle Tom's Cabin*. An American edition appeared in July. Less than two years later in the May of 1865 the Civil War was over and Fanny decided to return to America and resume her interrupted career. She was approaching her fifty-sixth birthday and the need to make money while she could remained with her.

Fanny returned to a very different America from the one that she had first known in 1832. In the twenty years between 1840 and 1860 a population of some seventeen million, in round figures, had been swollen to thirty-one and a half million. The United States was not only more populous, it was changing its character. Much of the increase was due to immigration from overseas. In search of new land and new opportunities foreign immigrants as well as native Americans had streamed west. Even before the end of the fighting the geographical and economic balance of the country had been changing in favour of the west, as Fanny had found when she had resumed her readings in America in 1857. With the end of the war the movement to the west coast was accelerated. Peace had released the potential of heavy industry, stimulated by the demand to equip the northern armies. This was now devoted to the construction of new railways and rolling stock. By 1869 the joining of the Union Pacific and the Canadian Pacific made it possible to travel by train 'from coast to shining coast'. After her return from England Fanny was struck by the changes that had taken place in her absence:

The country is no longer *English*. New England may be essentially still, but out of New England the English element has died out almost entirely. When I first came here thirty-four years ago, the whole country was like some remote part of England that I had never seen before, the people like English provincial or colonial folk; in short they were like *queer* English people.

Now, though American speech remained basically English, as did the foundation of their Law, Fanny thought that the new nation in both character and intellect would be more German than English. At that time she could hardly be expected to foresee the massive immigration that would come from Italy and the Mediterranean countries, but she was correct in supposing that the old America had gone and, with the ending of the Civil War, a new nation had been born.

NINE

Peaceful Pastures

During the early days of her marriage Fanny had told her friend Anna Jameson that her future resembled 'a level, peaceful landscape, through which I shall saunter leisurely towards my grave'. The turbulent years of Fanny's life since then were very different from what she had described as 'the pleasant probable future'. Nor, with her love of the wild and the dramatic in nature, is it easy to accept her bland statement that a 'level, peaceful landscape' could ever have contented her. But by the end of the Civil War, though she was only fifty-six, Fanny was losing some of her fire. The cause for which she had sacrificed so much of her personal happiness, and about which she had felt so deeply, had been won. The long separation from her daughters was over. She had a career which was profitable and which satisfied her pride and dignity. There was very little new or longed for that life had to offer. Moreover physically her tremendous energy was at last waning. The pace of living began to slow down for her; Fanny was preparing to accept the limitations of growing old. This did not mean that she was prepared to retire immediately, and for three more years she continued her money-making tours. The pattern of these seems to have been more or less standardized. She went west, 'reading as I run', as far as the Great Lakes and the Mississippi, and reaping a good financial reward if that of 1868 can be regarded as typical. In the spring of that year she netted 'four thousand pounds (all my expenses paid, three hundred pounds *given* away, and eleven hundred pounds *read away gratis* for charity)', a record on which she was inclined to preen herself, asking Harriet if she did not think it were a good 'three months' job'. Nevertheless, by now fifty-nine, Fanny was finding it a strain, telling Harriet in the same letter, 'It is time if ever, for me to rest, at least I think and feel so.' Her decision may have been partially influenced by the fact that Pierce Butler had died in 1867 and that Fan was now mistress of Butler Place, which she was busily getting into order with the intention of living there herself during the summer, when she was not in Georgia, and where Fanny was to spend the winter and spring before making her almost routine visit to her beloved Alps and presumably to England.

Fanny's chief anxiety after the close of the Civil War had been Fan's commitment to the Georgian plantation, with all the worries that this brought to her. In spite of her mother's dislike of the plan, as soon as hostilities had ceased Fan went back to the plantation with her father to see what could be salvaged, and if the estate could again be made a viable concern. This was the more important because Pierce's brother John had died leaving no heir, so that Pierce was now the sole owner. The journey itself, apart from the expectation of near chaos when Fan and her father finally reached Butler Island, was even worse than those which had faced Fanny when she had first gone south. Then the hazards and discomforts had come from the fact that railroads were still incomplete and bridges unsafe. Now the dislocation arose from the destruction of war, and the result was an appalling journey. Conditions when they reached the plantation were worse than Fanny had had to face. Then the overseer was ready to welcome them; simple though their accommodation was at least it was furnished; and the labour force was still under the discipline of slavery, while the routine of planting and harvest had been unbroken. Though their old slaves seem to have been genuinely delighted to see Fan and Pierce once more, exclaiming, 'T'ank the Lord, missis, we 's back and sees you and the massa again', the overseer, who had been left in charge, had absconded with most of their possessions, leaving the house bare of even essential furniture. Only those articles which had been entrusted to individual slaves had been safely hidden and were now restored to them. Fan, like her mother, kept a journal, which she later published under the title *Ten Years on a Georgian Plantation*. Like her mother's earlier journal, Fan's has both psychological and historical interest. The historical interest is obvious in that Fan's experiences illustrate the difficulties of transforming slave labour into wage labour; the psychological interest lies both in what Fan included and in what she left out, in the light that it throws on her relations with her mother. What she left out was any mention of her mother or of her mother's journal, and any allusion to Fanny's views on slavery. What she included was much evidence to show how devoted Mr Butler's slaves were to their old master, and how seriously he took his obligations towards them. Slaves who during the war had been scattered, and even those whom Pierce had been forced to sell, had in many cases spent what little money they had in getting back to their old home, which Fan wrote, in obvious contradiction to the picture which the publication of Fanny's journal had presented, 'speaks louder than words as to the feeling for their old master and their former treatment'. When Fanny reminded them that they were now free, the reply was, 'No, missus, we belong to you; we be yours as long as we lib.'

There was a reverse side to this coin. The older slaves had been utterly dependent on their master for so long that they could not even conceive the idea of standing on their own feet. However bad the old system had been, and however much Fanny's heart had been torn by the cases of neglect of the old, by the overworking of pregnant women, and the meagre care given to the sick, Mr Butler's slaves had a sense of belonging, of security. Even when he had been forced to sell them he told Bran (one of the drivers on the Hampton Point plantation whose likeness to the ex-overseer Mr King, and whose lightness of colour, had aroused Fanny's own suspicions in that distant past) that 'I am in great trouble; I have no money and I have to sell some of the people but I know where you are all going to, and will buy you back again as soon as I can.' As a further instance of Pierce's humane attitude towards 'his people', Bran added 'He told me Juba, my old wife, must go with me, for though she was not strong, and the gentleman who bought me would not buy her, the master said he could not let man and wife be separated.' At the end of the war the slaves of less concerned masters were free, but free to starve. Plantations had been ruined, capital was lacking, many of the old planter families were, like their estates, ruined also, while many of the freed slaves were in no position to make enough to keep their families. For those too young or too old to work, death by starvation seemed the probable future. Mr Butler's 'people' expected him to provide for them, and that they were still his responsibility was a view that he shared with them. He promised to support the children and the aged for three years until their own families could do so. As Fan explained, 'Fortunately as we have some property at the north, we are able to do this, but most of the planters are utterly ruined and have no money to buy food for their own families, so on their plantations I do not see what else is to become of the Negroes who cannot work except to die.' So it was natural that Fan should report with some pride that whereas other plantations could not get hands her father had as many as he wanted and 'nothing could induce our people to go elsewhere'.

There was another, less rosy, side to the picture. In the past the master had produced his crop with the aid of a discipline enforced by the lash. Now that that was no longer possible it was an appallingly uphill task to get the freed slaves to do steady and regular work. The Butlers tried to organize their erstwhile slaves as sharecroppers who, in return for the means of cultivation and provisions until the crop was ready, provided the labour, while both parties shared the crop. Fanny, who in spite of her deep concern that the slaves should be freed, took a realistic view of their limitations. She thought that, though by a mixture of scolding and coaxing her daughter might get the necessary work out of them when she was on the spot, once she and Pierce had gone north the crop would be neglected which, particularly in the case of rice, which needed constant cultivation, would be disastrous. This is exactly what happened. It was all but impossible to make the ex-slaves realize that as sharecroppers they too would suffer by this neglect. Fanny indeed thought that 'she, being there, has not helped to make them realize their new position as labourers, but has simply tended to prolong the dependent feeling of the old relation without the possibility of bringing back the former relations between the Negroes and their employers'. For two years Pierce and Fan struggled on, spending the winter months in Georgia and returning north in the summer.

In the July of 1867 Fan came back to the north. For years her father does not appear to have been a strong man, and in the following month he was taken ill, and died. It is clear that Fan grieved bitterly at her father's death and characteristically refused to give up the struggle and abandon something so dear to his heart. In the October of 1867, accompanied by her brother-in-law, Owen Wister, she went back with the intention of carrying on, though now alone. Obviously she found great comfort in what she described as 'their love for and belief in my father' which she found 'beyond all expression, and made me love them more than I can say. They never spoke of him without some touching and affectionate expression that comforted me far more than words uttered by educated lips could have done.' It would be interesting to know how Fanny reacted to her ex-husband's death when with her children.

Affection for their dead 'massa' Fan was to find did little to convert her loyal but unreliable black dependants into a disciplined force and though each winter she returned to Georgia it was both a lonely and a frustrating life for a woman in her early thirties. Pierce's death brought changes to Fanny's life also. With their father's death Butler Place passed to Sarah and Fan and, as Sarah was already living in Philadelphia with her husband and son, Fan decided to move into Butler Place which henceforth she intended to be her home in the north. After her return from the plantation in the late spring she was busy getting the house in order, and later Fanny joined her. The Perch was disposed of; after the death of Charles, Elizabeth and Catherine Maria Sedgwick, though Fan would always love Lenox and its hills and the many friends she still had there, she was the more prepared to let it go. The wheel had turned full circle; by the August of 1868 Fanny was back in Butler Place. When she wrote to Harriet on 30 August 1868 she told her 'Your letter reached me at this place, the home of my very sad married life, and I am writing to you now in the room where my children were born – in *my room* as it is now called. It is full twenty-six years since I last inhabited it.'

Three years later the pattern of Fanny's life was disrupted once again, this time by Fan's marriage. While she had been staying in New York in the November of 1869 she had met a young English clergyman, the Honourable James Leigh, who had taken time off from his clerical duties to tour America. Clearly Fan must have made an impression on him. In the course of his travels, accompanied by Sir Michael Hicks Beach and a couple of other friends, James Leigh contrived to include a visit to Butler Island before he returned to England in the next year. In the following spring, when Fanny and Fan were once again in England, Fan got to know his people, staying first at Stoneleigh Abbey and then with James Leigh's sister. It was there that he asked her to marry him and was accepted. The marriage however had to be delayed until she had made arrangements to appoint a suitable overseer and leave the management of the plantation in good hands; this meant returning to America. Then in the spring of 1871 Fan, her mother and her sister came back to England for the wedding; in June she became the Honourable Mrs James Leigh. It was a fashionable wedding; Fanny paid a guinea a metre for the three yards of Brussels lace that formed the sleeves and bodice of the dress she wore. The ceremony took place at St Thomas's, Portman Square. James's brother-in-law took the service and his great friend, the composer Arthur Sullivan, played the organ. It was a marriage that had Fanny's whole-hearted approval, both on personal and on social grounds. It must have been a great satisfaction to see her daughter allied to so old and con-siderable a family as the Leighs of Stoneleigh, and of her new son-in-law she was exceedingly fond. As she told Harriet, 'He has admirable common sense, excellent moral sense, great liberality of thought and sensibility of feeling and true sympathy with the poor and hardworking folk of this country,' adding that 'nobody endures hardship and priva-tion with such sweet tempered equanimity, but I hardly know anyone who has a keener relish for all the luxuries of the highest civilization – the civilization of Stoneleigh for instance.' There could hardly have been a combination more likely to endear him to his new mother-in-law. His friends called him Jumbo.

For a couple of years after their marriage the young couple – James was two years younger than his bride – stayed in Europe. A legacy that had come to the Owen Wisters had made this protracted stay possible and the whole family took the opportunity to stay with Adelaide and Edward in Rome. It was a visit which eventually brought Fanny the happiness of a new friendship that was to brighten the latter years of her life. Sarah, whom Fanny, after her return to America, had described to Harriet as 'so handsome and so clever', was now a magnificent, tawny-haired woman approaching forty, who made her mark on the brilliant, cosmopolitan company that gravitated to Rome where her Aunt Adelaide was a notable hostess. One of the people to be attracted by her was the young American novelist Henry James, with whom Sarah indulged in a flirtation that just escaped being labelled 'indis-creet'. It was there that he first met 'the terrific Kemble', Fanny herself, a passing acquaintance which later was to ripen into a warm and under-standing friendship. By the end of 1873 Fanny, her daughters and her sons-in-law returned to America. Dr Owen Wister had to go back to his practice and young Owen to St Paul's School in Concord after a two-year break in Europe. Fan was anxious to get back to the planta-tion where she hoped that with the help of her husband its management could be put on a sound foundation. In addition James Leigh, who had preached to the Negroes there and in Darien on his previous visit, hoped to be able to combine his Christian ministry with the pleasures of

a sportsman, riding, fishing and shooting. Fanny could not bear to be
once again separated from her children, in spite of an apprehension
that this time her exile might be permanent. Edward Fitzgerald did not
agree, telling her 'Oh, no! you will come back in spite of yourself,
depend upon it'. After a last visit to Harriet, a visit which both
friends must have realized might indeed be the last, the whole party
sailed on the *Celtic* which, despite Fanny's fears, did not go to the
bottom.

Fanny did not however return to her old quarters in Butler Place.
Fan and her husband departed for the south and it was decided that
Sarah and her family should take over Butler Place, now no longer
cut off from Philadelphia by the appalling roads of Fanny's early
married days. In order to accommodate Fanny, and provide a *pied à
terre* for Fan and James when they came north, it was further decided
to enlarge and modernize the farmer's house, York Farm, which was
separated from Butler Place only by the road. As this would take some
time Fanny rented a house in Rittenhouse square in Philadelphia,
where, with her devoted maid Ellen, who had accompanied her mistress
from England, Fanny led a somewhat dull life until her new home
could be got ready for her. Originally York Farm had been a characteristic small Pennsylvanian farmhouse, with four small rooms on
each floor built round a central chimney. When a new kitchen and a
bathroom had been added, Fanny declared it to be a 'very pleasant and
commodious dwelling in spite of the fact that the rooms were low and
small, as were the windows', though she hoped that the thickness of the
walls would moderate winter cold and summer heat. Fanny, as ever,
found the climate trying; in summer the heat was oppressive while in
winter the roads were so icy or so full of slush and snow that sometimes
she found it impossible even to walk over to Butler Place. Once she
told Harriet that 'my enduring this climate is a proof of my affection
for my children'. Her health was no longer good. In the April of 1874
she was complaining of sciatic rheumatism that had attacked her left
leg and extended down to her foot. This pain she told Harriet was not
'quite intolerable but quite bad enough to be very disagreeable'. Even
in the hot August weather she was still suffering this kind of discomfort
day and night. Sadly she wrote bemoaning the fact that she was
growing 'very old and very fat'. Possibly a modern doctor would have
prescribed dieting as a remedy for those aches and pains. She must have
been depressed indeed to add 'all the senses and the little sense I ever

had' was diminishing daily. Next year she confessed to being very deaf. In the spring of 1876, though she had to admit that her health was fairly good, she confessed that 'the thing I suffer most from is depression, languor, and debility, which I attribute partly to the climate and still more to anno domini.' Though she was only sixty-seven Fanny regarded herself as an old lady which, as Victorian reckoning went, she was perfectly entitled to do. She, who had once been so energetic, now found that 'a moderate stroll of between two and three miles once or twice a week, is pretty much all that I am good for, and after that I am glad to be on a sofa and rest'. Indeed she even confessed that she found such exertion so exhausting that she hardly felt up to the effort of spending the evening with Sarah and her family in spite of the short distance that separated their houses. It is difficult to know just what interest Fanny had ever had in her appearance; by 1875 apparently she had none. Faced with the summer heat she decided to get her hair cut short, telling Harriet that 'my hair is now short, a grizzled crop all round my head, and very dreadful indeed I look in that condition; but the relief is immense'. Harriet was horrified and in subsequent letters Fanny was able to reassure her friend that the hair had now grown sufficiently to be tied up with a ribbon and no longer looked quite so unattractive.

The cost of living in America was one of Fanny's constant preoccupations in retirement, as it had been when she was still earning money. Then she had complained bitterly that 'an income of seventeen hundred a year should be rendered, by the inordinate cost of living in this country, a very narrow one, not sufficient for me to live with a couple of servants in two rooms in a boarding house in Philadelphia'. She had some justification for so complaining. In England seventeen hundred pounds would have been considered a very comfortable income indeed. With less money coming in Fanny found it difficult to live in the 'decent comfort' which she considered indispensable. In respect of servants she was fortunate. She had her maid Ellen, whom she described as 'a very dear and devoted servant', confessing that all the comfort of her daily life depended on her. Ellen was obviously very competent as well as devoted, and the mainstay of Fanny's establishment, which included her manservant, Macfarland, and a little cook who had also come with her from England. These imported servants were the envy of all her American friends. Sarah in particular seems to have lived through a series of domestic crises; owing to its unpopularity with the native-born Americans domestic service attracted neither the able nor the hardworking and on occasions Sarah found herself almost without help. In addition to the servants which she brought with her Fanny also employed a gardener. She had therefore a staff of four. When she reviewed her financial position at the beginning of 1875 she found that she had spent £400 more in the previous year than she had spent running her own establishment in England with the same number of indoor servants, though admittedly without a gardener, travelling on the Continent for three months and indulging in a new Parisian outfit. Now she had found it difficult even to buy a piano for York Farm, though the fact that in 1874 Fanny had squandered a couple of hundred guineas in having portraits of Sarah and Fan painted had something to do with her inability to buy a piano immediately. It was with understandable relief therefore that she received a letter from the editor of the *Atlantic Monthly Magazine* offering her liberal terms for a series of articles based on her reminiscences. The necessary material was already at hand. Fanny had found life at Rittenhouse Square dull, for once again her hopes of finding congenial society in Philadelphia had disappointed her. The days often seemed long and Fanny would have welcomed evening calls from her friends, but American social habits were against this practice. As she explained to Harriet, the men worked so hard that 'they preferred sitting at home in their slippers and smoking' – a practice not confined to the nineteenth-century American male. On the other hand Fanny found that if friends were given a definite invitation they expected a hot supper, with oysters and champagne. This put up the housekeeping bills of which Fanny was so conscious. So invitations were not issued and her evenings were lonely. A creature of almost excessively regular habits, she dined at six, usually having changed into a black velvet dinner-dress. She then played patience for about an hour until the tea came in. The last ceremony of the day completed, Fanny took up her knitting, which included a shawl for her great friend Mary Fox of Champlost, whose kindness in sending Fanny gifts of fruit and flowers and in taking her for frequent drives did so much to relieve the tedium of her days in Philadelphia, and a coverlet for Fan's expected baby. At ten she retired to bed where she read for perhaps another hour. At York Farm, when she had finally acquired a piano, she would play by memory in the firelight, except on Sundays. Then, out of respect for other people's feelings she refrained, characteristically ending her week's music on

Saturday night by a rendering of *God Save the Queen*. In spite of the years she passed in America and her deep affection for that country Fanny never forgot that she was British.

It was the monotony of her life that first prompted her to start writing her reminiscences. She had abundant raw material at hand if her memory needed refreshing. Harriet, in failing health and almost blind, conscious too that she was Fanny's senior by twelve years, had returned to her the mass of letters which Fanny had written to her over the years in order to avoid either the risk of their falling into other hands on her death or the need to destroy them. To write her memoirs, Fanny told her friend, was 'an occupation which amuses me, but which I can put aside, of course, very frequently for other things, as I can always resume it at any time, and am not bound ever to finish'. When Harriet suggested that the depression from which Fanny was suffering was due to the reawakening of old, unhappy memories, she disagreed, explaining that she had already destroyed any letters that might distress her and that she was now finding both amusement and entertainment in this exercise of looking back. With an offer from the *Atlantic Monthly Magazine* she had now a financial incentive to persevere, though this meant much tedious copying because her original reminiscences had been written for her own pleasure; now they would have to be pruned of anything unsuitable for publication. At first she employed a bankrupt grocer to make a fair copy, but in the October of 1875 her son-in-law presented her with an early typewriter. At first Fanny was somewhat dubious about this machine, but later wrote with enthusiasm about it, describing it as 'the most delightful creature' and saying that she used it for copying all the articles that she sent to the *Atlantic Monthly Magazine* where, under the title of 'Old Woman's Gossip', they proved a popular feature.

In spite of the uneventful life that she was now leading, in spite of a climate that she hated and her worries about money, during these years of her retirement Fanny had one abiding joy: the company of her children and grandchildren. Sarah was so close at hand that Fanny, from York Farm across the dividing road, could almost look into her daughter's windows. Fan and James she saw less frequently, because of their winter absence on the plantation, but when they came north their home was with her. Indeed Fanny's first granddaughter was born during a violent thunderstorm in the July of 1874 at York Farm. Her father, who had undertaken some clerical duties at the small Anglican church nearby, took the christening service on 16 August, and the baby was given the names of Alice Dudley. For Fanny the christening was a day of mixed feelings, 'recalling with acute vividness memories of former days and rendering the church service of my little grand-daughter's christening full of conflicting emotions; recollections of past sorrows, combined with heartfelt thankfulness for all my present blessings'. Such feelings were not infrequent when Fanny found herself in Butler Place. When Sarah had first moved in it seemed very strange to be helping her daughter arrange the furniture 'in *my* old drawing-room, in *my* old home; and as I find myself thus once again all but inhabiting this my former "house of woe" I am occasionally seized with a bewildering sense of surprise, and overwhelmed with a sudden flow of reminiscences and associations, feel almost inclined to doubt my own identity.' It must also have come as something of a shock when memory brought back to her the picture of the two small children, first as babes in arms, then as toddlers, who had inhabited it with her in those far-off days, and then to look at Sarah, now a bustling matron of nearly forty, while she had been forced to tell a friend who had inquired after her younger daughter that 'The lady you call "dear little Fan" is no more. She is represented by a portly, personable body, little inferior to me in size and weight (Fanny now weighed fourteen stone) and with a comely double chin, which I have somehow or other avoided among my many signs of elderliness.'

Fanny had turned into a devoted grandmother, indeed where her grandson Owen was concerned, she might almost be described as doting. There was as yet little to suggest the budding novelist in the description which she sent to Harriet. 'His most decided tendency is to scientific objects and mechanics; all great works of engineering enterprise, all good and fine machinery and its results; his most remarkable gift is a real talent for music, which seems to me to approach to original genius. This is an unusual combination of unusual capacities, and cannot fail, I think, to make him a remarkable person in his day; he is at present, of course, a very chaotic *bundle of beginnings* but the natural endowments are full of promise – a promise profoundly inter-esting to me, though I can only look to his earliest entrance into man-hood, if even that.' Here his grandmother was unduly pessimistic; death was very far as yet from carrying her off. When he was away Fanny missed him. As she once confessed to Harriet, 'We are all rather depressed by the approaching departure of our boy for school. He

makes a wonderful light and warmth in our rather sad coloured existence and I think with dismay how terribly his poor mother will miss
him.' Fanny may have been feeling that her existence was somewhat
drab but there is little to suggest that this applied to Sarah, who in the
summer of 1875 was extremely busy organizing hospitality for the
forthcoming Centenary Exhibition to be held in Philadelphia to mark
the first hundred years of American independence. Perhaps however
young Owen agreed with Fanny in thinking his grandmother found
life monotonous because once, to her puzzlement, he told her that she
was like Mariana in the moated grange! Baby Alice was too young to
have any such fanciful notions but Fanny worried over her because she
considered that she looked delicate and was too slow in learning to
walk and talk. Her parents did not share this anxiety, repeatedly
reassuring her anxious grandmother that the child was perfectly healthy
in spite of her frail, delicate appearance. From Fanny's own description
Alice seems to have been an engaging infant, telling Harriet of her
'great spirit and vivacity, her quick, bright intelligence and sweet
temper', adding 'she never cries or frets and in spite of her sentimental
dark grey eyes and white skin' her grandmother thought her 'a
decidedly jolly baby'. Fan and James told Fanny that the Negroes on
the plantation idolized her and 'in spite of their newly obtained freedom
perpetuate on her the title of "Little missis" and are all her very devoted
slaves'. This too must have brought back memories of the way in
which Pierce's slaves had rushed to do Sarah's bidding, celebrating her
in one of their ad lib chants as

> Little missis Sally,
> That's a ruling lady.

Nevertheless, in spite of Fanny's telling Harriet in the October of
1875 'You cannot imagine how full of thankfulness to God I am at being
thus surrounded with my children', her letters to Harriet are filled with
trivia which suggest that she had very little about which to write. In
one, inspired by her inveterate hatred of the Philadelphian climate, she
gave her an account of the burden that this imposed on the housewife.
At the end of the winter she explained 'Every carpet had been taken
up, and every curtain taken down, and together with every woollen
table cover, rug, blanket, fur or similar object of furniture or apparel,
packed in rolls with pepper and camphor, in receptacles lined with
cedar wood.' This was because of the influx of moths and other summer

insects. For the same reason matting replaced carpets on the floor, and plain white muslin curtains the heavier fabric of winter. How different all this must have seemed from the country cottage of her girlhood at Weybridge; ice and snow and mud in winter, heat and flies in summer, and everywhere the parched brown grass instead of the lush meadows and velvet smooth lawns of England. Once she and Mary Fox tried to find fresher, cooler air by departing for the seaside, but so uncomfortable did these two fastidious ladies find boarding-house life that after two days they retreated to their own homes once again. Apart from Mary Fox, Fanny had few close friends in the neighbourhood, which to some extent explains the moods of depression from which at times she suffered. It was unfortunate that fate should once again have dictated that she must live so near Philadelphia, which she had never liked. Had she lived nearer to Boston she would have found congenial friends, intellectual interests, and a countryside with which she found some affinity. Generally during these last years of her sojourn in America Fanny managed to visit her beloved Berkshire, though the older generation of Sedgwicks were now dead, and to see her friends in Cambridge and Boston. Yet by now she, who had once travelled so regularly and so extensively on her money-making tours, found even the six-hour train journey something of an ordeal. Lenox was full of memories. When there she stayed at the inn kept now by the man who as a youth had rowed her on the lake when she went fishing, and there were still the younger members of the Sedgwick clan to give her a warm welcome. A visit to Boston was in some ways even more rewarding. Fanny told Harriet that it had been 'a most delightful visit, meeting again all my kind old friends and acquaintances'. They were a distinguished group, including the historians Prescott and Motley, Felton, the Professor of Greek, and a host of literary figures, Emerson, Oliver Wendell Holmes, Lowell and Longfellow, a friend by then of many years' standing. Much though she enjoyed this varied and stimulating company Fanny confessed to finding the pace of her Boston social life exhausting. The wheel of life here too was coming full circle; once it had been London society that had exhausted her after the isolation of Butler Place; now it was Boston.

In spite of Fanny's mournful pronouncement to Edward FitzGerald when she had sailed for America in 1873 that she never expected to come back to her native country, she does not seem to have contemplated her stay as being for more than a couple of years. Certainly her hope was that Fan and her husband would return sometime during 1875, in which case she would accompany them. When therefore James returned to England alone, leaving Fan and baby Alice at York Farm, Fanny realized with dismay that her time in the United States would be prolonged for at least another year. This delay was a matter of some concern to Fanny in that it threatened the smooth running of her household. Her maid Ellen had already been engaged to be married when she had agreed to come to America with Fanny on the understanding that her exile should last only two years. Now Fanny did not know what to do. She dreaded the idea of running York Farm without her capable help, yet was reluctant to put any pressure on Ellen that might cause her personal unhappiness and perhaps lead to her engagement being broken. Would it be fair to ask her to stay a little longer in the hope that the Leighs' departure might not be too long delayed? Fanny had another and more heartbreaking reason for wanting to get back to England as soon as possible. Harriet's health was failing, and Fanny was increasingly fearful lest she should not return in time to see her very dear friend alive. Now there was no hope of returning until at least 1876, and even that seemed uncertain, as Fan declared that she and James had always intended to give the experiment to get the plantations in good working order at least three winters. When Fanny had returned to Butler Place after her visit to Boston she discovered that Sarah had gone to visit her sister, leaving her husband, whom Fanny described as 'very forlorn', behind. At least he provided company for Fanny in the evenings as he always dined with her. As she told Harriet, her younger daughter 'was southern in all her views and sentiments' and Fanny realized that the pull of the south might make her and James delay their return to his native country once again. When Sarah returned she confirmed what to her mother must have been fears that both Fan and James found their life in Georgia pleasant and congenial. Indeed Sarah told her mother that in her opinion Fan was happier, better, more usefully employed and more content on the plantation than she could ever be elsewhere, and that the life they led there was equally congenial to her husband,

who finds duties enough everywhere to devote himself to, for the satisfaction of his conscience and his heart and who is actively interested in and eminently successful in the management of the estate, and to whom the freedom and ease of the life, the wild picturesqueness of the place, the fishing, the boating, the hunting are all elements of enjoyment, and that there is much in his apparent satisfaction in his existence there as well as his wife's passionate preference for the place [to account for their long stay].

For Fanny this was disquieting news. Her memories of Georgia were bitter, in spite of the beauty that had delighted her there; its influence on her life had been disastrous. Now, once again, the spell that it exercised over Pierce's daughter threatened to frustrate her own plans for returning to England.

The task of rehabilitating the Butler estates, dedicated though Fan and her husband were, was uphill and sometimes heartbreaking. In her letters to Harriet Fanny described their struggle to recreate on a basis of freedom what had been built on one of slavery. After four months herself in close contact with the Negroes Fanny was in a position to know how difficult this would be; they had been too long without any responsibility for their own lives to regard self-discipline as a virtue. In consequence the Leighs found it a major problem to secure a steady supply of labour, a requisite in the cultivation of rice, hitherto the most profitable of the estate crops. As Fanny explained,

The Negroes are gradually leaving the estates, buying morsels of land for themselves, where they knock up miserable shanties, and do a day's work, or a job here and there and now and then, but entirely decline the settled working by contract for the whole agricultural season which they have accepted for the last year or two since the war.

One of Fan's neighbours, in desperation, had even resorted to importing Chinese labour. The Leighs themselves had brought eight agricultural labourers out from England, an enterprise which was at least partly philanthropic in that James Leigh, during his stay in England, had in 1872 played a mediating part in the struggle of the farm workers to get better wages. The experiment had not been altogether successful. Two of the men returned home, two, more cooperative, had agreed to stay in the south and work at lumbering when the Leighs went north in the summer, and the remaining four had insisted on accompanying them. This involved the Leighs first in paying their fares and secondly in either maintaining them or finding them employment until it was time to return south. In addition to importing labour, in the struggle to increase the profitability of the estate the Leighs experimented with diversifying their crops, deciding to grow oranges on a commercial scale. In the spring of 1875 Fan had written hopefully to her mother 'I think that lovely and delicious fruit will come to be an important item in the return of the plantation.' In other ways things were not going so well. Parts of the plantation had been inundated with some danger to the domestic livestock, though apparently without damage to the crops. In addition the Savannah agent, who handled the rice crop, failed and the Leighs were uncertain how much loss this would entail. In any case the profits from rice were diminishing as many of the New Orleans and Louisiana planters were switching over to that crop. Whatever the problems connected with the running of the Georgian estates clearly both Fan and her husband were content with their way of life and it was fortunate for Fanny that James Leigh felt that he had obligations to his own country and to his cloth. Though during his time in Georgia he took his clerical duties seriously the scope that the black community offered to him was limited and in 1876 he was given the opportunity to return to England. Dr Collis, who had been head of the school at Bromsgrove when young James Leigh had been a curate, had now become vicar of Stratford-on-Avon, and invited James to take charge of the district church of St James there. As a result, to Fanny's great pleasure, she was able to tell Harriet that the Leighs were now talking of returning to England in the January of 1877.

In June Fanny started on a round of what she realized were her last visits. She was now sixty-eight and unlikely to cross the Atlantic from England again. First, as had been her custom, she went to Lenox, where she stayed at the Curtis Hotel, and from there took a nostalgic pilgrimage to her old haunts. These included the Perch, now in other hands. Fanny noted how the trees had grown, and all the changes made since first it had been her refuge in 1849. From Lenox she went to Boston for more last farewells. Now that she knew she would never return she made a pilgrimage to her long dead Aunt Dall's grave at Mount Auburn; where before she had come for comfort as her marriage was disintegrating, now she came to say goodbye. The place that she had chosen had been a little grove where during the days of their courtship she and Pierce had sat in remote seclusion. Now Fanny found the grave with difficulty in 'a marble wilderness of tombstones' instead of the solitude that had once reigned. Careful though Fanny always was to print nothing too intimate in her autobiography, her letter to Harriet, written after this visit to her aunt's grave, hints at the wave of memories that swept over her, memories not only of Dall but of the happy days when she and Pierce had been so much in love. It is one of the few mentions that in her published letters contains no hint of bitterness when she wrote of him. Nostalgia for the past did not preclude fear for the future, the fear that she was leaving one grave only to find another. Harriet, old and blind and now forced to dictate her letters, told her how she dreaded the alteration that Fanny would find in her when they met again. Just before Fanny left Butler Place for the last time she wrote on 13 January,

My dearest friend, I trust soon to see you again. I *know* that you will never be altered to me, and that I shall see you the same as I have known you from the first. Those we have loved *never alter* unless we cease to love them, and I am ever as ever your Fanny Kemble, as you will ever be to the last, ever as ever, my Harriet St Leger.

There were no more letters until March, a clear indication that Fanny must have hurried to Ireland to see her friend as soon as possible after landing in January.

Back in London it is not easy to follow her movements as the letters contained in her *Further Records* are either out of order or undated, but in order to provide some kind of headquarters both for herself and for Fan and Alice, until they could get settled in Stratford-on-Avon, Fanny rented a house in Connaught Square for a year. She found setting up house again in London a troublesome business, and that the capital had changed, not for the better. Ellen was now living in Italy with her husband, but her manservant Macfarland was still with her. Apart from him she had to engage a new domestic staff and was soon reporting ruefully that far from interviewing applications she felt that it was she who was being interviewed on her suitability as a mistress, adding 'I hear nothing but universal complaints of the insolence and want of principle of servants in the present day.' Indeed she felt that 'America is coming over here with a vengeance.' As summer approached Fanny made her annual visit to Switzerland. Her son-in-law remarked that she always departed on 1 June and returned on 1 September, but the dating of her letters from Switzerland, though far from reliable, indicate rather more elasticity in practice. Her first Christmas in England she spent with Fan and her family in their new home, the old manor house at Alverstan, which was convenient for James's parish. It was a charming house and both Fan and her mother were enchanted with it. (It is now a hotel, and one wonders if any among its guests remembers that Fanny Kemble once spent a Christmas there.) Already the Leighs' tenancy was likely to be brief as on the death of the Vicar of Leamington James was offered that living. As this would give him greater opportunities for pastoral work, he accepted. Fan loved her new home and was loath to leave it, so for a time her husband travelled between Stratford and his new parish.

Alverstan Manor provided a wonderful setting for a traditional family Christmas. There was a tree for little Alice, with presents and tiny packets of sweets which Fanny helped to put up. It was a merry, happy household, which included the novelist Henry James, then on a visit to England. The friendship which had developed between him and Sarah Wister when they had met in Rome had continued, and he had visited her at Butler Place. When he had first met Fanny he had found her formidable, but by the Christmas of 1877 the acquaintance was ripening into friendship; in his letters home she had become 'his sublime Fanny', and a very charming relationship developed between the rising young novelist and the old lady. In the latter years of her life this was to mean a great deal to her, after first Harriet and then her beloved sister Adelaide died. On both occasions Fanny was abroad. In the summer of 1878 she went as usual to Switzerland, whence she sent a stream of undated letters describing her travels to Harriet.

When she set out she was accompanied by her manservant Macfarland, and it must have seemed like old times when Fanny was able to arrange for Ellen to stay with them for a week at Stresa. Fanny considered that this would be less embarrassing for her old maid than for her to attempt to put them up in her own simple home. By now there was a baby, and it gave Fanny considerable satisfaction when it was agreed that he should be christened in accordance with the rites of the Protestant faith, Ellen's old fellow-servant acting as godfather.

In Switzerland Fanny was joined by her nephew Henry Kemble. How closely she had kept in personal touch with 'Harry's boy' after she had made herself responsible for his upbringing is one of those grey areas of uncertainty that are so tantalizing, but after her return to England in 1877 she saw a good deal of him. Physically he was very like her, short and solid in build and with a tendency to stoutness, though, born in 1848, he was still a young man. Showing more acting ability than his father, he had followed the family tradition and gone on the stage. Without achieving the stardom of the rest of the family, he was a sound actor of character parts and a good comedian. Like Fanny he too had a pronounced sense of the ridiculous. Ellen Terry described in her memoirs one incident when he was a member of the company with which she was touring the provinces in 1880. They were playing at Buxton and one evening, when Henry and his friend Charles

Brookfield were not in the current production, the two of them hired bath chairs and had themselves, along with other privileged invalids taking the waters, wheeled up the central aisle, pretending to be paralytic. Ellen Terry, suddenly, in the middle of a most pathetic scene, catching sight of them, dried up speechless with helpless amusement.

Fanny was fond of Henry, describing him as a good and affectionate nephew. Her other nephew, Adelaide's son Greville, who had married one of President Grant's daughters, had been killed in a riding accident in 1873, before her return to England, but her daughter May, now Mrs Gordon, was another of the younger generation of whom the elderly Fanny was very fond. One of her letters to Henry James contains a charming description of the Christmas that she spent with them while he was in America staying with the Wisters.

Yet, pleasant as it was to have Henry's company with her on her travels, Fanny was conscious that the shadow of death was hanging over her. Clearly Harriet was sinking fast; her friend and constant attendant told Fanny that the invalid was now too weak even to attempt to dictate a few lines to her friend. Then came what seemed like a reprieve. When Fanny was at Menton on her way home she received another letter in which Harriet had managed a message. The depth of Fanny's thankfulness is revealed in her reply, in which she wrote 'I cannot tell you how dark a curtain seemed to have fallen as last between me and my beloved Harriet, or how great the relief has been to see it once more lifted', going on, 'there seem some losses for which no length of preparation seems to avail, in spite of prolonged anticipation. Thank God for those words of *hers*, which I thought were never to reach me any more.' They were the last she was to receive; Harriet died before Fanny reached England. An even greater and less expected blow fell when Fanny was in Switzerland in 1879. This was the death of her sister Adelaide. Earlier in the year she had been sufficiently ill to make Fanny anxious but when she had gone down to Hampshire to stay with them before leaving for Switzerland, Adelaide had appeared so much better that it seemed safe to go. Then on 4 August Adelaide died. When the news reached Fanny she found it almost impossible to realize that, this side of the grave, she would never see her beloved sister again. For years they had been very close. Now of the older generation Fanny was the only Kemble left.

She was still active and energetic and was busy with her writing. The English publisher Richard Bentley had suggested that she should turn her autobiographical articles into a volume of reminiscences and the first fruits of enterprise, entitled *Records of a Girlhood*, was published in 1878. It had an immediate success. It is, in many ways, the most interesting of her books. Though the account of her childhood is based only on recollections, filtered through the haze of years, once the letters to Harriet commence these provide an authentic picture of Fanny as she thought and reacted up to her departure for America. Because in these early years Fanny had little to conceal they contain much fuller and less discreetly edited material than her subsequent volumes. Their success was sufficient to induce Bentley to press for further instalments, which were subsequently published under the title of *Records of a Later Life*. Now in her seventy-third year, Fanny often found the drudgery tedious; early in 1882 she told Henry James, now a close and intimate friend, that it was 'coming through the Press like glue'. This was partly because through kind-heartedness she was employing a poor clergyman's daughter to do the necessary copying and it took the poor woman an hour to do a folio page, 'writing with the point of her nose so close to her pen that I cannot tell the one from the other'. While on the topic of noses Fanny then proceeded to deliver a few sarcastic comments on the fact that Mrs Langtry, the reigning beauty queen, was paid £80 a week for what Fanny called 'the shape of her nose'. Plainly she did not consider that it was due to her prowess as an actress.

Fanny was not however altogether happy about her own literary activities. With her instinctive reserve she felt that to publish her own reminiscences was an indecency and she told Henry James that 'few people can think less agreeably of that proceeding than I do myself'. Her justification, she explained, was that as they were bound to be published sometime – here the old Kemble family pride peeps out – by undertaking the task herself she could make sure that 'only such portions as I thought would give less pains and offence to everyone' would be printed, while confessing 'this proceeding is one that for all that nauseated me a little – I do not speak of it.' This did not prevent Fanny from bringing out two volumes of *Further Records* in 1890. By then Fanny's memory, or her interest, or both, were failing. These last volumes are badly put together, many of the letters dealing with the period after 1874 being haphazardly arranged and often undated, particularly those that deal with her return to England and her travels in Switzerland up to Harriet's death. In order to pad them out to the requisite length Fanny added some earlier letters that she had written to Arthur Malkin, so that the final volume is disjointed and the train of events not easy to follow. It is a little ironic that Fanny should have achieved the literary reputation that she had so craved as a girl by writing in her seventies a series of volumes of which she only half approved. Her success did however have repercussions which must have given her more genuine satisfaction. In 1883 Bentley published both her critical *Notes on some of Shakespeare's Plays* and a revised edition of her poems, including some from the earlier volume of unhappy memories. Undeterred by growing age, an ageing that was physical rather than mental, Fanny continued to experiment with new literary forms. As a girl and as a young woman she had aspired to write tragedy. Now, in her old age, she turned to comedy, producing a lighthearted, satirical farce on the new type of tourist that was now flocking to Switzerland. *The Adventures of John Timothy Homespun in Switzerland* captures briefly in print that sense of fun and of the ridiculous that her friends found so engaging, and of which so little record necessarily remains. Her other venture, a novel, *Far Away and Long Ago*, was a more serious work. It was a sombre, moralistic tale set against the background of Fanny's favourite Berkshire Hills among a rural population still untouched by the modern world. Like its authoress it was something of a period piece. Even so, it is a testimony to Fanny's intellectual vigour. As Henry James pointed out, it is not many people who produce their first novel at the age of eighty.

Physically her energy was beginning to flag and each year, on her annual visit to Switzerland, she found that she could do less and less. This was a great deprivation to her. Years ago, writing about the Berkshires, she had told Harriet, 'I do believe mountains and hills are kindred of mine, larger and smaller relations, taller and shorter cousins, for my heart expands and rejoices and beats more freely among them.' One of her more endearing tricks was to express this exhilaration by bursting into song so that the Swiss guides, who had come to know her well, nicknamed her *'la dame qui va chantant par les montagnes'*. Fanny felt that Switzerland, like England, was not changing for the better. Past were the days when the English visitor could wander at will, without plans or reservations, always sure of a bed and a welcome. By the seventies tourists were discovering its delights and its beauties, which in earlier days had been the preserves of the well-born or the adventurous. When the St Moritz hotel-keeper asked how long she intended to stay, Fanny was furious. Commercialism was rapidly replacing the spontaneous hospitality of the past. Fanny was convinced that the hotelier in question was quite capable of letting her room over her head if it suited his purpose. No wonder she castigated the new tourist breed, American as well as English, in her farce. In 1878 Fanny was still fit enough not only to walk but even on occasion to scramble, as when she negotiated fifteen hundred feet of a dry torrent bed, climbing down from Axenstein to Brunnen, though she confessed to Harriet that she was forced to go on because to turn and try to get back the way she had come would have been even worse and that she was very glad to return to her hotel more comfortably in a carriage. She also in the same year achieved her ambition, which was to have been over all the great Swiss passes, by adding the Stelvio to her bag. At least now no niggling regret could assail her as each year her travels became more and more restricted to places easier of access, to lakes rather than to mountains. Increasingly all Fanny could do was to go 'from one charming *hill top* to another, always lifting mine eyes to the mountains in loving worship'. Only those who love mountains can know how much they meant to her. Even to be near them was some refreshment to her spirit, though most of her time was now spent looking at whatever beauty could be seen from her hotel balcony. In a letter which she wrote to Henry James in 1885 she reported that she had found comfortable quarters where the cooking was good and where from her covered balcony, on which she spent many hours, she had the spectacle of several waterfalls. In an article that he wrote after her death he described her as sitting on such balconies looking with wistful eyes at 'her paradise lost', until finally her travels were confined to the Italian lakes, staying at Orta and at Stresa near her devoted Ellen. At the age of eighty she made her last pilgrimage. When Fanny accepted the fact that her travels were over she presented her travelling-clock to Henry James, accompanied by the following touching verses:

> *When thy sweet voice shall tell my hours no more*
> *Asking with each what did'st thou with the last*
> *When spent or lost is all thy precious store*
> *And time is but a phantom of the past,*

> *Go count the days of him my faithful friend*
> *And make the hours thou measureth him be glad,*
> *With memory of the help he oft did lend*
> *To make the hours thou measureth me less sad.*

Bid him give heed unto thy silver chime
Nor scorn the gentle counsel of thy voice
So shall he safely to life's summit climb
And then look Heavenwards only to rejoice.

After the Christmas which they had spent together at Alverstan Manor, a very pleasant relationship had developed between the novelist and Fanny, a friendship which, particularly after the deaths of Harriet and Adelaide, helped to lessen some of the loneliness of her London days. Stimulation had always been the breath of life to her and, in spite of the time that she spent on her writing, Fanny found her days solitary and stagnant. She, who had once known everybody and gone every-where, now complained that 'I might be in the moon as well as Westminster for all I know of London gossip'. In particular she missed congenial neighbours; for a brilliant conversationalist life was dull when there was no one to provide an audience or throw back the verbal ball. When he was in London this was something that Henry James was most willing to do. For Fanny these years of her retirement may have dragged but to him, listening, they were 'years of anecdote and eloquence and commentary, and of a wonderful many-hued retrospective lucidity'. Indeed he felt that even if Fanny had been a less remarkable person

she would still have owed a distinction to the far away past to which she gave continuity . . . She had been in short a celebrity in the twenties, had attracted the town while the nineteenth century was almost as immature as herself. She had figured in the old London world, which lived again in her talk and, to a great degree in her habits and standards and tone. It was this background, embroidered with her theatrical past, so unassimilated but so vivid in her handsome hereditary head and unflagging drama of her manner, was helped by her agitated, unsettled life to make her what I call historic.

Fanny provided Henry James with perpetual interest and entertain-ment. Sometimes they went to the theatre together and when the play had been one of Shakespeare's, driving home in the brougham, Fanny, commenting on the interpretations they had just seen, would give her own with vivid gesture and voice until the character lived again. Of her love for Shakespeare he declared 'She was so saturated with Shakespeare that she had made him, as it were, the air she lived in.' If they went to a French comedy then the subsequent commentary would be in that language which he pronounced 'rose to her lips as quickly and as racily as English'. When he was on the continent or back in his native America he and Fanny wrote to one another. Often he either sent her books or recommended them and they exchanged criticisms. Having read Rhoda Broughton's latest novel she said that she did not think it as good as her earlier ones but that she had been enchanted with *Treasure Island*. At the moment she told him she was taking a course of Balzac. Fanny was a thorough reader; once she had started a book she invariably finished it and her taste, even in old age, was catholic. According to Henry James, the only source of information that she never read was the newspapers. A letter which she wrote to him in January 1882, when he was in America, bears witness to the almost playful affection with which she regarded her young friend. When suffering from a cold she told him, obviously in response to an inquiry as to whether she was missing him,

As for you, you are a Puppy! No, I am not languishing for you – or sick of your absence – unless a sore throat and obstructed bronchial tubes and a heavy drowning cold in the head are symptoms of sentimental sorrow. It is true I have my handkerchief oftener in my hand than I could wish it to be but it is to blow my nose and not wipe away regretful tears.

Afterwards, as if to soften her feigned indifference she added 'I beg you to believe that I am very sincerely attached to you and think of you almost as if you belonged to me.'

Another young man to be fascinated by Fanny in her old age was Nathaniel Beard, who, while working for her publisher, was a frequent caller at Queen Anne's Mansions, where she was living when he first met her in 1882. He described her as 'a rather stout and short lady of about seventy, clad in black silk, with a noble grey head, guiltless of any cap or ornament, finely set upon her shoulders, and a pair of the most gleaming and beautiful dark eyes I ever beheld'. Soon Fanny was calling him 'my dear child', sometimes starting her letters to him with 'My Dear Young Man, or Young Gentleman – which ever you like best.' She even tried to persuade him to come to Switzerland with her in order to remedy what she called his 'untravelled condition'. Once, when in the course of conversation he happened to say that both his parents had been particularly good-looking, glancing mischievously at his own plain features she remarked, with a humorous twinkle in her eye, 'My dear child, they ought to have done better by you!' Whereupon they both dissolved into laughter. Like Henry James he admired her immensely, declaring her to be 'the most remarkable woman living within the last two or three decades'. Like every one who knew her he found her conversation

positively dazzling in its quality. No ordinary mind could keep pace with it, and after an interview with her one came away amazed at the amount of her far-reaching knowledge, her acute wisdom and her fascinating humour. It was an education divested of all educational qualities but charm.

She certainly charmed Nathaniel Beard, but he held her in some awe. Fanny had never been good at suffering fools gladly; her likes and dislikes were equally strong. Beard's affection for her did not blind him to her 'uncompromising manner of displaying her dislike or indifference'. Even he came occasionally under her displeasure for making some unfortunate remark which earned him a sharp verbal rap, though, with her usual impulsive generosity, he would hardly be out of the room before she dashed after him, full of warm apologies for her hasty tongue. In spite of her shortcomings, to him to count Fanny as a friend 'was an honour of which the greatest might feel proud'. In many ways throughout the years of their friendship he tried to show his regard for her, never failing to bring her flowers on her birthday. On her eightieth birthday he brought her a print of Lawrence's portrait of her as young girl, which he had discovered and bought. Looking at it, she told him 'I had quite forgotten it; dear me! I was a pretty girl then-eheu!' When she autographed it, Beard thought he saw 'something suspiciously like tears in her eyes'. The last time he saw Fanny was on her eighty-third birthday, when both her eyes and her hearing were failing. Yet even then she could still make fun of her ear-trumpet with its rubber tubing which she was struggling to use. That was in the November of 1892, when her end was very near.

Much as Fanny enjoyed the company of her young friends, her emotional anchorage was still her family. Adelaide's death had left a gaping hole, but she still had her daughters and the younger generation, her nephew Henry, for whom she had done so much since his father's death, and Adelaide's daughter, her 'dear May Gordon', whose house was always open to her. Fan and James were at Leamington until 1883 when Mr Gladstone offered him the living of St Mary's, Bryanston Square. After that they too were in London except when they returned to Georgia to spend some time on the plantation. They were still living in Leamington when Fan's second child, a son, was born in the autumn of 1879 and Fanny spent some time with them after his birth.

Was it a sign of some strain between mother and daughter that Fan, twelve years after her father's death, had him christened Pierce Butler Leigh? Even so, Fanny must have grieved for Fan for her only son was a sickly infant and died in early childhood. Fanny never returned to America but in 1882 she had the great happiness of being able to be again with Sarah and her much loved grandson Owen. 'That bundle of beginnings', as his grandmother had once called him, had done well After graduating from Harvard *summa cum laude*, he decided, following his early bent, to study music at the Paris Conservatoire. This was in 1882 and to Fanny's delight Sarah came with him. After spending some time in England the trio went back to Paris. From there Fanny and Sarah made a trip to Tours where they were joined by Henry James, now deeply attached to both mother and daughter.

When Fanny had first returned to England in 1877 she was still sufficiently full of energy to lead a full and busy life. As well as old friends, both in England and in Scotland, enthusiastic supporters of reforming causes looked to her for support and sympathy. Francis Power Cobbe in particular hoped to enlist her aid in the anti-vivisection campaign. Occasionally she exerted herself to make new friends as when, at Henry James's request, she went to call on his sister, but generally she eschewed morning calls, preferring that people should come to see her. The pattern of her days was still an odd mixture of routine and change. Beard thought her 'whole life was a succession of impulses except where her daily routine was concerned' and nowhere was this unsettled quality better shown than in the way in which she kept up the family tradition of continually changing houses. 'The same held good with Fanny Kemble', he wrote, 'at any rate during the last ten years of her life. I first met her at Queen Anne's Mansions, then she would go abroad and return, or take up her abode at some hotel; then perhaps at another hotel, and even another, then take a house for a short time.' In 1881 she wrote to Henry James from Cavendish Square, in 1882 from Queen Anne's Mansions, in the January of 1883 she was living at 27 Grosvenor Street where she could remain for the next six weeks, after which she hoped to find a 'more permanent resting place'. This is something that she apparently did not achieve until she was no longer able to lead her old peripatetic life. Then at last she was forced to exchange a hotel balcony in Switzerland for a donkey chair in Bournemouth, sometimes varied by a drive out in a carriage, and to find a final home with Fan and James, now living at 86 Gloucester

Place. Here for the last years of her life she was joined by her old servant Ellen.

To the world Fanny continued to show a brave face. One of the younger friends with whom she had kept in touch, and whom Fanny had so embarrassed in the days when she drove with her across the Campagna singing at the top of her voice, Anne Thackeray Ritchie, writing after Fanny's death, said of her 'She grew to be old indeed, but it was only for a little while that she *was* an old woman', she still remained almost to the very last, 'stately, upright, ruddy and brown of complexion, mobile, expressive in features, reproachful, mocking, humorous, heroic, uplifted in turn.' This was no old woman but someone who could still feel the throb of life 'with an intensity far beyond that of younger people, splendid in expression, vehement and yet at times tender with a tenderness such as is very rare'. It was with both affection and admiration that she remembered Fanny, 'stitching in her armchair, dressed in her black silk Paris dress and lace cap she sits upright by the window, with flowers on the table beside her while her birds are pecking in their cage'. In the evenings she still played a few games of patience before retiring to bed. It was a quiet and ordered existence. One day she received a letter from the past, from her old friends Mr and Mrs Sam Ward, and in her reply she sketched the routine of her day, 'I go out every day in a wheel chair, see a few old and attached friends, read a little, and knit a little and have a dog to whom I am devoted. This is my history,' adding, 'I have much cause for gratitude.' One of the things for which she was grateful was her niece Alice, whom she described as 'an excellent nurse and amiable young girl'. Another was the presence of her dear Ellen.

Gradually she grew weaker; her eyesight failed, so that Ellen wrote many of her letters, and her hearing grew worse. To the end she showed a gallant courage. Nathaniel Beard, when he saw her on her eighty-third birthday, noticed that she never allowed herself to 'talk sadly', though he felt that during the last years she 'never felt other than sad'. Once, and only once, did he hear her allude to the sadness of her married life, and it was then but to reproach herself for her own shortcomings of temper and intolerance.

Fanny Kemble died on 13 January 1893. The end was peaceful and quick. As she was being put to bed she collapsed and died in the arms of her faithful Ellen. She was buried near her father's grave in Kensal Green Cemetery under a mound of the flowers she had so loved in life.

Fan was in America, but her niece Alice, her son-in-law James Leigh, Henry James and a few old friends stood at the graveside on that soft January morning. Fanny's long, turbulent life was over. She went in peace, leaving a world that had changed almost beyond recognition since that November day in 1809 when she had entered it. She left behind her a memory that eighty years later has become faint and blurred. Yet in the fullness of her experience perhaps she was the most human and the most worth remembering of all the Kembles. Henry James's pronouncement that 'there was no convenient or handy formula for Mrs Kemble's genius, and one had to take her career, the juxta-position of her interests, exactly as one took her disposition, for a remarkably fine cluster of inconsistencies', may well stand as her epitaph. To those of her family who remained, and to her friends, the world was the poorer for her passing.

Index

Abbott, William 42
Adventures of John Timothy Homespun (FK) 264
Alabama (ship) 241
Albert Edward, Prince of Wales 233–4
Aleck (slave) 134, 145, 155
Altamaha river, FK crosses 157
Anthony and Cleopatra 224
Appleton, Fanny (Mrs Henry Longfellow) 108, 159, 181, 187, 203, 224
Appleton, Mary (Mrs MacIntosh) 171, 179, 192
Astley's Amphitheatre 37
Atlantic Monthly Magazine 252, 253

Baltimore, Maryland 89, 99, 130
Bath: ladies school 14; Theatre 9, 35, 55, 207
Beard, Nathaniel 4, 267–8, 269, 270
Belvoir 46, 173
Bentley, Richard 262–3, 264
Berkeley, Lady 173
Bessborough, Lady 207
Birmingham 56
Blackwood's 200
Boston 202; memoir to FK published in 44; FK in 74, 91–2, 94, 100, 159, 180; FK gives reading at 235; final visits to 256, 259
Bournemouth 269
Bran (slave driver) 246
Brandon, Henry 11

Brenner, Fredrica 201
Bridgewater House 45, 60, 62, 174
Bristol 66–7, 208
Brookfield, Charles 261–2
Broughton, Rhoda 267
Brown, John (abolitionist) 232–3
Browne, Mrs, of Boston 81
Brunswick, Georgia 157
Burnham 197–8
Butler, Frances (aunt of Pierce) 97, 109, 123
Butler, Frances Anne (Fan, daughter of FK): birth 127, 158–9; childhood 176, 180–1, 184, 185–95, 218–21, 223–4, 228, 231, 254; character 228, 234; becomes twenty-one 231; in Georgia 237–8, 245–8, 249–50, 253, 257–9, 268, 271; Georgian Journal 245–7; in Europe 231–2, 240, 260, 269–70; marriage 248–9; children 253–4, 255, 257, 268–9
Butler, Gabrielle (wife of John) 108–9
Butler, John (brother of Pierce) 97, 108–9, 193, 245; and Georgian estates 120, 123, 143, 147, 164, 168
Butler, Major (grandfather of Pierce) 97, 133, 143
Butler, Pierce: meets FK 94, 97–8; family and personality 97–8; courtship 95, 97, 98–104, 105–8; marriage 104, 105–7, 108–23; collects FK from England 126–8;

273

Butler, Pierce—*contd.*
travels to Georgia 129–32; on Georgian estates 132–3, 135–6, 138–157, 164–8, 245–7; marriage breakdown 158–69, 170–95; in England 169–80; after separation 196–7, 199, 204, 231, 238; divorce proceedings 217–21; financial difficulties 175, 179–80, 221, 231; arrested 237; death 245, 247–8; FK's memories of 259; FK's letters to 106, 114, 115, 158, 160, Statement 110, 117, 153, 167, 183, 195, 199

Butler, Sarah (mother of Pierce) 97

Butler, Sarah (daughter of FK): birth 115, 117; childhood 126, 128, 129–130, 164–5, 176, 180–1; on parents' break-up 184, 185–95, 218–21, 223–4, 231; at twenty-one 228; marriage and children 231–2, 233, 237, 238, 248, 249, 251–2, 253, 254–5, 257, 269

Butler Island, Georgia 132–52, 154, 157, 245; Fan Butler on 245–7, 257–9

Butler Place, near Philadelphia: FK and Pierce's home 109, 112–17, 126, 159, 164, 166; let 180; daughters inherit 245, 248, 250, 254

Byron, Lord 94; biography of 31; plays 27, 31; poetry 7, 17–18, 19, 27, 31, 32, 33, 73

Cadwallader, John 217
Cambridge, Trinity College 24–5
Cambridge, Mass. 100, 256
Canada 94, 101
Chadwick, Edwin 214
Channing, Dr William 93–4, 121, 124
Charleston, S. Carolina 132, 140
Chartists 198, 213, 214
Chesterfield, Lord 199
child labour, 19c England 138–9
Childe, Maria 170–1
Clifford, Henry 11
Cobbe, Frances Power 269
Collis, Dr 259
Combe, Dr Andrew 31–2, 208
Combe, Cecilia (*née* Siddons) 32, 165, 208

Combe, George 31–2, 72, 167, 208; FK's letters to 19, 23, 25, 33, 51, 56, 57, 75, 78, 86, 92, 93–4, 99, 102, 103, 106, 109, 226

Cork, Lady 63

Cornhill Magazine 224

Covent Garden Theatre: fire 9; rebuilt 10–11; riots 10–12, 35–6; Charles Kemble manages 12, 25, 26, 28, 34–8, 42–4, 69, 174, 209; FK's debut at 42–4; FK at 38, 47, 50–5, 58–9, 69, 96, 174; farewell to 71

Craven, Augustus 60, 207–8

Craven Hill, Kembles home at 16–17

Dacre, Lady 46, 61, 124, 197; FK's letters to 170, 176

Darien, Georgia 132, 143, 144, 146, 153, 157, 249

Davis, Jefferson 235, 239

Dawkins, Major 50

de Camp (FK's grandfather) 9–10

de Camp, Adelaide (FK's Aunt Dall): in FK's childhood 13, 16–17, 21; FK's chaperone 43, 55, 67, 68, 96–7, 206; goes to America 71, 73, 82, 84, 88, 98–9; death 101–3, 104; grave 180, 259

de Ros, Lord 165–6

Dickens, Charles 224

Dorchester 66

Drury Lane Theatre 8, 9, 27, 35, 36

Edinburgh 28–33, 55, 71–2, 76, 103, 208

Egerton, Lord and Lady Francis 46, 60, 124, 169, 170, 174, 205

Ellen (FK's maid) 250, 251, 257, 260, 261, 265, 270

Ellesmeres, the 227

Ellsler, Fanny 168

English Tragedy, The (FK) 166, 200

Eton College 216

Factory Acts 138–9, 214

Far Away and Long Ago (FK) 264

Fatal Marriage, The (T. Southerne) 9, 54–5

Faudier, Mme 15–16

Fazio (Milman) 54, 58–9, 83–4
Firth of Forth 20
Fisher, Joshua 220, 221
Fisher, Sidney 97, 166
FitzClarence, Augustus 47
FitzGerald, Edward 25, 225, 250, 256
Fitzhugh, Emily 46, 62, 118, 126, 133, 205
Florida (ship) 241
Forrester (horse) 186–7, 204
Fox, Mary 252, 256
Fozzard (riding-master) 66
France: FK educated in 15–16, 17–19; travels in 131, 232, 269; political events in 63, 213
Francis I (FK) 26–8, 58, 65, 201
Furness, Mr (Unitarian minister) 182, 185, 188
Further Records (FK) 231, 260, 263–4

Gamester, The 53
Garrick, David 8, 42, 54
Garrison, William Lloyd 119–20
George IV, King, death of 63
George Society 223
Georgia: Butler estates in 97, 120–3, 164, 169, 220, 255; FK journeys to 129–32; FK lives on 132–57; and Civil War 237, 245–8; slaves sold 231, 237, 246; Fan Butler on 237–8, 245–8, 249–50, 253, 257–9, 268, 271; white society of 156–7, 238
Gerhard, Mr (lawyer) 184
Germany 25–6, 126, 168
Glasgow 55
Glyn, Mrs 226
Great Russell Street 58, 76
Greathead, Lady Mary 8
Grecian Daughter, The (A. Murphy) 53
Greville, Charles 54, 111, 170, 216; criticism 53–4, 174; diary 3, 178
Greville, Henry 54, 205–6, 207, 216, 217, 223, 240–1; Diary 3, 4, 236; FK's letters to 232, 233–4, 235–6, 239–40
Grey, Lady, Barbarina 61, 208
Grey, Lord 61, 64
Grote, Mrs, of Burnham 197

Hall, Miss (governess) 176, 180, 186, 189, 190, 191–3
Hallam, Arthur 65
Hamlet 212, 224
Harness, Dr 216
Harris, Henry 36, 55
Harris, Thomas 35, 36
Hayes (maid) 200, 206
Henry VIII (Shakespeare) 205
Hernani (Victor Hugo) 60, 62, 207, 210
Hicks Beach, Sir Michael 248
Highgate Institute 216, 217
Hoboken 78
Holland, Lady 82–3, 116
Holland House 45, 82
Hone, Philip 4, 76, 79–80, 84–5, 95, 111, 112, 220
Honeymoon, The 206
horses, American 86–7; Forrester 186–7, 204
hotels: American 229; English 225; French 131
House of Commons; structure of 63–4; *see also* Parliament
House of Lords 45, 64, 65; *see also* Parliament
Hull 213, 216
Hunchback, The (Sheridan Knowles) 59, 170, 174, 207; at Manchester 205–6

Ireland 225–6, 260; tours in 37, 55–6, 207
Irving, Henry 224
Italy 118, 200–4, 226–7, 249

Jackson, Andrew 90–1
James, Henry 1, 2, 4, 6, 158, 249, 261, 262, 263, 264, 265–7, 269, 271
Jameson, Anna 42, 103, 109, 114, 118, 119, 124, 125, 244
Jenner, Edward 39
Johnson, David Claypole, cartoons by 111–12
Journal of a Residence in America, The (FK) 75, 77, 80, 87, 95, 108, 110, 201; decision to publish 101–2; reception 110–12

Journal of a Residence on a Georgian Plantation (FK) 169, 171, 174; published 4, 241–2

Keely (actor) 43
Kemble, Adelaide (sister of FK): childhood 14, 21, 39; adult 60, 101, 223, 228; operatic career 66, 124, 126–7, 168, 169; marriage 176, 178; and break-up of FK's marriage 187, 191–2, 194; in Italy 200–1, 202–4, 226–7, 249; and FK 124, 176, 203–4, 209; death 262
Kemble, Charles (father of FK) 7; as actor 9, 37, 44, 209, 224; manager 12, 25, 27, 28, 34, 36–8, 42–4, 69, 174; family life 14–15, 19, 24, 25, 26, 30–1, 34, 37; in France with FK 18; puts FK on stage 38, 41–4; on tour 55–6, 66–8; American tour 64, 69, 71–3, 79, 84–6, 88–9, 99, 101, 103–5, 120; returns to England 105–6; health 68–9, 169, 223, 227–8; re FK's Journal 111; on FK's return to England 124, 126, 127; retirement 124; and FK's divorce 194, 195; FK lives with 196–7, 199–200, 204; play readings 209, 216; old age 226, 227–8; death 228; grave 270
Kemble, Elizabeth (aunt of FK; Mrs Whitelock) 7, 23–4, 69
Kemble, Fanny (Frances Anne; Mrs Pierce Butler): birth 6, 12; family 7–12; childhood 12–19; education 14–19, 31–3; youth 19–33, 34; and mother 13–14, 29, 163; appearance 38–40, 49, 251; posture 39–40; smallpox 39; first writing 26–8; turns to stage 37–43; debut 42–4; success 46–69, 96–7; and Sarah Siddons 49, 50, 52, 53, 224; tours English provinces 55–6, 66–8; leaves London stage 71; goes to America 69, 70–95; social manners 80–3; engagement 95, 97; considers marriage 96–104; marries 104; married life 105–23; motherhood 115, 117; visit to England 123–7; returns to America 127–8; travels to Georgia 129–32; on Butler estates 132–57; marriage breaks up 158–69, 170–95; in England 169–80, 195, 196–200; Italy 200–4, 226–7, 249; returns to stage 204–12; *1848*, 213–15; play readings 215–17, 220, 222–5, 228–9; divorce proceedings 217–21; in America 218–21; *1852* 225–6; family deaths 227–8; on Sarah's majority 228–31; brings Fan to England 231–2, 240; tours America 228–9, 230–1, 232, 242, 244; and Civil War 232–43; last years 244–70; last American visits 259; death 270–1; verse 21, 60–1, 70–1, 104, 105–6, 265–6; biographies, *listed*, 5; books, availability, 4; *see also* titles of books and plays; letters, *see under recipients*
Kemble, Henry (brother of FK): childhood 14, 21, 28, 58; acting 42; career 66; health 163, 226, 227–8; in Ireland 207, 225–6; children 225–6, 228
Kemble, Henry (nephew of FK) 261–2 268
Kemble, John Mitchell (brother of FK) 21, 24–6, 34, 228
Kemble, John Philip (uncle of FK) 7–8, 17, 22; acting 8, 9, 10, 11, 209; manager 9, 10–12, 35–6
Kemble, Maria Theresa (*née* de Camp; mother of FK) 12–15, 19, 25, 26, 30–1, 37–9, 58, 71–2, 111; early life 9–10; appearance and character 12–14, 163; relations with Fanny 13–14, 29, 163; puts Fanny on stage 40–4, 59; acts 9, 43, 44, 68; death 24, 163
Kemble, 'Pop' (aunt of FK) 22, 23
Kemble, Roger (grandfather of FK) 7–8, 9, 35
Kemble, Sally (*née* Ward, grandmother of FK) 7–8
Kemble, Sarah *see* Siddons, Mrs Sarah
Keppel (actor) 83–4
King (overseer on Georgia estate) 143, 147, 150, 152, 153, 157, 246

King John 42, 52, 62
King Lear 224
King's Theatre, Haymarket 35

Lancashire, labouring conditions in 39–40
Langtry, Lily 40, 263
Lansdowne, Lord and Lady 125, 127, 170, 217
Laporte, Mrs 71
Lausanne 12, 36
Lawrence, Sir Thomas 6, 41, 48–50; portrait of FK 49, 268
Leamington 260–1, 268
Leeds Mercury, letter in 138
Leigh, Alice Dudley (granddaughter of FK) 253–4, 255, 257, 260, 261, 270, 271
Leigh, James (son-in-law of FK) 83, 248–50, 253–4; in Georgia 248, 249–50, 255, 257–9; vicar in England 253–4, 260–1, 268–9, 269, 271
Leigh, Pierce Butler (grandson of FK) 268–9
Lenox, Mass. 93, 123, 159, 164, 166, 181, 194, 195, 202–3, 216, 218; Court 218; FK buys house in 220–1; sells 248; returns to 228, 231, 238, 256, 259
Lincoln, Abraham 234–5, 237, 238, 241
Linton, Mrs Lyn 83
Liverpool, Lord 24, 44
Liverpool 56, 72, 172–3, 206; labourers of 139, 198; Collegiate Institution 217
London, Frank 144–5, 146
London, 19c. 30, 76, 77, 87, 155; *1831* social structure 63–5; *1836* 124–6; *1841* 169–70, 173–4, 180; *1845* 196; *1848* 213–15; *1877* 260; aristocracy 44–5; Clarendon Hotel 169, 175–6, 191; Opera 80; sanitation 68; shopping 81–2; Theatres 10–12, 34–7, 41–2; FK returns to stage of 207, 209–12
Longfellow, Mrs Fanny *see* Appleton, Fanny
Longfellow, Henry 108, 181, 224,

256; FK reads *The Building of the Ship* 235

Macadam, John L. 86
Macaulay, Thomas B. 170
Macbeth 11, 52, 205, 206; with Macready 210–11, 212
Macdonald, Lawrence 32
MacIntosh, Mrs Mary 171, 179, 192
McLaren, Duncan 32
Macready (actor) 27, 166; in America 181; FK acts with 209–12
Maddox (manager) 207, 208, 210, 215, 217
Mademoiselle de Belle-Isle (Dumas) 174
Malkin, Dr Arthur 19, 21, 217, 223, 229, 264
Manchester 30, 33; labourers of 139, 198; FK returns to stage in 205–6
Mandeville, *Fable of the Bees* 145
marriage laws 116, 175, 217, 219
Martin, Anne 169, 173, 191, 193
Martineau, Harriet 109
Maurice, Frederick 25
Merchant of Venice, The 40, 217
Mill, John Stuart 24, 31
Milwaukee Sentinel, letter to 229
Minot, Mrs Kate *see* Sedgwick, Kate
Mitchell (manager) 216, 217
Morgan, Lady 56
Mount Auburn burial ground 100–1, 103, 259
Much Ado About Nothing 59, 88, 170, 217
Murray, Hannah *see* Siddons, Mrs Henry
Murray, John (publisher) 27, 58, 65
Murray, William 28–9

New York 91, 92, 94, 232, 248; Theatre in 69; FK's impression of 75–81; FK acts in 83–5, 88; Butlers together in 181; FK reads in 220; hotel 229
Newport, R. I. 108, 184, 185–6
Niagara Falls 94–5
Norwich 208, 216
Notes on some of Shakespeare's Plays (FK) 264

O'Brien, Margery 126, 129, 131–2, 150, 165
Othello 211–12
Pacific (ship) 72–3
Paley, Evidences of Christianity 25, 26
Paris 131, 176, 232, 269; FK at school at 17–19
Parliament, British, 19c. 36, 45, 77; 1831 63–4; 1836 124–5; and divorce 116; licensing of plays 34–5; Reform 24, 64, 65, 69, 125; Victoria first opens 125–6
Philadelphia: shopping in 82; Kembles on tour in 87–8, 88–9, 91, 97; FK meets Butler in 97, 98–9; married in 104; attitude to FK 108, 219–20; married life in 108–9, 158, 164, 168, 180, 181–94; Court of Common Pleas 217–18; University committee 219–20; Butler daughters live in 232, 233; FK in 1874–5 250–6; Centenary Exhibition 255; see also Butler Place
Plymouth 66, 67–8
Poor Law 213
Portland Bill 68
Potocki, Count 205
Princes Theatre 207, 208, 209–12
Proctor, Mrs 226
Provoked Husband, The 59

Quarterly Review 65

Racine, plays of 17, 18
railways: American 129–31, 231, 242; British 56–8, 107, 208
Recollections (FK) 21
Records of a Girlhood (FK) 119, 263
Records of a Later Life (FK) 105, 109–10, 263
Richmond, Yorkshire, Theatre 67, 209
Robinson, Crabbe 54, 59, 65, 224, 228
Rogers (poet) 124, 170
Rome 200, 202, 227, 249
Romeo and Juliet 33, 50–1; FK's debut in 40–4; at Bath 55; in America 84–5
Romilly, John 25

Rowden, Mrs (schoolmistress) 17
Russell, Lord John 61, 64, 170
Rutland, Duke of 46, 173

Sadler's Wells 37
St James Theatre 207, 210
St Leger, Harriet 21–3, 26, 56, 72, 118, 123–4, 127, 169, 225, 250, 253, 257, 260, 262; FK's letters to 16, 21, 22, 24, 27, 28, 29, 38, 41, 43, 47, 50, 51, 56, 58, 59, 60, 62, 63, 64–5, 69, 263, 264, 265; from America 73, 92, 96, 100, 101, 109, 113, 117, 118, 121, 122, 159, 164, 165, 166, 168, 180, 185, 186, 248, 249, 250, 251, 252, 254–5, 256, 258, 259, 260; from Georgia 133–4; from Italy 201, 202, 203; from England later 172, 174–5, 196–7, 199, 200, 205, 207, 208, 209, 211
St Simon's Island, Georgia (Hampton Point) 132–4, 137, 146, 148, 152–7, 246
Sartoris, Edward (brother-in-law of FK) 176, 178, 188–9, 190, 209; in Italy 202, 226–7, 249
Sartoris, Greville 262
Sartoris, May (Mrs Gordon) 262, 268
School for Scandal, A 59
Schuylkill river, rail crossing 130
Scott, Sir Walter 31
Sedgwick family 93, 256; Butler bans FK from seeing 184, 188, 189–90; reunited 195
Sedgwick, Catherine Maria 20, 78, 92–3, 94, 111, 159–60, 189, 220, 248; writings 92–3, 201; Letters from Abroad 76
Sedgwick, Charles 93, 114, 218, 248
Sedgwick, Elizabeth (Mrs Charles) 182, 248; school 93, 216; Pierce confides in 158–63; writes to FK 161, 162–3, 166–7, 168; FK's letters to 133, 140, 141, 147, 148–9, 153–4, 155, 156, 171, 218
Sedgwick, Kate (daughter of Elizabeth; Mrs Edward Minot) 93; FK's letters to 2, 104, 105, 172, 179, 189
Sedgwick, Theodore (brother of

Catherine) 93, 166, 175; and Butlers' divorce 182–3; FK's letters to 180

Senior, Nassau 197–8

Shaftesbury, Lord 214

Shakespeare, William 51–2, 266; FK's readings from 215, 216, 217, 220, 222–5; *see also names of plays*

Siddons, Cecilia (Mrs George Combe) 32, 165, 208

Siddons, Henry (cousin of FK) 28–9

Siddons, Mrs Henry (*née* Hannah Murray) 28–31, 33, 51, 72

Siddons, Maria (cousin of FK) 15, 48–9

Siddons, Sally (cousin of FK) 15, 48–9, 72

Siddons, Mrs Sarah (*née* Kemble; aunt of FK): early life 7–8; marriage 8; actress 8–9, 10, 11, 42, 50, 52, 53, 54, 59, 209, 224; retires 12; after 14, 15; and Thomas Lawrence 48–9; death 49

slavery, Negro: abolitionists 119–21, 170–1, 232–3; and American Civil War 232–3, 235–8, 241–2; British attitude 119, 138; FK's attitude 119–23, 160, 170–2, 235–7; in W. Indies 119, 120

slaves: on Butler estates 132–57; sold off 231, 237, 246; women 135–9, 147–52; after Civil War 245–7, 255

Smith, Sydney 61, 124

Stafford House, concert at 169–70

Stanley, Dean 83

Star of Seville, The (FK) 58, 201

Stephenson, George 56–7, 107

Stranger, The (Kotzebue) 95, 174

Stratford-on-Avon 259, 260–1

Sullivan Arthur 249

Switzerland, visits to 232, 240, 260, 261, 262, 264–5, 267, 269

Ten Years on a Georgian Plantation (F. Butler) 245–7

Tennyson, Alfred 25–6

Terry, Ellen 224, 261–2

Thackeray, Anne (Ritchie) 4, 176, 203, 227, 270

Thackeray, Henry 226

Thackeray, Mary Anne 78, 81–2, 216

Thackeray, William M. 26, 204

Times, The 11, 240

tours, theatrical: British 55–6, 66–8; American 85–91, 94, 244; play readings 224–5, 228–9, 230–1, 232, 242, 244

Townsend, Charles 80

Trelawny, Edward 94–5, 101, 109

Trent (ship) 239

Turner, Nat 120

Twiss, Mrs (Aunt of FK) 14

United States of America: in *1832* 74–5; Civil War 91, 235–42; *19c.* development 229–31, 242–3; *see also* railways, slavery, tours and place names

Venice Preserv'd (Otway) 42, 52–3, 66

Vesuvius, Mount 227

Victoria, Queen 66, 80, 91, 234; opens Parliament 125–6; FK meets 173

Walpole, Sir Robert 34

Ward, John (great grandfather of FK) 7

Ward, Sam, FK's letters to 83, 194 204, 219, 220, 221, 270

Washington, D.C. 89–91, 120

Weber, Carl 26

Webster, Daniel 90

Weldon, US, staging post 130–1

Wellington, Duke of 57, 64

Weybridge, Surrey 19–20, 24, 28, 30

Whatley, Thomas 8

Whitelock, Elizabeth (*née* Kemble) 7, 23–4, 69

Wilkinson, Tate 9

William IV, King 47, 64, 65, 125

Willoughby, Lord and Lady 173

Wilson, Dorothy 197

Wilton, Lord and Lady 56

Wister, Fanny Kemble (great granddaughter of FK) 1–2

Wister, Dr Owen (son-in-law of FK) 231–2, 238, 247, 249, 257

Wister, Owen (grandson of FK) 233, 238, 249, 254–5, 269

Witkoff, Henry 80, 86, 99

Yarmouth 208

Year of Consolation (FK) 201, 206

Yellow Springs, US spa 180–1

York Farm, near Philadelphia 250–3, 257